APOCALYPSE WITHOUT GOD

Apocalypse, it seems, is everywhere. Preachers with vast followings proclaim the world's end. Apocalyptic fears grip even the nonreligious amid climate change, pandemics, and threats of nuclear war. As these ideas pervade popular discourse, grasping their logic remains elusive. Ben Jones argues that we can gain insight into apocalyptic thought through secular thinkers. He starts with a puzzle: Why would secular thinkers draw on Christian apocalyptic beliefs – often dismissed as bizarre – to interpret politics? The apocalyptic tradition proves appealing in part because it theorizes a relation between crisis and utopia. Apocalyptic thought points to crisis as the vehicle to bring the previously impossible within reach, offering resources for navigating challenges in ideal theory, which involves imagining the best, most just society. By examining apocalyptic thought's appeal and risks, this study arrives at new insights on the limits of utopian hope. This title is available as open access on Cambridge Core.

Ben Jones is the Assistant Director of Penn State's Rock Ethics Institute and has a Ph.D. in political science from Yale University. His research has appeared in *the Journal of Applied Philosophy, European Journal of Political Theory, Political Research Quarterly*, and other venues, including popular outlets like *The Washington Post*.

Apocalypse without God

APOCALYPTIC THOUGHT, IDEAL POLITICS, AND THE LIMITS OF UTOPIAN HOPE

BEN JONES

The Pennsylvania State University

Shaftesbury Road, Cambridge CB2 8EA, United Kingdom

One Liberty Plaza, 20th Floor, New York, NY 10006, USA

477 Williamstown Road, Port Melbourne, VIC 3207, Australia

314–321, 3rd Floor, Plot 3, Splendor Forum, Jasola District Centre, New Delhi – 110025, India

103 Penang Road, #05–06/07, Visioncrest Commercial, Singapore 238467

Cambridge University Press is part of Cambridge University Press & Assessment, a department of the University of Cambridge.

We share the University's mission to contribute to society through the pursuit of education, learning and research at the highest international levels of excellence.

www.cambridge.org
Information on this title: www.cambridge.org/9781009017039

DOI: 10.1017/9781009037037

© Ben Jones 2022

This work is subject to copyright protection. Reuse of any part of this work not permitted under the Creative Commons license detailed below, a statutory exception, or the provisions of relevant collective licensing agreements may not take place without written permission of Cambridge University Press.

An online version of this work is published at doi.org/10.1017/9781009037037 under a Creative Commons Open Access licence CC-BY-NC 4.0 which permits re-use, distribution and reproduction in any medium for non-commercial purposes providing appropriate credit to the original work is given and any changes made are indicated. To view this license, visit https://creativecommons.org/licenses/by-nc/4.0

All versions of this work may contain content reproduced under license from third parties. Permission to reproduce this third-party content must be obtained from these third parties directly.

This book is freely available in an open access edition thanks to TOME (Toward an Open Monograph Ecosystem)—a collaboration of the Association of American Universities, the Association of University Presses, and the Association of Research Libraries—and the generous support of the Pennsylvania State University. Learn more at the TOME website, available at: openmonographs.org.

When citing this work, please include a reference to the DOI 10.1017/9781009037037

First published 2022
First paperback edition 2025

A catalogue record for this publication is available from the British Library

ISBN   978-1-316-51705-5   Hardback
ISBN   978-1-009-01703-9   Paperback

Cambridge University Press & Assessment has no responsibility for the persistence or accuracy of URLs for external or third-party internet websites referred to in this publication and does not guarantee that any content on such websites is, or will remain, accurate or appropriate.

For Peggy Jones, my mother, who first taught me how to hope

Contents

List of Figures	*page* ix
Preface	xi
Acknowledgments	xii

Introduction   1

PART I   SECULAR APOCALYPTIC THOUGHT

1 The Hazards of Studying Secular Apocalyptic Thought   21

2 The Paradox of Secular Apocalyptic Thought   39

PART II   HISTORICAL CASE STUDIES

3 Apocalyptic Hope's Appeal: Machiavelli and Savonarola   61

4 Tempering Apocalyptic Ideals: Hobbes and Pretenders to God's Kingdom   92

5 Reimagining God's Kingdom: Engels and Müntzer   119

PART III   IMPLICATIONS FOR IDEAL THEORY

6 Ideal Theory as Faith   145

7 Limiting the Dangers of Utopian Hope   175

   Conclusion   191

Appendix: Argument against Ideal Theory's Plausibility   198
Bibliography   203
Index   222

Figures

2.1	The catch-22 of ideal theory	*page* 50
3.1	Execution of Savonarola	89
4.1	Execution of King Charles I	97
5.1	East German stamp of Thomas Müntzer	133
7.1	Angels of death from Revelation 9	178
C.1	Separation of the sheep and the goats	195

Preface

Apocalypse, it seems, is everywhere. Preachers with vast followings proclaim that the world will soon end. Motivated by apocalyptic visions, terrorist groups carry out acts of unspeakable violence. Apocalyptic fears even grip the non-religious faced with the dangers of climate change, deadly pandemics, and nuclear war. But as apocalyptic ideas pervade popular discourse, grasping their logic remains elusive. They increasingly have become disconnected from the religious traditions in which they arose, obscuring the hopes and anxieties that first gave birth to them.

Apocalypse without God argues that we can gain insight into apocalyptic thought by studying it through the eyes of secular thinkers. It starts with a puzzle: Why would secular thinkers find in Christian apocalyptic beliefs – often dismissed as bizarre – appealing tools for interpreting politics? To answer that question, it examines how three theorists with secular conceptions of politics – Machiavelli, Hobbes, and Engels – engage with Christian apocalyptic thought and how such thought still influences politics today. The apocalyptic tradition proves appealing, in part, because it theorizes a special relation between crisis and utopia. A persistent challenge in political philosophy is imagining a path from the imperfect present to the seemingly unattainable ideal society. To solve this challenge, apocalyptic thought points to crisis as the vehicle that creates new opportunities and brings the previously impossible within reach.

Though apocalyptic thought brings to mind doomsday visions, its appeal for political philosophy lies just as much in its visions of utopia. Apocalyptic thought offers apparent resources for navigating challenges that arise in ideal theory, which tries to imagine the best and most just society. By examining apocalyptic thought's appeal and risks, this study ultimately arrives at new insights on the limits of ideal theory and utopian hope.

Acknowledgments

Research for this book began during my time in graduate school at Yale University. There Karuna Mantena and Steven Smith provided helpful feedback and guidance from the start when I was just brainstorming ideas. I also benefited from conversations with John Collins and John Grim, whose wealth of knowledge on religion proved invaluable. I am especially grateful to Bryan Garsten who advised my dissertation, which through much transformation eventually became this book. The Beinecke Scholarship Program deserves special thanks for helping fund my graduate studies during early work on this project.

I am indebted to William Altman, Roland Boer, Daryl Cameron, Chris Costello, Greg Crofford, Kyle Haines, Robynn Kuhlmann, Ben Laurence, Désirée Lim, Lorraine McCrary, Alison McQueen, Shmuel Nili, John Parrish, Emily Ray, Don Thompson, David Wiens, and Arthur Williamson, who all read parts of the manuscript and provided valuable feedback on it. Burke Hendrix, whose work on ideal and nonideal theory deeply influenced my own thinking, was incredibly generous in providing extensive comments on sections of the manuscript and talking through ideas I was wrestling with.

Sheila Denion proofread the entire manuscript, and I greatly appreciate her assistance and attention to detail. Chapter 4 benefited from conversations and correspondence with Patrick Callahan, Harro Höpfl, Al Martinich, and Stefania Tutino. That chapter partly draws on arguments from my article "The Natural Kingdom of God in Hobbes's Political Thought," *History of European Ideas* 45, no. 3 (2019): 436–53, © 2018 Taylor & Francis, available online: www.tandfonline.com/doi/figure/10.1080/01916599.2018.1548810.

I presented research from this project at a number of venues: the New England Political Science Association Annual Meeting (2015), American Political Science Association Annual Meeting (2015 and 2016), Great Plains

Political Science Association Annual Meeting (2015), American Philosophical Association Eastern Meeting (2017), Department of Political Science at the University of Kansas (2017), Western Political Science Association Annual Meeting (2017), Midwest Political Science Association Conference (2018), and Moral Agency Workshop at Penn State (2020). Those audiences introduced me to new perspectives and pushed me to develop what hopefully is a more compelling account of apocalyptic thought's relationship to politics.

Sections of Part I, in particular much of Chapter 2, previously appeared in my article "The Challenges of Ideal Theory and Appeal of Secular Apocalyptic Thought," *European Journal of Political Theory* 19, no. 4 (2020): 465–88, © 2017 Ben Jones, DOI: 10.1177/1474885117722074. The review process for that article played a key role in sharpening the book's argument. I am grateful to the journal's editors and two anonymous reviewers for the care they showed in evaluating the manuscript and for their detailed suggestions.

At Cambridge University Press, I have been fortunate to have a terrific editor in Robert Dreesen. His guidance helped transform my manuscript into the book you see today and improve it in countless ways. Two anonymous reviewers offered extensive and valuable suggestions, which helped bring the different strands of my argument together in more cogent form. I am thankful to the reviewers, Robert, and the rest of the team at Cambridge University Press for their significant investments in the project.

I completed work on this book at the Rock Ethics Institute at Penn State, which provided a rich intellectual environment and could not have been more supportive. Ted Toadvine, the institute's director, deserves special thanks for his encouragement and sage recommendations. A grant from the TOME (Toward an Open Monograph Ecosystem) Initiative at Penn State made this book available in an open access edition. I am thankful for that generous support, and in particular to Ally Laird of the Penn State University Libraries for all the help she provided in answering questions about the grant and application process.

I could imagine no better partner on the journey of writing this book than my wife Mackenzie Jones. As I wrote and rewrote the manuscript, she read various parts of it, which benefited from her insights and suggestions. She also provided the image in Chapter 5. Beyond those specific contributions, her compassion, patience, and encouragement were constant throughout the project's development – both its high and low points – for which I am deeply grateful.

I would be remiss not to mention one other member of our family, our dog Barlow. It's hard to imagine anyone matching his enthusiasm for joining writing sessions in my home office. He spent many hours and long nights at my feet as this manuscript slowly took form, making the lonely task of writing a bit less so.

Introduction

THE PARABLE OF HILLSIDE

With little warning, the rustic kingdom of Hillside found itself under attack from its powerful neighbor to the north, Acadia. The Acadians started raiding Hillside, stealing its resources, inflicting casualties, and filling the kingdom with fear. Acadia had not conquered Hillside yet, but many worried it was only a matter of time.

Meanwhile, a prophet named John roamed the streets of Hillside, preaching that the end was near. Acadia's attack, he claimed, was a sign that God would soon intervene to wipe away corruption and establish his perfect kingdom. In the past, John had attracted large crowds with his message of hope in the midst of crisis. But his prophecies had failed too many times. By now, most of his followers had abandoned him.

Three wise men in Hillside – Nicholas, Thomas, and Frederick – closely studied John's preaching. They rejected the idea that God was about to intervene but still found power in John's message. Drawing on it, each developed his own vision for saving Hillside.

Nicholas spoke first to the people. Like John, he emphasized the opportunity presented by the current crisis, which had the potential to renew Hillside. Having gone years without a crisis to test it, Hillside had grown weak and vulnerable. Now was the time to commit to building its military strength. If serious about this commitment, Hillside could fend off attacks, expand, and become more glorious than ever. This plan appealed to many, but others pressed for more details. If the people sacrificed their time, resources, and lives as Nicholas called for, could he assure them that Hillside would face no more crises and achieve lasting peace? Unfortunately, Nicholas could make no such promise. He knew that, even after conquering Acadia, Hillside would face more tests. The people found this message discouraging and rejected his plan.

Thomas went next. He scolded the people for exaggerating their troubles. Yes, the raids had hurt the kingdom, but the real danger was allowing the crisis to foster internal strife. Already, some were questioning the authority of Hillside's king and suggesting rebellion. Thomas stressed that they must obey the king and respect his authority. He went so far as to flip John's prophecy on its head, saying that the kingdom of God *already* existed in Hillside under the king's rule. The people of Hillside found this message preposterous. The Acadians were maiming, killing, and stealing from them on a regular basis – how could *this* be God's kingdom?

Frederick took a different tack. Hillside's current crisis *was* the king's fault, he said. For too long, the ruling class had oppressed the people, weakening the kingdom. The latest crisis had made the king so weak that revolution against him could succeed. Following John's example, Frederick portrayed the current crisis as one of historic importance: if the people seized this opportunity and threw off their chains, they could defeat their enemies and create in Hillside a lasting utopia. This is the future that prophets like John *actually* had in mind when they spoke of God's perfect kingdom. Frederick's hopeful vision – and a path for getting there – was what Hillside longed for! The people rebelled, overthrew the king, and defeated Acadia.

Despite the revolution, utopia sadly never came to Hillside. There is still hunger, suffering, and occasional violence. Reportedly, prophets and revolutionaries continue to visit Hillside, always managing to find some eager for their message.

THE MORAL

The parable introduces three of the main protagonists in the pages to come: Niccolò Machiavelli (Nicholas), Thomas Hobbes (Thomas), and Friedrich Engels (Frederick). None of these thinkers stand out as likely suspects to embrace apocalyptic thought. Engels, one of Marxism's founders, was an atheist.[1] The religious beliefs of Machiavelli and Hobbes – the respective authors of the classic texts *The Prince* and *Leviathan* – are a matter of dispute. Without question, they criticized aspects of Christianity, and for that reason some suspect them of atheism.[2] What is clear for all three is that they had no illusions that divine intervention would solve the woes afflicting political and

---

[1] For more on Engels's religious views, see Roland Boer, *Criticism of Earth: On Marxism and Theology IV* (Chicago: Haymarket Books, 2013), 233–306.

[2] For the dispute over Machiavelli's religious views, see Leo Strauss, *Thoughts on Machiavelli* (Chicago: University of Chicago Press, 1958); Clifford Orwin, "Machiavelli's Unchristian Charity," *American Political Science Review* 72, no. 4 (1978): 1217–28; Sebastian de Grazia,

social life. Their theories are secular in the following sense: they make prescriptions for political institutions without the hope that God will assist in perfecting them. That view stands in contrast to apocalyptic hopes throughout history that divine forces soon will intervene to wipe away earthly corruption and establish a lasting utopia – the kingdom of God. Given the apparent chasm between that idea and these thinkers' perspectives, it would be reasonable to expect Machiavelli, Hobbes, and Engels to dismiss apocalyptic hopes as nonsense.

Yet their writings reveal a different attitude. Their engagement with apocalyptic figures and texts reveals a sincere interest in apocalyptic thought and appreciation of its power. Machiavelli grapples with how to assess a central figure of Florentine politics from the 1490s, the Dominican Friar Girolamo Savonarola, whose apocalyptic preaching helped usher in a brief revival of republican rule. Though at times critical of Savonarola, Machiavelli recognizes the power of his apocalyptic preaching in helping establish new political orders. Hobbes takes a harsher view of the apocalyptic prophets and sects that flourished during the English Civil War of the mid-1600s, yet responds by

---

Machiavelli in Hell (Princeton, NJ: Princeton University Press, 1989); Vickie Sullivan, "Neither Christian nor Pagan: Machiavelli's Treatment of Religion in the *Discourses*," *Polity* 26, no. 2 (1993): 259–80; and Maurizio Viroli, *Machiavelli's God*, trans. Antony Shugaar (Princeton, NJ: Princeton University Press, 2010). For the dispute over Hobbes's religious views, see Leo Strauss, *The Political Philosophy of Hobbes: Its Basis and Its Genesis*, trans. Elsa Sinclair (Chicago: University of Chicago Press, 1952); Howard Warrender, *The Political Philosophy of Hobbes: His Theory of Obligation* (Oxford: Clarendon Press, 1957); Willis Glover, "God and Thomas Hobbes," *Church History* 29, no. 3 (1960): 275–97; J. G. A. Pocock, "Time, History and Eschatology in the Thought of Thomas Hobbes," in *Politics, Language, and Time: Essays on Political Thought and History* (New York: Atheneum, 1971), 148–201; Edwin Curley, " 'I Durst Not Write so Boldly,' or How to Read Hobbes' Theological-Political Treatise," in *Hobbes e Spinoza*, ed. Daniela Bostrenghi (Napoli: Bibliopolis, 1992), 497–593; A. P. Martinich, *The Two Gods of* Leviathan: *Thomas Hobbes on Religion and Politics* (New York: Cambridge University Press, 1992); Richard Tuck, "The 'Christian Atheism' of Thomas Hobbes," in *Atheism from the Reformation to the Enlightenment*, ed. Michael Hunter and David Wootton (Oxford: Clarendon Press, 1992), 111–30; Paul Cooke, *Hobbes and Christianity: Reassessing the Bible in* Leviathan (Lanham, MD: Rowman & Littlefield Publishers, 1996); Devin Stauffer, " 'Of Religion' in Hobbes's *Leviathan*," *Journal of Politics* 72, no. 3 (2010): 868–79; Agostino Lupoli, "Hobbes and Religion without Theology," in *The Oxford Handbook of Hobbes*, ed. Al Martinich and Kinch Hoekstra (New York: Oxford University Press, 2016), 453–80; Sarah Mortimer, "Christianity and Civil Religion in Hobbes's *Leviathan*," in *The Oxford Handbook of Hobbes*, ed. Al Martinich and Kinch Hoekstra (New York: Oxford University Press, 2016), 501–19; Steven Smith, *Modernity and Its Discontents: Making and Unmaking the Bourgeois from Machiavelli to Bellow* (New Haven, CT: Yale University Press, 2016), 67–87; Arash Abizadeh, "Hobbes's Agnostic Theology before *Leviathan*," *Canadian Journal of Philosophy* 47, no. 5 (2017): 714–37; and Arash Abizadeh, "Hobbes's Conventionalist Theology, the Trinity, and God as an Artificial Person by Fiction," *Historical Journal* 60, no. 4 (2017): 915–41.

co-opting apocalyptic ideals to advance an alternative vision. In *Leviathan*, he calls earthly commonwealths a manifestation of the kingdom of God, essentially telling his readers to stop looking for God's kingdom – it is already in front of them and can be theirs if they just obey the civil sovereign. Engels exhibits an enduring fascination with apocalyptic thought, evident from his writings on the book of Revelation and the apocalyptic figure Thomas Müntzer, a leader of the German Peasants' War in the 1520s. Rather than entirely reject the Christian concept of the kingdom of God, he transforms it into a Marxist ideal.

Each develops a distinct strategy for responding to apocalyptic hopes, which is closely tied to how they approach theorizing about the ideal state. Machiavelli longs for a perpetual republic, which Savonarola's apocalyptic message promises. But despite recognizing the appeal of this ideal, Machiavelli ultimately rejects it, unable to accept the idea that any republic could survive the vicissitudes of politics and endure forever. Hobbes adopts a different strategy when confronted with the idealism of apocalyptic beliefs. He dramatically tempers this idealism by equating God's perfect kingdom with imperfect commonwealths that command the worship of false gods, kill the innocent, and engage in other evils. Engels goes further than Hobbes and embraces the apocalyptic tradition's utopian hopes. Though he envisions a secular ideal different from that envisioned by Christian apocalyptic thought, he shares with this tradition the belief that utopia will come after a period of crisis and upheaval. Appreciation of apocalyptic thought's political power leads Machiavelli, Hobbes, and Engels to three different strategies for handling its idealism: rejecting it, tempering it, and embracing it.

These thinkers' engagement with apocalyptic thought offers insights into this book's central question: Why do secular thinkers find in Christianity's apocalyptic doctrines appealing tools to interpret politics? By exploring apocalyptic thought's appeal even to those skeptical of its underlying theology, we can better understand its persistent influence in politics. More broadly, this analysis sheds light on strategies for overcoming the challenge of how to reconcile deeply held hopes for a more perfect political future with a world seemingly hostile to it.

THE PUZZLE OF SECULAR APOCALYPTIC THOUGHT

On its face, why secular thinkers would find apocalyptic thought appealing is somewhat puzzling. Such thought enjoys a less-than-stellar reputation among both believers and nonbelievers. Many Christians find apocalyptic beliefs – predictions of coming plagues and judgment, the resurrection of the dead, an

Antichrist who will persecute the righteous, and a millennial kingdom on earth – to be the most bizarre elements of their faith. This discomfort with their faith's apocalyptic heritage has led many Christians to downplay it, from urging allegorical interpretations of apocalyptic texts to skipping over them in church services.

The perceived link between apocalyptic thought and violence exacerbates these concerns. In both the past and present, there have been violent manifestations of apocalyptic thought. During the Crusades, Christians used apocalyptic texts like the book of Revelation to justify a brutal holy war aimed at taking Jerusalem.[3] Today, apocalyptic themes and rhetoric from Christian sources appear in the ideologies of right-wing militia movements in the United States and have influenced domestic terrorists like Timothy McVeigh.[4] The violent potential of apocalyptic beliefs also was on display with the rise of the Islamic State or ISIS. Through selectively drawing on Islamic sources, ISIS embraced apocalyptic beliefs that provided the logic for its shocking and violent tactics.[5] For some, these groups embody everything wrong with apocalyptic thought – bizarre and violent beliefs.

Indeed, the baggage associated with apocalyptic thought creates barriers to understanding it. One reaction is that only the crazy or deluded could sincerely embrace and act on apocalyptic belief. Many who study apocalyptic groups, however, caution against dismissing their members as irrational or brainwashed, pointing out that their actions are often rational when interpreted from the perspective of their belief system. So little is gained from dismissing members of apocalyptic groups as crazy. Instead, it is more productive to study their beliefs so that we can respond to them in constructive ways that minimize violence.[6]

---

[3] John Hall, *Apocalypse: From Antiquity to the Empire of Modernity* (Malden, MA: Polity Press, 2009), 44–78; and Frances Flannery, *Understanding Apocalyptic Terrorism: Countering the Radical Mindset* (New York: Routledge, 2016), 38–50.

[4] Michael Barkun, "Religion, Militias and Oklahoma City: The Mind of Conspiratorialists," *Terrorism and Political Violence* 8, no. 1 (1996): 50–64; Michael Barkun, "Millennialism on the Radical Right in America," in *The Oxford Handbook of Millennialism*, ed. Catherine Wessinger (New York: Oxford University Press, 2011), 649–66; and Martin Durham, "Preparing for Armageddon: Citizen Militias, the Patriot Movement and the Oklahoma City Bombing," *Terrorism and Political Violence* 8, no. 1 (1996): 65–79.

[5] William McCants, *The ISIS Apocalypse: The History, Strategy, and Doomsday Vision of the Islamic State* (New York: St. Martin's Press, 2015); and Graeme Wood, "What ISIS Really Wants," *The Atlantic*, March 2015, www.theatlantic.com/magazine/archive/2015/03/what-isis-really-wants/384980/.

[6] Catherine Wessinger, "Introduction: The Interacting Dynamics of Millennial Beliefs, Persecution, and Violence," in *Millennialism, Persecution, and Violence: Historical Cases*, ed. Catherine Wessinger (Syracuse, NY: Syracuse University Press, 2000), 15, 39.

These recommendations make sense, yet putting them into practice is a challenge. The idiosyncratic and often exotic nature of apocalyptic belief makes it difficult for outsiders to overcome the bizarre impression they initially have of it. After all, the gap between an apocalyptic belief system and that of an outsider can seem vast. Even if one sincerely *wants* to understand apocalyptic beliefs, they can appear disconnected from reality and anything familiar.

One benefit of studying secular apocalyptic thought is that it helps overcome this disconnect. Examining secular thinkers who take an interest in apocalyptic figures and texts allows us to see their appeal in a new light. This approach reveals thinkers who, while skeptical of apocalyptic belief, still find aspects of it appealing. In fact, some secular thinkers draw on apocalyptic thought and incorporate elements from it into their own political philosophy. Exploring why they make this move helps us better understand apocalyptic thought's appeal.

When we examine apocalyptic thought from the perspective of secular thinkers, it becomes harder to dismiss it as foreign and disconnected from the world we inhabit. Apocalyptic thought springs from persistent human hopes – notably, a longing for the ideal society and end to the evils that have plagued the world for too long. If we move past the assumption that apocalyptic thought's appeal is limited only to fringe groups, that shift in perspective forces us to recognize that the hopes bound up in it are not so radically different from ones long present in political thought.

WHAT IDEAL THEORY TEACHES US ABOUT APOCALYPTIC THOUGHT

This study draws on a strand of political philosophy known as ideal theory, often understood as theorizing about what the best, most just society would look like. Ideal theory often gets a bad rap. The arcane debates characterizing it, over visions of society with seemingly little hope of being realized, give the impression that ideal theory lacks any connection to advancing justice in the real world.[7] Though ideal theory deserves its fair share of criticism, it is

---

[7] For more on the debates over ideal theory, see Alan Hamlin and Zofia Stemplowska, "Theory, Ideal Theory and the Theory of Ideals," *Political Studies Review* 10, no. 1 (2012): 48–62; Zofia Stemplowska and Adam Swift, "Ideal and Nonideal Theory," in *The Oxford Handbook of Political Philosophy*, ed. David Estlund (New York: Oxford University Press, 2012), 373–88; Laura Valentini, "Ideal vs. Non-ideal Theory: A Conceptual Map," *Philosophy Compass* 7, no. 9 (2012): 654–64; Kwame Appiah, *As If: Idealization and Ideals* (Cambridge, MA: Harvard University Press, 2017), 112–72; and Michael Weber and Kevin Vallier, eds., *Political Utopias: Contemporary Debates* (New York: Oxford University Press, 2017).

important to appreciate the motivations behind it. The persistence of cruelty, suffering, and violence makes clear that the world is not what it should be. Moreover, many of these evils exist in complex interrelationships, where alleviating one could exacerbate others. Faced with that dilemma, ideal theory seeks to outline a vision of society whose institutions and foundational principles fit together in a cohesive whole that best advances justice. This vision offers a goal to aim for. Ideal theory is thus more than mere intellectual curiosity: it springs from legitimate concerns over how best to advance justice in a world where the answer is rarely straightforward.

On its face, ideal theory seems like an odd lens for studying apocalyptic thought. Today apocalypse is synonymous with catastrophe, bringing to mind wide-scale disaster and doom. Given how the term is often used, nothing about the apocalypse seems ideal. Apocalyptic thought's link to ideal theory becomes clearer, though, by looking at the Jewish and Christian traditions from which such thought emerged. Apocalyptic texts in these traditions anticipate crisis, but interpret it as a necessary step to realizing utopia. So apocalyptic thought is more than theorizing about crisis: *it is theorizing about the special relation between crisis and utopia.*

This claim requires some qualification. Apocalyptic thought is incredibly diverse, and generalizations inevitably fail to capture all its forms. Much of this study focuses on what I call *cataclysmic apocalyptic thought*. That particular strand of apocalyptic thought sees crisis as a key force to wipe away corruption and make way for a utopian society, in what will be a radical break from the past. Cataclysmic apocalyptic thought does not represent all of the apocalyptic tradition but is certainly a significant part of it. Notably, the apocalyptic text of Revelation expresses the hope that divine intervention will bring about earthly upheaval and eliminate corrupt ruling powers. When these rulers meet their demise, the kingdom of God – a perfect kingdom to last forever – will rise in their place.

This apocalyptic perspective has proved influential throughout the history of political thought. The appeal of cataclysmic apocalyptic thought partly lies in offering resources to navigate a problem that has long plagued ideal theory: How can we get to the ideal society when it seems so hopelessly removed from the present? Ideal theory faces the competing demands of specifying a *feasible* ideal that we can actually achieve, but also a *utopian* ideal that remains appealing and worth sacrificing for. These competing demands create a catch-22: a more utopian ideal is less feasible, which diminishes our reasons to strive for it and its moral force, yet a more modest and feasible ideal lessens its appeal, which also diminishes our reasons to strive for it and its moral force. Machiavelli, Hobbes, and Engels all encounter this dilemma when considering hopes for utopia. Cataclysmic apocalyptic thought offers a solution to ideal theory's catch-22: embrace a utopian ideal and declare it feasible by pointing to a coming crisis that will bring it about. Rather than abandon hope for utopia, cataclysmic apocalyptic thought proclaims that crisis will finally make this hope a reality. It thus fashions a narrative of political change to explain how the seemingly impossible becomes possible, which makes cataclysmic apocalyptic thought attractive to those who want to go beyond imagining the ideal and actually realize it.

Though Machiavelli and Hobbes recognize cataclysmic apocalyptic thought's appeal for politics, they stop short of embracing it. Engels goes further and embraces this perspective, providing an example of how cataclysmic apocalyptic thought takes secular form. In the hands of secular thinkers, apocalyptic thought becomes transformed by identifying human or natural forces – as opposed to divine ones – as the drivers behind crisis that will realize the ideal society. For Engels, economic forces will spark a crisis that leads to the collapse of capitalism and gives way to an ideal society grounded in Marxist principles. Both Christian and secular versions of cataclysmic apocalyptic thought take a hopeful view of crisis since only crisis can remove entrenched corruption in society and create a path to the ideal.

Cataclysmic apocalyptic thought remains thoroughly utopian even in conditions that seem hopeless. This worldview proves appealing to theorists who are acutely aware of the present's imperfection but refuse to let it shake their hopes for the ideal society. When understood from this perspective, secular apocalyptic thought becomes less puzzling. Its appeal comes from offering a rationale for holding on to utopian hope in the midst of corruption and crisis. Even in trying conditions, one can draw on such thought to instill hope and motivate action in pursuit of the ideal.

WHAT APOCALYPTIC THOUGHT TEACHES US ABOUT IDEAL THEORY

Beyond just using ideal theory as a tool to understand apocalyptic thought, this study asks what insights apocalyptic thought can provide into ideal theory.[8] It is a novel approach to ideal theory and one that stands in contrast to the ahistorical nature of most scholarship on the subject.

---

[8] In how I approach the history of political thought for insights into contemporary political philosophy, I am deeply sympathetic to the recommendations in Adrian Blau, "How (Not) to Use the History of Political Thought for Contemporary Purposes," *American Journal of Political Science* 65, no. 2 (2021): 359–72.

John Rawls's 1971 work *A Theory of Justice* sparked much of the current interest in ideal theory. The book introduces that term to describe its approach of outlining principles of justice for ideal circumstances (ideal theory), which then are necessary to determine what justice demands under less-than-ideal circumstances (nonideal theory).[9] The bulk of scholarship on ideal theory focuses on how Rawls understands it and the debates he generated. By itself, this scholarship can give the impression that the ideal theory debate started with Rawls. But as some rightly point out, ideal theory has a long and rich history predating Rawls.[10] In the Western tradition, there are examples as early as Plato's *Republic* of political philosophers theorizing about what the ideal, most just society would look like.[11]

By examining that history, we gain new perspectives on current challenges for ideal theory. A common frustration is trying to imagine a path to an ideal that seems hopelessly far away. Apocalyptic thought offers a strategy to overcome that obstacle: interpret crisis as an opportunity to realize an ideal that previously seemed beyond reach, while encouraging dramatic action to seize the opportunity at hand. It is a strategy that, like most things in politics, comes with risks. Crises open up new opportunities, but almost always fall short of fulfilling utopian hopes. And when people try to force the end and realize apocalyptic expectations by any means necessary, their efforts often backfire and move society further from utopia.

That danger looms over ideal theory generally, not just apocalyptic thought. Given the world's immense complexity and human limitations, we cannot know the full consequences of implementing proposed principles of justice. That problem is especially acute for ideal theory since most people envision the ideal society as being markedly different than the present. The ideal theorist proposes principles of justice without being able to know what they would look like in a future world – one perhaps radically different than our own – which leaves them in no position to plausibly defend their theory. After all, for an ideal theory to be compelling, we need reason to believe that its principles would have normative force under the conditions in which they would be implemented.[12] Unfortunately, we lack that knowledge. If we still

---

[9] John Rawls, *A Theory of Justice*, rev. ed. (Cambridge, MA: Harvard University Press, 1999), 8.
[10] Lea Ypi, "On the Confusion between Ideal and Non-ideal in Recent Debates on Global Justice," *Political Studies* 58, no. 3 (2010): 537–38; and Gerald Gaus, *The Tyranny of the Ideal: Justice in a Diverse Society* (Princeton, NJ: Princeton University Press, 2016), 2–3.
[11] Plato, *The Republic*, ed. G. R. F. Ferrari and trans. Tom Griffith (New York: Cambridge University Press, 2000), 471c–73b.
[12] For this point, I draw on Amartya Sen, *The Idea of Justice* (Cambridge, MA: Harvard University Press, 2009), 18–22; and Gaus, *The Tyranny of the Ideal*, 23.

push forward with adopting these principles on a wide scale, we risk unforeseen consequences that could exacerbate the very injustices we seek to remedy.[13]

Though cataclysmic apocalyptic thought often heightens this danger, other resources in the apocalyptic tradition help address it. This tradition may seem like an odd place to turn, given its links to violence by those determined to realize utopia by force. It is this explosive potential in apocalyptic thought that spurred theologians and others to interpret it in ways that neutralize its dangers. Jewish and Christian thought both developed strategies to preserve apocalyptic thought's utopian hope, while emphasizing human ignorance of utopia and how to bring it about. That knowledge rests with God alone.

What results is a somewhat counterintuitive idea – utopian hope that largely rejects claims to knowledge about utopia. This humble approach has certain advantages: it recognizes the epistemic limitations inherent in ideal theorizing and guards against political visions that ignore them. It also understands belief in the ideal as resting on faith in contrast to the dominant view in political philosophy, which treats ideal theory as something that its defenders can give plausible grounds for. If ideal theory rests on faith, it is a mistake to think that anyone must embrace ideal theory and the utopian hope it offers in light of certain evidence. People still are welcome to embrace this hope, but its basis in faith counsels humility about any claims regarding what the ideal society would look like.

This study departs from previous ones by focusing on apocalyptic thought's insights for ideal theory. The most significant recent work on the relationship between apocalyptic and political thought is Alison McQueen's *Political Realism in Apocalyptic Times*. It specifically analyzes how political realism engages with apocalyptic thought and responds to fears about the end of the world.[14]

The focus of McQueen's study, political realism, often stands in opposition to ideal theory.[15] Though definitions vary, political realism generally refers to a tradition of thought that understands the political sphere as having distinctive challenges and evaluative standards, and therefore criticizes attempts to simply apply moral philosophy to political life. Political realists also see

---

[13] For an insightful discussion of this danger, see Burke Hendrix, "Where Should We Expect Social Change in Non-ideal Theory?" *Political Theory* 41, no. 1 (2013): 116–43.

[14] Alison McQueen, *Political Realism in Apocalyptic Times* (New York: Cambridge University Press, 2018).

[15] It is important to note that political realism's opposition to ideal theory, though common, is not inherent to it. See Matt Sleat, "Realism, Liberalism and Non-ideal Theory or, Are There Two Ways to Do Realistic Political Theory?" *Political Studies* 64, no. 1 (2016): 27–41.

conflict and disagreement as inescapable parts of politics. According to the realist account, politics is about managing conflict, not eliminating it.[16] So political realists are often critical of ideal theory and its harmonious vision for politics. Indeed, some of the most trenchant criticisms of ideal theory come from those writing in the tradition of political realism.[17]

This difference between McQueen's approach and mine – the former focusing on political realism, the latter on ideal theory – stems in part from which aspect of apocalyptic thought we emphasize. McQueen recognizes that the apocalyptic tradition includes both visions of catastrophe and utopia,[18] but puts more attention on its catastrophic elements. This approach makes sense for a study on political realism, which has little interest in pursuing utopia and instead is concerned with how to keep disaster at bay.[19]

It is important, though, not to lose sight of the utopian hope present in apocalyptic thought, which is easy to do when apocalypse so often brings to mind doomsday. This study puts the focus on the other side of the apocalyptic coin, so to speak, by examining its utopian hope and relevance to ideal theory. With regard to McQueen's approach and mine, one is not right and the other wrong. Rather, both approaches complement each other and provide a fuller picture of apocalyptic thought's relevance to political theory.[20]

APOCALYPSE, EVERYWHERE AND NOWHERE

One feature of apocalyptic thought that stands out, which this book grapples with, is its apparent ubiquity. Talk of the apocalypse seems to be wherever one turns.[21] There is no shortage of apocalyptic preachers who use select biblical passages as a lens for interpreting current events and predicting the rapture,

---

[16] William Galston, "Realism in Political Theory," *European Journal of Political Theory* 9, no. 4 (2010): 385–411.
[17] See, e.g., Bernard Williams, *In the Beginning Was the Deed: Realism and Moralism in Political Argument*, ed. Geoffrey Hawthorn (Princeton, NJ: Princeton University Press, 2005); and Raymond Geuss, *Philosophy and Real Politics* (Princeton, NJ: Princeton University Press, 2008).
[18] McQueen, *Political Realism in Apocalyptic Times*, 12.
[19] See, e.g., Judith Shklar, "The Liberalism of Fear," in *Liberalism and the Moral Life*, ed. Nancy Rosenblum (Cambridge, MA: Harvard University Press, 1989), 21–38.
[20] McQueen and I also differ in our methodological approaches, which *do* come into conflict. Chapter 1 explains and defends my approach to studying secular apocalyptic thought.
[21] See Nicholas Guyatt, *Have a Nice Doomsday: Why Millions of Americans Are Looking Forward to the End of the World* (New York: HarperCollins Publishers, 2007); and Richard Kyle, *Apocalyptic Fever: End-Time Prophecies in Modern America* (Eugene, OR: Cascade Books, 2012).

tribulation, and fulfillment of other end-time prophecies.[22] Despite their failed track record, many continue with their predictions. And it is not just televangelists who warn of apocalypse. Scholars and reporters concerned about nuclear war, climate change, deadly pandemics, and other threats often describe them in apocalyptic terms.

Media coverage of Donald Trump's presidency provided its fair share of examples. In the lead-up to the 2016 presidential election, the online magazine *Slate* posted a "Trump Apocalypse Watch" to track the likelihood of the apocalypse – that is, a Trump victory. The morning after the election, *Slate* gave its final update: "4 Horsemen."[23] The outbreak of the COVID-19 pandemic during Trump's presidency further encouraged the conclusion that America found itself in apocalyptic times.[24] "Welcome to the Trumpocalypse" declared *Rolling Stone* as the pandemic ravaged the United States over the Easter holiday in 2020.[25]

Such language – sometimes meant to be humorous, sometimes meant to emphasize the gravity of a threat, and sometimes both – frequently appears in news, movies, art, literature, and scholarship. Apocalyptic themes and concepts have migrated from religious contexts to largely secular ones, and now are applied to a much wider range of phenomena. This shift comes at a cost. When apocalypse becomes synonymous with any disaster, the concept loses much of the nuance and complexity it possessed in the religious traditions from which it emerged.

The evolution of the term's meaning in English illustrates this point. When it first entered English in the Middle Ages, "apocalypse" referred to the book of Revelation (i.e., the Apocalypse of John). The adjective "apocalyptic" came several centuries later and also referred to the book of Revelation and its contents. Near the end of the nineteenth century, apocalypse took the broader meaning of referring to wide-scale disaster or cataclysm (not just the events described in Revelation).[26] This is how many use the term today. It has a vague religious resonance, but this connection is often tenuous, as many using the term have limited familiarity with religious apocalyptic thought. So as

---

[22] See, e.g., Scott James, "From Oakland to the World, Words of Warning: Time's Up," *New York Times*, May 19, 2011, www.nytimes.com/2011/05/20/us/20bcjames.html.

[23] Ben Mathis-Lilley, "The Last Trump Apocalypse Watch," *Slate*, November 9, 2016, https://slate.com/news-and-politics/2016/11/the-last-trump-apocalypse-watch.html.

[24] See Elizabeth Dias, "The Apocalypse as an 'Unveiling': What Religion Teaches Us about the End Times," *New York Times*, April 2, 2020, www.nytimes.com/2020/04/02/us/coronavirus-apocalypse-religion.html.

[25] Bob Moser, "Welcome to the Trumpocalypse," *Rolling Stone*, April 11, 2020, www.rollingstone.com/politics/politics-features/trump-evangelicals-apocalypse-coronavirus-981995/.

[26] *Oxford English Dictionary*.

apocalyptic language shows up in more contexts, it loses much of its richness, particularly the utopian hope initially bound up in it. Apocalypse is seemingly everywhere, yet stripped of aspects of its original meaning.

This development creates challenges for studying *secular* apocalyptic thought. If any prediction of disaster qualifies, such a broad understanding fails to ensure a meaningful connection between secular apocalyptic thought and the religious traditions it supposedly stems from. Calling texts or ideologies apocalyptic usually implies that they are indebted to religious traditions due to their preoccupation with disaster. But such fears can come from other sources, like the threat of war. An overly broad conception of apocalyptic thought makes it easy to read into secular works religious influences that are not there.

In the 1960s, two influential theorists – Judith Shklar and Hans Blumenberg – raised this concern. Shklar found many claims about purportedly secular apocalyptic thought to be baseless and insensitive to important distinctions between religious and secular thought.[27] Blumenberg shared these concerns, and raised the additional point that labeling secular thought apocalyptic often serves the goal of undermining its legitimacy. By characterizing modern ideologies as apocalyptic, critics suggest that these ideologies are not what they claim to be – paradigms of reason – and instead rely on bizarre beliefs.[28] Together, Shklar and Blumenberg cast doubt on the concept of secular apocalyptic thought and its value for studying the history of ideas.

Curiously, these objections have gone unnoticed by most scholars of secular apocalyptic thought, who largely have proceeded without grappling with them.[29] That oversight raises the risk of drawing spurious connections in the history of ideas. To minimize that risk and put claims about secular apocalyptic thought on firmer ground, this study offers a proposal to address Shklar's and Blumenberg's concerns. It argues that research on secular apocalyptic thought should focus on cases where religion's influence is clear because secular thinkers explicitly mention religious apocalyptic texts, figures, or

---

[27] Judith Shklar, "The Political Theory of Utopia: From Melancholy to Nostalgia," *Daedalus* 94, no. 2 (1965): 367–81.

[28] Hans Blumenberg, *The Legitimacy of the Modern Age*, trans. Robert Wallace (Cambridge, MA: MIT Press, 1983).

[29] See, e.g., Michael Barkun, "Divided Apocalypse: Thinking about the End in Contemporary America," *Soundings: An Interdisciplinary Journal* 66, no. 3 (1983): 257–80; John Gray, *Black Mass: Apocalyptic Religion and the Death of Utopia* (New York: Farrar, Straus and Giroux, 2007); Hall, *Apocalypse: From Antiquity to the Empire of Modernity*; and McQueen, *Political Realism in Apocalyptic Times*. One notable exception that considers Blumenberg's objection when discussing secular apocalyptic thought is Klaus Vondung, *The Apocalypse in Germany*, trans. Stephen Ricks (Columbia, MO: University of Missouri Press, 2000), 36–49.

concepts. This approach ensures a stronger link between what we label secular apocalyptic thought and religious apocalyptic traditions.

The history of political thought offers various examples where secular thinkers directly engage with religious apocalyptic traditions. Engels, for instance, shows a deep interest in apocalyptic figures and texts, drawing parallels between the apocalyptic worldview of early Christians and the socialist movement of his day. In such cases, where secular thinkers explicitly discuss, praise, and appropriate elements from apocalyptic traditions, it is harder to dismiss the concept of secular apocalyptic thought as merely an invention of later interpreters. Given the undeniable links between some secular thinkers and religious apocalyptic beliefs, there is strong reason to preserve secular apocalyptic thought as a conceptual tool.

A NOTE ON TERMINOLOGY

For the sake of clarity, it is helpful here at the start to explain and distinguish some key terms that will be used throughout. The terms fall into two groups. The first are common in scholarship on apocalyptic thought – apocalypse, chiliasm, eschatology, millennialism, and millenarianism – but are not always used consistently. The second are traditions of thought – prophetic, utopian, and secular – that are distinct from apocalyptic thought but intersect with it.

Let's begin with apocalypse, which comes from the Greek and originally meant revelation or unveiling. For scholars of religion, apocalypse refers to an ancient genre of literature, in which a supernatural messenger provides revelation about a transcendent reality and salvation that awaits a chosen group at the end of time.[30] Perhaps the best-known example of this genre is the final book of the Christian canon, Revelation. Because of the catastrophic events described in Revelation, apocalypse eventually came to also mean catastrophe.

Apocalypses like the book of Revelation contribute to a branch of theology called eschatology. This term derives from the Greek word *eschatos*, meaning "last things." Eschatology refers to the study of last things at the individual (death) or global level (end of the world).[31] Apocalyptic literature offers perspectives within eschatology, but not all eschatology is apocalyptic. Eschatology includes a variety of texts and meditations on last things that fall outside the apocalyptic tradition and genre.

---

[30] John Collins, "Introduction: Towards the Morphology of a Genre," *Semeia* 14 (1979): 9.
[31] Catherine Wessinger, "Millennial Glossary," in *The Oxford Handbook of Millennialism*, ed. Catherine Wessinger (New York: Oxford University Press, 2011), 719.

The related terms of millennialism, millenarianism, and chiliasm – the latter derived from the Greek term for millennium – stem from a reference in Revelation 20:1–6. These verses speak of Satan's being bound for a thousand years, during which time those killed for their Christian faith "came to life and reigned with Christ" (Revelation 20:4).[32] In the Christian tradition, this passage has spawned hopes of a millennial kingdom on earth where Christ will rule. Millennialism in the field of religious studies has come to take on the broader meaning of referring to belief systems that anticipate the imminent salvation of the faithful, who will inhabit a utopian society on earth or in heaven. Used in this way, millennialism applies to religious groups beyond just Christians.[33]

This study generally opts for the term apocalyptic thought over millennialism. The primary reason is that the focus here is on the influence of Christian apocalyptic texts and their interpreters on political thinkers, less so on the influence of the specific doctrine of Christ's millennial kingdom. Political thinkers can draw on apocalyptic beliefs and find valuable elements within them without embracing belief in a millennial kingdom. Moreover, though millennialism's meaning has broadened, in many contexts it remains closely tied to debates over how to interpret the millennial kingdom discussed in Revelation.[34] The term apocalyptic thought avoids some of those implications and thus seems more apt.

Let's turn to the second group of terms, starting with prophetic thought. A prophet is someone who receives a message from God and then communicates it to a particular person or group. Prophecy occupies a central place in the Jewish and Christian traditions, with prophetic books comprising much of the Hebrew Bible. In the Old Testament, prophets often deliver messages that call for repentance and predict societal flourishing or destruction, depending on whether the audience heeds God's commands.[35] Though works of prophecy need not be apocalyptic – most prophetic books in the Old Testament are not – they can be. For example, the author of Revelation describes his words as prophecy inspired by the God of the prophets (Revelation 1:3, 22:6–7).[36] So prophetic and apocalyptic thought are not mutually exclusive, since authors of

---

[32] New Revised Standard Version.
[33] Wessinger, "Millennial Glossary," 720.
[34] For example, premillennialism claims that Christ will return before establishing his millennial kingdom, whereas postmillennialism claims that his return will follow this kingdom. See Craig Koester, *Revelation and the End of All Things* (Grand Rapids, MI: Eerdmans, 2001), 12–13.
[35] Deborah Rooke, "Prophecy," in *The Oxford Handbook of Biblical Studies*, ed. J. W. Rogerson and Judith Lieu (New York: Oxford University Press, 2008), 385–96.
[36] Collins, "Introduction: Towards the Morphology of a Genre," 269.

apocalyptic texts often understand themselves as part of the prophetic tradition.

Similarly, utopian thought is distinct from apocalyptic thought but overlaps with it in important ways. Utopia commonly is understood as referring to the best and most just society, which is the definition adopted here (at some points, utopia specifically will refer to the best and most just society *possible*).[37] Thomas More coined the term in 1516 with his book *Utopia*, and inspired a genre of literature – fictional accounts of ideal societies – that would flourish after its publication.[38] Yet the tradition of ideal theorizing long precedes More. Notably, he understands *Utopia* as continuing rather than inventing a tradition, evident in the book's claim that its account of the ideal society surpasses Plato's *Republic*.[39] Accounts of the ideal society also appear in ancient religious texts, including Jewish and Christian apocalyptic literature, which highlights the close links between apocalyptic and utopian thought.[40]

The last term requiring explanation is secular thought. One understanding avoided here is that such thought stands in contrast to modes of thought grounded in faith. According to this view, secular thought has its foundation in reason, science, and evidence, whereas beliefs relying on faith espouse a worldview colored by superstition and irrationality. Reliance on faith is a misleading criterion for distinguishing secular from religious thought, since all first principles are insusceptible to proof and require some level of faith. With regard to apocalyptic thought, what distinguishes secular and religious varieties of it is not the presence of faith, but rather its object. By placing its faith in God, religious apocalyptic thought looks toward divine intervention to realize utopia. Secular apocalyptic thought, on the other hand, places its faith in human forces, natural forces, or some combination of the two. It prioritizes earthly over heavenly ends, and emphasizes that it is up to human action – perhaps with help from nature – to advance history toward its intended end of the ideal society. In short, secular apocalyptic thought seeks to achieve the ideal without any room for divine intervention.

---

[37] For more on the different ways utopia has been understood, see Ruth Levitas, *The Concept of Utopia* (Syracuse, NY: Syracuse University Press, 1990).

[38] See Susan Bruce, ed., *Three Early Modern Utopias* (New York: Oxford University Press, 1999); Gregory Claeys, ed., *Utopias of the British Enlightenment* (New York: Cambridge University Press, 1994); and Frank Manuel and Fritzie Manuel, eds., *French Utopias: An Anthology of Ideal Societies* (New York: The Free Press, 1966).

[39] Thomas More, *Utopia*, trans. Paul Turner (New York: Penguin Books, 1965), 27, 33.

[40] See Eric Gilchrest, *Revelation 21–22 in Light of Jewish and Greco-Roman Utopianism* (Leiden: Brill, 2013).

WHAT'S TO COME

To summarize, this book makes three main arguments – one methodological, one interpretive, one normative.

(1) *Methodological argument:* The study of secular apocalyptic thought would place itself on firmer ground by focusing on cases where secular thinkers explicitly reference religious apocalyptic texts, figures, or concepts.
(2) *Interpretive argument:* Apocalyptic thought's political appeal partly lies in offering resources to navigate persistent challenges in ideal theory.
(3) *Normative argument:* Ideal theory and apocalyptic thought both rest on faith and are best suited to be sources of utopian hope, not guides for collective action by a society.

The book fleshes out these arguments over three parts. Part I (Chapters 1 and 2) closely analyzes the concept of secular apocalyptic thought, the challenges of studying it, and the paradox it poses. In popular culture and scholarship, apocalypse has taken on the expansive meaning of referring to any catastrophe. It is common to attribute religious influences to a text that may rely on nonreligious sources for its catastrophic language and imagery. Part I proposes a more rigorous approach. Specifically, the study of secular apocalyptic thought should restrict its focus to cases where it can offer evidence of secular thinkers explicitly referencing religious apocalyptic traditions. After outlining that methodological proposal, Part I turns to the question of why secular thinkers would find the Christian apocalyptic tradition appealing for politics, given its baggage and seemingly bizarre doctrines. The answer to this puzzle lies partly in apocalyptic thought's value to ideal theory. Apocalyptic thought, with its emphasis on crisis as the path to utopia, offers a vision for bringing the ideal society within reach.

Part II (Chapters 3, 4, and 5) puts into practice the methodological recommendation of Part I and presents three historical cases studies. These case studies feature thinkers with secular conceptions of politics who directly engage with Christian apocalyptic figures and texts. The first looks at how Machiavelli grapples with the appeal of Savonarola's apocalyptic message and its promise of an eternal republic, which helped foster a brief period of republican rule in Florence. Our attention then shifts to Hobbes, who confronts apocalyptic ideas during the English Civil War, as many looked for the arrival of Christ's kingdom in the midst of political strife. The final case study investigates Engels's interest in the book of Revelation and in the apocalyptic figure Müntzer as sources of insight into socialism's hopes and challenges.

These historical case studies reveal three strategies for responding to apocalyptic thought's idealism – rejecting, tempering, and embracing it – and reflect contrasting attitudes toward utopian hope.

Part III (Chapters 6 and 7) asks what insights the study of secular apocalyptic thought offers for current debates over ideal theory. Here I argue that political philosophy needs to rethink ideal theory's role. For figures like Rawls, ideal theory outlines a realistic utopia that individuals have reasonable grounds to accept and pursue. This idea of giving a plausible defense of ideal theory runs into insurmountable challenges, for it requires predictions about society that we cannot have confidence in, given uncertainty about the future. Ideal theory, if we choose to hang on to it, ultimately rests on faith and shares more in common with apocalyptic thought than political philosophy tends to admit. Some may embrace ideal theory for the utopian hope it offers, which gives meaning to the difficult and always incomplete work of advancing justice by linking it to a loftier goal. But this hope comes with risks, since those yearning for utopia sometimes try to force it into existence without true knowledge of how to achieve it. It is in addressing this danger, and emphasizing that utopian hope must be paired with epistemic humility, that the apocalyptic tradition proves to be a surprising source of wisdom for ideal theory today.

PART I
SECULAR APOCALYPTIC THOUGHT

1

The Hazards of Studying Secular Apocalyptic Thought

It is not uncommon for studies of apocalyptic thought to open with an apologetic tone. In his history of apocalyptic belief in America, *When Time Shall Be No More*, Paul Boyer starts by relating awkward encounters he had while researching the book. During his travels, Boyer's choice of reading material – popular prophecies on the rapture and Antichrist – would prompt strangers to share their predictions regarding the end times, as well as eagerly ask for his.[1] Such anecdotes reinforce the impression that the beliefs studied by scholars of apocalyptic thought are, well, a bit nutty. Some may wonder whether these beliefs are worth anyone's time. Sensing this skepticism, Boyer goes out of his way to offer a defense "for devoting so many pages to a belief system seemingly so marginal and fantastic."[2] Like Boyer, those who study apocalyptic ideas find that a hazard of their research is encountering friends and colleagues puzzled by why anyone would dedicate so much time to such a bizarre topic. Inevitably, there is skepticism to overcome in persuading others of the value of studying apocalyptic beliefs.

On that front, researchers appear to be having some success. Many disciplines – from theology to literary studies to political science – now take an interest in apocalyptic thought, and literature on the topic continues to proliferate. Apocalyptic thought's enduring influence in various secular and religious contexts, including politics, makes it difficult to dismiss as a fringe phenomenon unworthy of serious scholarship. With apocalypse seemingly everywhere, those who study it are finding audiences interested in their

---

[1] Paul Boyer, *When Time Shall Be No More: Prophecy Belief in Modern American Culture* (Cambridge, MA: Harvard University Press, 1992), 1, 11.
[2] Boyer, *When Time Shall Be No More*, 17. For a similar attempt to allay readers' skepticism, see Richard Landes, *Heaven on Earth: The Varieties of Millennial Experience* (New York: Oxford University Press, 2011), xiv.

research and its connection to contemporary challenges, such as terrorism and the threat of nuclear war.[3]

But though scholars are keen to counter skepticism about the value of studying apocalyptic thought, other hazards of their research receive less attention. In particular, there has been insufficient reflection on what methods and approaches are best for studying *secular* apocalyptic thought. The very nature of such thought poses a dilemma for researching it. On the one hand, secular apocalyptic thought departs in important ways from religious thought – after all, that is what makes it secular and distinct. On the other hand, calling secular thought "apocalyptic" implies that it retains some connection to the religious traditions that gave birth to apocalyptic ideas. These two aspects of secular apocalyptic thought exist in tension with one another and prompt the question: How strong of a connection must secular thought have with religious apocalyptic traditions for it to count as apocalyptic? When scholars fail to address this question, they end up with haphazard approaches that leave the concept of secular apocalyptic thought vague and ill defined.

More than a half century ago, two prominent theorists – Judith Shklar and Hans Blumenberg – recognized this danger.[4] They criticized the idea of secular apocalyptic thought for blurring important distinctions in the history of ideas. Rather than clarify, the concept too often functioned as a rhetorical weapon against certain ideologies. Unfortunately, the study of secular apocalyptic thought largely has proceeded as if these critiques were never raised. As a result, the concept of secular apocalyptic thought has become so expansive that it risks becoming a largely empty one with little value in tracing the development of different traditions of thought. Though there are potential strategies for overcoming Shklar's and Blumenberg's concerns, research on secular apocalyptic thought suffers so long as it ignores their critiques.

To better understand these critiques, this chapter first examines the context in which they arose. It specifically looks at some of the early pioneers who studied secular apocalyptic thought, such as Eric Voegelin, Karl Löwith, and Norman Cohn. They all took an interest in the topic during the mid-twentieth century, at a time when potent political ideologies like communism and

---

[3] See, e.g., Zack Beauchamp, "ISIS Is Really Obsessed with the Apocalypse," *Vox*, April 6, 2015, www.vox.com/2015/4/6/8341691/isis-apocalypse; and Alison McQueen, "How to Be a Prophet of Doom," *New York Times*, May 11, 2018, www.nytimes.com/2018/05/11/opinion/nuclear-doomsday-denial.html.

[4] Judith Shklar, "The Political Theory of Utopia: From Melancholy to Nostalgia," *Daedalus* 94, no. 2 (1965): 367–81; and Hans Blumenberg, *The Legitimacy of the Modern Age*, trans. Robert Wallace (Cambridge, MA: MIT Press, 1983).

Nazism prompted growing fears that apocalyptic aspirations were invading politics. For many, this research captured the disruptive political forces at the time, but it also prompted critiques from Shklar and Blumenberg. After discussing these early studies and criticisms of them, the chapter turns to more recent treatments of secular apocalyptic thought. Studies today often fall victim to the very problems Shklar and Blumenberg identify: reading into texts apocalyptic themes that are not there and using the concept as a rhetorical weapon. To address these concerns, the chapter concludes with a modest proposal. Despite its current shortcomings, research on secular apocalyptic thought has the opportunity to put itself on more solid ground. It can do so by limiting its focus to cases where religious apocalyptic thought's influence on secular thinkers is clear because they *explicitly* mention such thought and its appeal. In this way, research can avoid much of the speculation that currently leaves it vulnerable to criticism.

EARLY PIONEERS

Today there is clear interest in secular apocalyptic thought. That is evident in the three-volume *Encyclopedia of Apocalypticism*, which dedicates six of its forty-three articles to the topic "Secularization of Apocalypticism."[5] Current research on secular apocalyptic thought builds on a longer tradition going back at least to the first half of the twentieth century. There one finds burgeoning interest in secular apocalyptic thought, not coincidentally after the rise of communism and National Socialism. As these movements emerged, a number of scholars identified what they saw as apocalyptic hopes bursting into politics and taking secular form.

One of the first thinkers to bring attention to secular apocalyptic thought during this period is Voegelin. In *The Political Religions* – published in Vienna in 1938, the year Nazi Germany invaded Austria – Voegelin points to the secularization of religion, and particularly apocalyptic thought, as part of the appeal of fascist and totalitarian regimes. Apocalyptic thought helps satisfy people's desire for perfection and transcendence. When religion loses its hold, Voegelin argues, political ideologies step into the void as a source of meaning. The apocalyptic symbolism of the Middle Ages, which envisioned a perfect empire on the horizon, "lives on in the symbolism of the nineteenth and twentieth centuries: in ... Marx and Engels's philosophy of history, in the

---

[5] John Collins, Bernard McGinn, and Stephen Stein, eds., *The Encyclopedia of Apocalypticism* (New York: Continuum, 1998).

Third Reich of National Socialism, and in the fascist third Rome."[6] For Voegelin, apocalyptic thought takes secular form and, in the process, unleashes disruptive effects on politics.

A decade later, Löwith in his influential work *Meaning in History* draws a connection between apocalyptic thought and modern conceptions of history and politics. For many, Löwith's analysis hits closer to home because he sees apocalyptic thought's influence not only in fascist and communist ideologies but also in the widespread faith in human progress. Löwith makes the bold claim that a concept central to modernity, progress, has its roots in Jewish and Christian eschatology: "We of today, concerned with the unity of universal history and with its progress toward an ultimate goal or at least toward a 'better world,' are still in the line of prophetic and messianic monotheism; we are still Jews and Christians, however little we may think of ourselves in those terms."[7] According to Löwith, Jewish and Christian thought's conception of linear time moving toward an ideal end grounds modern understandings of history. The secularization of apocalyptic thought produces the widely held belief in human progress, while leaving many unaware of its religious heritage.

Cohn's 1957 classic *Pursuit of the Millennium* also contributed to heightened interest in secular apocalyptic thought in the mid-twentieth century. The study focuses on medieval apocalyptic sects and the chaos they caused. Cohn ends it, though, by noting similarities between these sects and revolutionary movements such as communism. Like apocalyptic sects of old, modern revolutionaries are motivated by "phantasies of a final, exterminatory struggle against 'the great ones'; and of a perfect world from which self-seeking would be for ever banished." Cohn continues: "The old religious idiom has been replaced by a secular one, and this tends to obscure what otherwise would be obvious. For it is the simple truth that, stripped of their original supernatural sanction, revolutionary millenarianism and mystical anarchism are with us still."[8] So after detailing the death and destruction perpetrated by past apocalyptic sects and the sad ends they met, Cohn closes with a somber warning – similar threats remain with us today. His history serves as a cautionary tale of the dangers society faces when apocalyptic sects flourish.

Together, Voegelin, Löwith, and Cohn represent an earlier generation of researchers who brought attention to how apocalyptic thought becomes

---

[6] Eric Voegelin, *The Political Religions*, trans. Virginia Ann Schildhauer, in *Modernity without Restraint*, The Collected Works of Eric Voegelin, vol. 5, ed. Manfred Henningsen (Columbia, MO: University of Missouri, 2000), 52.
[7] Karl Löwith, *Meaning in History* (Chicago: Chicago University Press, 1949), 19.
[8] Norman Cohn, *The Pursuit of the Millennium: Revolutionary Millenarians and Mystical Anarchists of the Middle Ages*, rev. ed. (New York: Oxford University Press, 1970), 286.

secular and its continued influence in the modern world. But though some greeted their research with enthusiasm, it also had its critics, which we turn to next.

NEGLECTED CRITIQUES

Early researchers of secular apocalyptic thought made bold and sweeping claims about its impact. They argued that some of the most influential and disruptive forces of the twentieth century – communism and National Socialism – had apocalyptic beliefs at their core. The 1960s, though, produced two important critiques that pushed back on these claims and cast doubt on whether secular apocalyptic thought even made sense as a conceptual tool for political theorists.

The first critique comes from Shklar's 1965 essay "The Political Theory of Utopia." Here she makes the case for emphasizing distinctions rather than continuities between political ideologies and apocalyptic thought. She writes: "It has of late been suggested that the radicalism of the last century was a form of 'messianism,' of 'millennialism,' or of a transplanted eschatological consciousness." Shklar resists this claim on the grounds that political movements like communism do not make promises of eternal salvation, which for her is an essential element of millennialism.[9] She thus concludes:

> Neither the view of history as a dualistic combat of impersonal social forces nor the confident belief in a better future which would at last bring rest to mankind was a "millennial" fancy, nor was either really akin to the chiliastic religious visions that inspired ... apocalyptic sects .... The desire to stress similarities, to find continuities everywhere, is not always helpful, especially in the history of ideas, where the drawing of distinctions is apt to lead one more nearly to the truth.[10]

Looking for connections between religious apocalyptic thought and secular political movements strikes Shklar as misguided – an approach liable to lead theorists astray by pushing them to make spurious links among very different traditions of thought. Her argument implies that political theorists might be better off abandoning the concept of secular apocalyptic thought altogether.

Blumenberg raises similar concerns in his book *The Legitimacy of the Modern Age*, first published in 1966. Part I focuses on the ever-growing list of features of modernity that purportedly reflect the secularization of theological

---

[9] Shklar, "The Political Theory of Utopia," 376.
[10] Shklar, "The Political Theory of Utopia," 377.

concepts. Blumenberg criticizes the loose way in which theorists apply the idea of secularization. As scholars continue to draw one tenuous connection after another, the result in his words is "secularization 'run wild.'"[11]

One of the many examples that Blumenberg objects to is the "fashionable pastime to interpret expectations of political redemption, like those typified by the *Communist Manifesto*, as secularizations either of the biblical paradise or of apocalyptic messianism."[12] In particular, Blumenberg takes issue with Löwith's characterization of the modern idea of progress as being a vestige of Jewish and Christian eschatology. According to Blumenberg, Löwith overlooks critical distinctions among different traditions of thought: "It is a formal, but for that very reason a manifest, difference that an eschatology speaks of an event breaking into history, an event that transcends and is heterogeneous to it, while the idea of progress extrapolates from a structure present in every moment to a future that is immanent in history."[13] For Blumenberg, Christian eschatology presents a dramatically different vision for the future – marked by abrupt supernatural intervention – than that offered by the idea of progress, which envisions the gradual perfecting of what is already present.[14]

In addition to sharing Shklar's concern that the concept of secular apocalyptic thought blurs important distinctions, Blumenberg makes the further critique that it often serves as a rhetorical weapon. Secularization, he writes, is among "the weapons with which the legitimacy of the modern age is attacked."[15] This line of attack argues that modern ideologies and political traditions are the "inauthentic manifestation" of religious beliefs. Though indebted to these beliefs, modernity purposefully avoids acknowledging them. That charge leaves modern political ideologies with a taint of illegitimacy that they have difficulty escaping.[16] The label "apocalyptic" undermines the legitimacy of modern ideologies by associating them with bizarre and seemingly irrational beliefs. Blumenberg worries that many claims about secularization, while popular ways to express discontent over the present, ultimately provide a misleading account of the relation between religious concepts and modern thought.[17]

---

[11] Blumenberg, *The Legitimacy of the Modern Age*, 15.
[12] Blumenberg, *The Legitimacy of the Modern Age*, 14–15.
[13] Blumenberg, *The Legitimacy of the Modern Age*, 30.
[14] Not all scholars of eschatology would agree with this distinction by Blumenberg. See Ernest Tuveson, *Millennium and Utopia: A Study in the Background of the Idea of Progress*, (Berkeley, CA: University of California Press, 1949); and Theodore Olson, *Millennialism, Utopianism, and Progress* (Toronto: University of Toronto Press, 1982).
[15] Blumenberg, *The Legitimacy of the Modern Age*, 125.
[16] Blumenberg, *The Legitimacy of the Modern Age*, 18.
[17] Blumenberg, *The Legitimacy of the Modern Age*, 118–19.

To summarize, Shklar and Blumenberg level two criticisms against the concept of secular apocalyptic thought: (1) it blurs important distinctions in the history of ideas and (2) it functions more as a rhetorical weapon against modern ideologies than as a device for clarifying their development. Their critiques identify potential dangers that can undermine the study of apocalyptic thought. To ensure the credibility of their research, scholars of secular apocalyptic thought have good reasons to address these concerns. But in practice, they rarely do. As the next section discusses, too often studies repeat the errors Shklar and Blumenberg warned against.

APOCALYPSE WITHOUT BOUNDS

In his wide-ranging study *Heaven on Earth*, Richard Landes uses the term "semiotic arousal" to describe how many with apocalyptic beliefs interpret the world. Their anticipation of the apocalypse colors everything they see. Developments near and far reinforce one another as further evidence of the coming apocalypse. Even events with little ostensible connection to the end times – at least from an outsider's perspective – take on significance for believers.[18] In short, those anxiously looking for the apocalypse can find traces of it wherever they turn.

What Landes fails to add is that those holding apocalyptic beliefs are not the only ones in a state of semiotic arousal. That description also seems apt for many scholars on the lookout for apocalyptic thought. Primed to see apocalyptic influences, they claim to find them in all sorts of unanticipated contexts. From their perspective, apocalyptic thought not only migrates into secular contexts but also pervades them. Such heightened interest among scholars has the benefit of bringing to light examples of secular apocalyptic thought previously overlooked. But it also runs the risk of drawing tenuous connections and making questionable claims about the far-reaching influence of apocalyptic thought.

Vague and overly broad conceptions of apocalyptic thought by their very nature give the impression that it is everywhere. Some scholars raise this concern, especially as more disciplines outside theology and religious studies take an interest in apocalyptic thought. "Millennialism has perhaps appeared ubiquitous," notes church historian James Moorhead, "because scholars have been reluctant to explain precisely what they mean by the term."[19] Rather than

---

[18] Landes, *Heaven on Earth*, 14.
[19] James Moorhead, "Searching for the Millennium in America," *Princeton Seminary Bulletin* 8, no. 2 (1987): 22.

provide clear criteria for what constitutes millennialism or apocalyptic thought, the trend has been to multiply their meanings. Literary critic Frank Kermode goes so far as to equate apocalypse with any sort of ending.[20] Armed with such an expansive understanding of the apocalypse, scholars can find traces of it in just about any narrative.

Indeed, it is common for scholars to adopt understandings of apocalypse that stretch its meaning. Consider Alison McQueen's recent study *Political Realism in Apocalyptic Times*. In it she focuses on what she calls the "apocalyptic imaginary." The apocalypse is best understood as an imaginary, according to McQueen, because it emphasizes that the concept is more than just an ancient genre of literature. It persists today in images, narratives, and sets of meanings that influence how people interpret their world.[21]

On its face, that approach makes sense. Apocalyptic ideas take various forms today and are not just confined to ancient religious texts. It is important to note, though, that McQueen's characterization of apocalypse as an imaginary lowers the bar for identifying apocalyptic thought and its influence. She cautions against limiting "ourselves to overtly scriptural expression" of apocalyptic ideas when tracing their "trajectories ... in the works of modern and purportedly secular thinkers."[22] Because its influence often operates in insidious ways, the apocalyptic imaginary "rarely rises into complete awareness by those who draw upon its resources."[23] It thus can "resonate for people with no knowledge" of apocalyptic texts like "Daniel and Revelation" in the Bible.[24]

As with all ideas and images, those derived from the apocalyptic tradition certainly can influence people in unconscious ways. But in such cases, if even the person being influenced is not aware of it, one wonders how often later interpreters will be in a better position to make that determination. More generally, in cases where individuals make no explicit reference to apocalyptic texts or figures, it can be difficult to know with any certainty whether they are in fact drawing on those sources. After all, imagery in non-apocalyptic sources – say, accounts of war – can resemble imagery in apocalyptic literature, which creates obstacles to knowing whether the former, the latter, or both influence a particular text.

---

[20] Frank Kermode, *The Sense of an Ending: Studies in the Theory of Fiction* (New York: Oxford University Press, 2000). See also Paul Corcoran, *Awaiting Apocalypse* (New York: St. Martin's Press, 2000).
[21] Alison McQueen, *Political Realism in Apocalyptic Times* (New York: Cambridge University Press, 2018), 51–62.
[22] McQueen, *Political Realism in Apocalyptic Times*, 19.
[23] McQueen, *Political Realism in Apocalyptic Times*, 56.
[24] McQueen, *Political Realism in Apocalyptic Times*, 52.

Ultimately, these obstacles do not deter McQueen and others from identifying apocalyptic thought in the midst of ambiguous evidence. Their approach certainly broadens the scope for potential research on secular apocalyptic thought, but also leaves itself vulnerable to criticisms that it relies on questionable and spurious claims.

An example from McQueen's study illustrates this point. To show apocalyptic thought's influence in politics today, McQueen points to President George W. Bush's speech announcing military strikes in Afghanistan after the September 11 attacks. In the speech Bush says: "Initially, the terrorists may burrow deeper into caves and other entrenched hiding places. Our military action is also designed to clear the way for sustained, comprehensive and relentless operations to drive them out and bring them to justice."[25] McQueen sees in this statement coded references to Revelation 6:15–17, which speaks of God's wrath against the unrighteous at the end of time:

> Then the kings of the earth and the magnates and the generals and the rich and the powerful, and everyone, slave and free, hid in the caves and among the rocks of the mountains, calling to the mountains and rocks, "Fall on us and hide us from the face of the one seated on the throne and from the wrath of the Lamb; for the great day of their wrath has come, and who is able to stand?"[26]

McQueen recognizes that the "apocalyptic undertones of Bush's speeches may not be ... obvious," but stresses that "they are there for those able and willing to hear them."[27]

This interpretation by McQueen revives an earlier one by Bruce Lincoln from his book *Holy Terrors*. Lincoln shares McQueen's confidence that there are references to Revelation 6:15–17 in Bush's speech, which are "plainly audible" to those familiar with the Bible's apocalyptic texts.[28] In fact, despite no explicit references to scripture, Bush's short speech contains several biblical references according to Lincoln. He also points to one phrase Bush uses for terrorists – "killers of innocents" – as "surely gestur[ing] toward Herod's slaughter of the innocents in Matthew 2."[29] Stories of the killing of innocent people are virtually endless throughout history. Lincoln, though, is

---

[25] George W. Bush, "Appendix B: George W. Bush, Address to the Nation, October 7, 2001," in Bruce Lincoln, *Holy Terrors: Thinking about Religion after September 11* (Chicago: Chicago University Press, 2003), 99.
[26] New Revised Standard Version.
[27] McQueen, *Political Realism in Apocalyptic Times*, 4.
[28] Bruce Lincoln, *Holy Terrors: Thinking about Religion after September 11* (Chicago: Chicago University Press, 2003), 30.
[29] Lincoln, *Holy Terrors*, 31.

certain that these three words by Bush indicate that he had Herod on his mind when announcing military action against the Taliban.

It is safe to say that these alleged biblical and apocalyptic references in Bush's speech would come as a surprise to most Americans who watched or read it. Even for many familiar with Christian apocalyptic beliefs, the phrase Lincoln and McQueen focus on – "terrorists may burrow deeper into caves" – fails to register as apocalyptic imagery. After all, the caves mentioned in Revelation 6:15–17 are by no means one of the images most commonly associated with apocalyptic thought. Revelation's images of plagues, two beasts, and Christ's millennial kingdom are far more distinctive and better suited for bringing to mind apocalyptic hopes and fears. Bush's speech lacks such imagery. The most straightforward interpretation of the cave reference is that, rather than convey some deep apocalyptic meaning, it merely emphasizes that the Taliban's practice of hiding in caves will be futile against American military might.

Perhaps Bush and his advisors purposefully chose subtle imagery so that they could plausibly deny charges of apocalyptic influences in the speech, while still speaking to fundamentalist supporters. Politicians do sometimes employ subtle messages that speak to portions of their base while aiming to avoid the attention of others. In some cases, we can be pretty sure that hidden motivations were at work because the architects of the ads and speeches later say so.[30] In other cases, it is easy to recognize, say, racist dog whistles because they appear in a long-standing pattern of speech that includes less subtle messages (e.g., the demonization of certain racial and ethnic groups).[31] Such explicit admissions and patterns provide compelling evidence to confirm suspicions about the presence of coded messages in political speech.

Lincoln and McQueen, however, offer no evidence along these lines. When the apocalypse is understood as an imaginary, the discovery of any phrase or image resembling those in apocalyptic texts can become the basis for making claims about apocalyptic influences in politics. Sometimes there may be truth to these claims. Perhaps Bush really did draw on Revelation in his speech announcing military action. But it is hard to have confidence in that claim – other interpretations of the speech seem just as plausible, if not more so. By focusing on ambiguous imagery rather than more explicit

[30] See, e.g., Rick Perlstein, "Exclusive: Lee Atwater's Infamous 1981 Interview on the Southern Strategy," *The Nation*, November 13, 2012, www.thenation.com/article/exclusive-lee-atwaters-infamous-1981-interview-southern-strategy/.

[31] See, e.g., Karen Grigsby Bates, "'Rapists,' 'Huts': Trump's Racist Dog Whistles Aren't New," NPR, January 13, 2018, www.npr.org/sections/codeswitch/2018/01/13/577674607/rapists-huts-shitholes-trumps-racist-dog-whistles-arent-new.

references, Lincoln and McQueen advance claims about apocalyptic thought's role in politics with only tenuous evidence to back them up.

This approach to studying apocalyptic thought often takes a polemical tone, as in John Gray's *Black Mass: Apocalyptic Religion and the Death of Utopia*. There Gray mounts a wide-ranging critique of utopian projects in politics, while wielding the concept of apocalyptic thought as a rhetorical weapon. In particular, his book illustrates how motivations to discredit certain ideological views can lead to expansive claims about apocalyptic thought's influence in politics.

Gray takes aim at a diverse array of historical and contemporary targets: Jacobins, Bolsheviks, Nazis, Islamic terrorists, neoconservatives, and just about any prominent supporter of the Iraq War. In his view, all these groups suffer from deluded and destructive utopian hopes. When faced with the reality that their impossible visions for politics cannot be realized, these groups resort to violence in a futile effort to realize utopia by force. Gray specifically sees apocalyptic beliefs as playing "a central role in state terror from the Jacobins through the Bolsheviks and the Nazis."[32] Now in the forms of neoconservatism and Islamic terrorism, "apocalyptic religion has re-emerged, naked and unadorned, as a force in world politics."[33]

It certainly is possible that apocalyptic ideas are present in many of the ideologies singled out by Gray. But it often takes little evidence for Gray to reach sweeping generalizations about apocalyptic thought's role in politics. As a case in point, he approvingly cites Lincoln's interpretation of Bush's speech announcing military strikes in Afghanistan as evidence of apocalyptic influences in the war on terror.[34] Highlighting such examples in his brisk tour of modern ideologies, Gray sees apocalyptic beliefs as a potent force wherever he turns. In one of his more hyperbolic remarks, he writes: "If a simple definition of western civilization could be formulated it would have to be framed in terms of the central role of millenarian thinking."[35] Clearly no fan of apocalyptic beliefs, Gray is more than ready to attribute their influence to everything he finds wrong with politics today.

Together, these studies highlight that current approaches to secular apocalyptic thought often involve expansive understandings of it. First, many lower the bar for what counts as secular apocalyptic thought. Any imagery loosely resembling that found in religious apocalyptic texts can count as apocalyptic

---

[32] John Gray, *Black Mass: Apocalyptic Religion and the Death of Utopia* (New York: Farrar, Straus and Giroux, 2007), 176–77.
[33] Gray, *Black Mass*, 3.
[34] Gray, *Black Mass*, 115.
[35] Gray, *Black Mass*, 6.

thought in secular form, even when the imagery appears in a context with no explicit religious references and there are other plausible explanations for it. Second, the desire to undermine the legitimacy of certain ideologies leads some to see secular apocalyptic thought everywhere in politics. Calling a secular ideology apocalyptic taints it by association. Shklar and Blumenberg identify both these moves as pitfalls common to the study of secular apocalyptic thought. The following section explores why these approaches prove so problematic.

PROBLEMS WITH CURRENT APPROACHES

Though critics like Shklar and Blumenberg have concerns with expansive understandings of apocalyptic thought, some may push back and attribute their concerns to a matter of taste. One way to categorize historians (as well as scholars in other fields) speaks to this difference in taste: some are "splitters," others "lumpers." Splitters look for opportunities to draw distinctions among different thinkers and traditions of thought, whereas lumpers look for opportunities to make connections.[36] Historical evidence is often ambiguous, and when scholars encounter it, some lean toward lumping ideas together while others have the opposite inclination. For whatever reason, many lumpers find their way into the study of secular apocalyptic thought, and their style may not be to everyone's taste. Understandably, some may be skeptical of methodological critiques of lumpers and see them as merely reflecting a difference in taste.

I hope to overcome that skepticism and show how expansive understandings of secular apocalyptic thought mislead. When secular texts contain imagery similar to that found in religious apocalyptic texts, many treat it as evidence of apocalyptic thought in secular form. That conclusion, though, rests on a flawed argument:

(1) If a religious apocalyptic tradition influenced a secular text – whether directly or indirectly, consciously or unconsciously – the text will use images or language resembling those found in that tradition (e.g., images of catastrophe).
(2) A secular text uses images or language resembling those found in a religious apocalyptic tradition (e.g., images of catastrophe).
(3) Therefore, a religious apocalyptic tradition influenced the secular text in question.

---

[36] J. H. Hexter, "The Burden of Proof," *Times Literary Supplement* 3841 (1975): 1251–52.

The problem, of course, is that this conclusion does not follow from its premises. The argument commits a common fallacy known as affirming the consequent. An example is someone who says that, if it rains, their neighbor's driveway will get wet, and when they see that their neighbor's driveway is wet, they conclude it must have rained. Perhaps it rained, but it could also be the case that there's not a cloud in the sky and the driveway is wet from a sprinkler.

Similarly, just because a text uses catastrophic images does not mean that apocalyptic influences are at work. After all, the apocalyptic tradition that emerged from religious belief has no monopoly on catastrophe. Fears of wide-scale catastrophe are common throughout human history, and it is easy to experience such fears absent direct or indirect contact with religious apocalyptic traditions. Histories of war, for instance, can inspire a writer to use catastrophic imagery. For this reason, simply looking for the apocalyptic imaginary, as McQueen calls it, sets an insufficiently low bar for identifying secular apocalyptic thought.

McQueen's discussion of apocalyptic influences in Thomas Hobbes's political thought illustrates how this approach can result in questionable claims. During the English Civil War when Hobbes wrote, clergy, scholars, soldiers, and government officials often drew on Christian apocalyptic texts as a lens to understand the political upheaval around them. Hobbes finds many faults with these interpretations, especially when they use apocalyptic belief to justify rebellion.[37] McQueen argues that, to counter apocalyptic prophecies, Hobbes adopts a strategy where he "fights apocalypse *with apocalypse*."[38] In her view, Hobbes specifically carries out this strategy through his imagery of the state of nature and the state that emerges in its place, described as a powerful Leviathan that keeps violence at bay.

Famously in *Leviathan*, Hobbes describes life outside of government as "solitary, poore, nasty, brutish, and short,"[39] and uses this dismal portrait of the state of nature to motivate obedience to the civil sovereign. McQueen sees in this political argument the staging of "a secular apocalypse, in which the terror and chaos of the state of nature are the narrative prelude to an enduring commonwealth ruled by a mortal God." She then adds: "Hobbes does not reject the apocalyptic imaginary. He redirects it."[40] McQueen goes further than just pointing out similar imagery in Hobbes's writings and Christian apocalyptic texts. She makes the stronger claim that Hobbes draws on

---

[37] See Chapter 4.
[38] McQueen, *Political Realism in Apocalyptic Times*, 14.
[39] Thomas Hobbes, *Leviathan*, ed. Noel Malcolm (New York: Oxford University Press, 2012), XIII: 192.
[40] McQueen, *Political Realism in Apocalyptic Times*, 106.

apocalyptic thought when formulating his description of the state of nature: "Both the imagery and narrative structure of [Hobbes's] secular political argument appropriate elements of the seventeenth-century English apocalyptic imaginary."[41]

What evidence, though, is there that apocalyptic influences contribute to Hobbes's account of the state of nature? In his various descriptions of the state of nature – in *The Elements of Law*, *De Cive*, and *Leviathan* – he never directly references Christian apocalyptic texts, contemporary interpretations of these texts, or distinct concepts from these texts.[42] Moreover, Hobbes explicitly names several sources for his understanding of the state of nature, all of which fall *outside* the apocalyptic tradition. Conditions resembling the state of nature, according to Hobbes, characterize how "savage" peoples in America live and how "inhabitants of Germany and other now civil countries" used to live.[43] In addition, the Latin *Leviathan* mentions the Genesis story of Cain's killing Abel to illustrate the anarchic violence characterizing the state of nature.[44] So Hobbes does not leave his readers in the dark as to the sources that influence his thinking about the state of nature.[45] This textual evidence undermines rather than strengthens the claim that apocalyptic influences play a central role in Hobbes's account of the state of nature.

Of course, there could be influences Hobbes fails to mention. Even so, it is far from clear that apocalyptic thought stands out as the most likely source for the catastrophic imagery in Hobbes's state of nature. Though apocalyptic texts often include catastrophic imagery, other texts do, too. Accounts of war and their devastating effects provide rich resources for theorizing about catastrophe. Notably, Hobbes uses the term "war" to characterize conditions in the state of nature.[46] Given this evidence, Hobbes very well could have had in mind accounts of war, not the Christian apocalyptic tradition, when developing the catastrophic imagery in his state of nature.

---

[41] McQueen, *Political Realism in Apocalyptic Times*, 145.
[42] Hobbes, *The Elements of Law*, ed. Ferdinand Tönnies (Cambridge: Cambridge University Press, 1928), I.14; *On the Citizen*, ed. and trans. Richard Tuck and Michael Silverthorne (New York: Cambridge University Press, 1998), I; and *Leviathan*, XIII.
[43] Hobbes, *The Elements of Law*, I.14.12. See also Hobbes *On the Citizen*, I.13; and *Leviathan*, XIII: 194.
[44] Hobbes, *Leviathan*, XIII: 194–95.
[45] For more on the sources for Hobbes's accounts of the state of nature, see Ioannis Evrigenis, *Images of Anarchy: The Rhetoric and Science in Hobbes's State of Nature* (New York: Cambridge University Press, 2014).
[46] Hobbes, *The Elements of Law*, I.14.11; *On the Citizen*, I.12; and *Leviathan*, XIII: 192.

McQueen notes that Hobbes translated Thucydides's *History of the Peloponnesian War*,[47] and that it "provided him with a rhetorical and visual vocabulary with which to both imagine and describe an apocalyptic moment of uncreation."[48] This history certainly offers vivid accounts of catastrophe. Yet it fails to qualify as an apocalyptic text like Daniel or Revelation. Hobbes's deep familiarity with texts like the *History of the Peloponnesian War* points to resources outside the apocalyptic tradition that could have shaped his vision of the state of nature.

Since it is impossible to know the full scope of influences left unmentioned by Hobbes, it could be the case that the apocalyptic tradition informed his account of the state of nature. Hobbes does explicitly reference apocalyptic concepts and texts in his writings.[49] But the specific claim that his description of the state of nature draws on apocalyptic thought is highly speculative, resting on a vague resemblance between imagery in Hobbes's writings and imagery in the Christian apocalyptic tradition. And that is the problem with expansive understandings of secular apocalyptic thought: they treat mere speculation with greater certainty than it deserves. The root of this problem goes back to the low bar used by many to identify secular apocalyptic thought. If a text contains any imagery reminiscent of the apocalyptic tradition – say, it describes some catastrophe – that suffices as evidence that apocalyptic influences are at work.

Such loose criteria are ill-suited to meaningfully check the inevitable biases that affect scholars when studying secular apocalyptic thought. A longstanding methodological concern in the history of ideas is that scholars, when looking for a concept, read it into historical texts. They interpret any ambiguous evidence as confirmation of what they are looking for.[50] Confirmation bias gets the best of them and too often they fail to seriously consider alternative explanations. In the case of research on secular apocalyptic thought, additional motivations exacerbate that risk, as some use the label apocalyptic to undermine political ideologies they dislike. Such motivations, combined with lax evidentiary standards, lead to understandings of secular apocalyptic thought so broad that a clever interpreter can find it just about anywhere they want.

---

[47] See Thucydides, *The History of the Grecian War*, trans. Thomas Hobbes, in *The English Works of Thomas Hobbes of Malmesbury*, vol. 8–9, ed. William Molesworth (London: John Bohn, 1843).

[48] McQueen, *Political Realism in Apocalyptic Times*, 135.

[49] See Chapter 4.

[50] See Quentin Skinner, "Meaning and Understanding in the History of Ideas," *History and Theory* 8, no. 1 (1969): 3–53.

Tackling this problem is no easy task. Confirmation bias is well documented and no one is immune to it.[51] Given its pervasive and stubborn nature, scholars are unlikely to ever fully avoid it. So they have to be on constant guard against confirmation bias and adopt strategies to minimize it. More rigorous criteria can advance that goal – such as requiring explicit references to religious apocalyptic traditions when looking for secular transformations of them. By relying on less ambiguous evidence, such an approach has the potential to limit opportunities for confirmation bias to influence interpretive decisions, as the following section explains.

A MODEST PROPOSAL

Shklar and Blumenberg raise legitimate concerns about the study of secular apocalyptic thought. Overly broad conceptions of such thought do mislead by blurring important distinctions. But though Shklar and Blumenberg identify real problems with the study of secular apocalyptic thought, their critiques do not necessarily doom it.

In fact, it is difficult to fully abandon the idea of secular apocalyptic thought. Too many thinkers with secular theories of politics directly reference religious apocalyptic texts, figures, or concepts while finding aspects of them appealing. Part II of this book focuses on such cases. For instance, Friedrich Engels praises Thomas Müntzer – a Christian apocalyptic figure from the Reformation – and interprets his vision of the kingdom of God as a communist ideal. The appreciation that an atheist like Engels has for Christian apocalyptic thought makes clear that it can offer resources for secular theories of politics. In light of such examples, it would be a mistake to dismiss secular apocalyptic thought as a confused concept. Studying these examples offers insight into why the apocalyptic tradition proves to be a persistent force in politics.

Given that apocalyptic thought clearly does influence some secular thinkers, the question then becomes how best to study it. My modest proposal is for a more focused approach that reins in some of the more ambitious claims about apocalyptic thought's influence. By trying to find apocalyptic influences everywhere, scholars often end up making shaky arguments vulnerable to criticism. I suggest instead the following alternative: to focus on cases where secular thinkers *explicitly* mention religious apocalyptic texts, figures, or concepts, so that the link between secular thought and the apocalyptic tradition is clear.

---

[51] See Raymond Nickerson, "Confirmation Bias: A Ubiquitous Phenomenon in Many Guises," *Review of General Psychology* 2, no. 2 (1998): 175–220.

This approach studies secular apocalyptic thought in a way sensitive to the critiques raised by Shklar and Blumenberg. Since explicit references to apocalyptic thought are necessary to make claims about its influence, there is no place for speculative claims based, say, solely on a text's remark about catastrophe. By raising the level of evidence needed to make claims about secular apocalyptic thought, this proposal limits opportunities for reading apocalyptic influences into a text based on ambiguous evidence (e.g., the cave remark in Bush's speech after September 11). Such constraints help check confirmation bias, a risk that scholars inevitably face when searching for secular apocalyptic thought in historical and contemporary texts.

Some might raise the following objection: this chapter's proposal addresses one error only to heighten the risk of another. By raising the standard of evidence required, the proposal reduces the risk of a false positive – claiming to find apocalyptic influences that are not there. Yet this higher bar increases the risk of false negatives – not detecting apocalyptic influences because the evidence required is lacking. Certainly, some thinkers draw on apocalyptic thought without directly recognizing their debt to it. Isn't it important not to overlook such examples?

Admittedly, the proposal suggested here limits the scope of cases that clearly count as secular apocalyptic thought. But in excluding cases that do not explicitly reference religious apocalyptic thought, this proposal does not mean to imply that apocalyptic influences are necessarily absent from such cases. It rather says that we cannot know. In these cases, scholars can note similarities between imagery found in secular and apocalyptic texts. Yet they should be careful to avoid concluding that the latter influenced the former. That claim would go beyond the available evidence. A key to ensuring the credibility of research is being frank about its limitations. Unfortunately, some of the more ambitious claims about secular apocalyptic thought overlook the limitations of available evidence, which undermines their credibility.

The negative connotations often associated with apocalyptic thought give scholars further reason to avoid applying this label to political thinkers and texts unless they have strong evidence of its influence. As Blumenberg points out, many claims about secular apocalyptic thought have the effect of casting doubt on the legitimacy of political beliefs. Since calling political thought apocalyptic can leave the impression that it is bizarre and irrational – even if that is not one's intention – it is irresponsible to use that label loosely. Doing so risks damaging others' reputation as a result of claims based on mere speculation. Scholars need stronger evidence before making claims about secular apocalyptic thought.

What follows in the text is an attempt to put into practice this modest proposal for studying secular apocalyptic thought. In particular, Part II adopts this approach as a guide for selecting cases that illustrate how apocalyptic thought makes its way into politics and takes secular form. But before turning to specific case studies, we first will try to understand more generally what draws secular thinkers to apocalyptic thought.

2

The Paradox of Secular Apocalyptic Thought

Christianity's apocalyptic doctrines strike many – believers and nonbelievers alike – as its most bizarre elements. Despite apocalyptic doctrines' presence in the Christian canon, there is a tendency to minimize their importance, which stretches all the way back to the early church. In the fifth century, the Church Father Augustine urged an allegorical interpretation of Revelation and criticized predictions of Christ's imminent return to establish a millennial kingdom.[1] Today, many churches rarely include passages from Revelation in their services, evident from the book's scant presence in the lectionary.[2] As Glenn Tinder puts it, the Bible's apocalyptic themes are among the "most outworn vestments of religious faith."[3]

Yet attempts to suppress apocalyptic thought's influence never wholly succeeded. Apocalyptic prophecies and themes continue to emerge and impact various spheres of life, including politics. Part of apocalyptic thought's potency in politics stems from its ability to migrate beyond the confines of religion and take on new, secular forms – a somewhat puzzling development. If many Christians are embarrassed by their faith's apocalyptic heritage, why would thinkers hostile or agnostic toward Christianity find in its apocalyptic doctrines appealing tools for interpreting politics?

This chapter aims to unpack that puzzle. A helpful approach for understanding apocalyptic thought's appeal in politics is the lens of ideal theory – commonly understood as theorizing about the best, most just society, rather than just a marginal improvement over the present.[4] When ideal theory aspires to have navigational value and be a moral guide to action, it faces a daunting

---

[1] Augustine, *City of God*, trans. Henry Bettenson (New York: Penguin Books, 1984), esp. XX.7, XX.9, XXII.30.
[2] Craig Koester, *Revelation and the End of All Things* (Grand Rapids, MI: Eerdmans, 2001), 32.
[3] Glenn Tinder, "Eschatology and Politics," *Review of Politics* 27, no. 3 (1965): 311.
[4] There are other understandings of ideal theory, which Chapter 6 discusses.

task: outlining a goal that is both utopian and feasible. To be worth striving for, the ideal must be utopian and possess sufficient moral appeal to justify the transition costs needed to achieve it. Yet at the same time, the ideal must be feasible – otherwise, there is little reason to dedicate limited resources chasing after something outside the realm of possibility. These competing goals result in a catch-22 for ideal theory: a more utopian ideal is a less feasible moral goal, which diminishes reasons to strive for it and its normative force, but a more modest and feasible ideal is a less appealing moral goal, which also diminishes reasons to strive for it and its normative force. Within the apocalyptic tradition, a particular strand of it – what I call *cataclysmic apocalyptic thought* – proposes a way out of this dilemma. And that feature of apocalyptic thought contributes to its appeal in politics.

Specifically, cataclysmic apocalyptic thought identifies crisis as the path to the ideal society. It embraces a utopian goal and declares it feasible by pointing to crisis as the vehicle to wipe away corruption and bring the seemingly impossible within reach. This perspective has a prominent place in Christian texts like the book of Revelation, which envisions plagues and upheaval that precede the arrival of God's perfect kingdom. Cataclysmic apocalyptic thought takes secular form with the belief that natural or human forces, not divine ones, will direct crisis toward utopia. That way of interpreting the world gives a particular crisis meaning and creates a sense of urgency to take advantage of the historic opportunity at hand. Some secular thinkers find this view especially attractive. For them, apocalyptic thought offers resources to navigate persistent challenges in ideal theory, show how utopia is possible, and make the case for urgent action in pursuit of a utopian vision for politics.

CATACLYSMIC APOCALYPTIC THOUGHT IN THE CHRISTIAN TRADITION

Apocalyptic thought can take secular forms, but its roots go back to the Jewish and Christian traditions. For scholars of ancient religious texts, apocalypse refers to a genre of literature in which the author shares a divine revelation they received. Apocalyptic writers recount visions of a hopeful and just conclusion to history, and establish their authority by citing divine messengers as the source of their inspiration.[5] Apocalyptic literature emerged in the Jewish tradition following the Babylonian exile,[6] functioning as resistance literature

---

[5] John Collins, "Introduction: Towards the Morphology of a Genre," *Semeia* 14 (1979): 9.
[6] See John Collins, *The Apocalyptic Imagination: An Introduction to Jewish Apocalyptic Literature*, 2nd ed. (Grand Rapids, MI: Eerdmans, 1998); and Paul Hanson, *The Dawn of*

during a period of persecution.[7] Perhaps the most influential apocalypse, the book of Revelation or Apocalypse of John, continued this tradition but shifted to a Christian vision in which Jesus, the Lamb of God, would conquer the forces of sin and idolatry to realize his perfect kingdom, the new Jerusalem.

In Revelation and many apocalyptic writings, crisis plays a central role. Crisis has a redemptive quality due to its ability to bring about ideal conditions never before experienced and believed to be beyond reach. Though crisis prompts fear, it also opens up new opportunities. Rather than seeing crisis as something to avoid, the apocalyptic mindset welcomes it as a disruptive event necessary to wipe away corruption and perfect society. Crisis is part of a larger plan to overcome evil once and for all.

For this worldview, I opt for the term *cataclysmic apocalyptic thought*, which consists of four principal beliefs:

(1) Present corruption
(2) Impending crisis
(3) A divine force guiding crisis
(4) Finally, lasting utopia in the form of the kingdom of God[8]

A helpful illustration of cataclysmic apocalyptic thought comes from examining these elements in the book of Revelation.

(1) *Present corruption*. The apocalyptic mindset sees societal institutions and values as morally bankrupt and in need of radical change. There is desperate need for renewal, yet attempts to spark it seem unlikely to succeed. Nothing is how it should be: those deserving honor are powerless, persecuted by a ruling class motivated by idolatry, cruelty, self-glorification, and greed.[9] In Revelation, the Roman Empire embodies this entrenched corruption. Revelation's author, John, calls the Roman Empire the "beast" to communicate its overwhelming power. "Who is like the beast, and who can fight against

---

Apocalyptic: The Historical and Sociological Roots of Jewish Apocalyptic Eschatology (Philadelphia, PA: Fortress Press, 1975).

[7] See Richard Horsley, *Revolt of the Scribes: Resistance and Apocalyptic Origins* (Minneapolis, MN: Fortress Press, 2010); and Anathea Portier-Young, *Apocalypse against Empire: Theologies of Resistance in Early Judaism* (Grand Rapids, MI: Eerdmans, 2011).

[8] This list overlaps with some of the elements of apocalyptic rhetoric outlined in Frank Borchardt, *Doomsday Speculation as a Strategy of Persuasion: A Study of Apocalypticism as Rhetoric* (Lewiston, NY: Edwin Mellen Press, 1990). I, however, omit Borchardt's idea of a golden age that is restored. Hope of a restored golden age is sometimes present in apocalyptic worldviews. Yet Borchardt misses the important point that apocalyptic thought often envisions a truly novel ideal, superior to anything that ever existed before.

[9] Adela Yarbro Collins, *Crisis and Catharsis: The Power of Apocalypse* (Philadelphia, PA: Westminster Press, 1984), 123.

it?" ask those who worship it (Revelation 13:4).[10] In this environment of pervasive corruption, many become numb to it. Apocalyptic writing seeks to awaken people from blind acceptance of the status quo, so it is often gritty, shocking, and unrelenting in its attacks on social and political structures. John exemplifies this style, calling Rome the " 'mother of whores and of earth's abominations' ... drunk with the blood of the saints" (Revelation 17:5–6). What should be revolting – killing the righteous – has become normal and widely accepted. Though New Testament scholars question whether Christian persecution was as widespread as Revelation implies, John certainly *perceives* it as ubiquitous.[11] This conviction leads to a damning portrait of Rome: its corruption has reached such a point that, for Christians, compromising with it is not an option.

(2) *Impending crisis*. Surrounded by corruption, believers hold on to the hope that, though the ruling authorities appear dominant, their hold on power is actually tenuous. A coming crisis will disrupt the status quo, rooting out corruption at its source. In Revelation, an angel proclaims that such a crisis will engulf Rome (referred to as Babylon): "With ... violence Babylon the great city will be thrown down, and will be found no more" (Revelation 18:21). Rome's persecution of the righteous has put it on a path that will culminate in its destruction. Importantly, the apocalyptic crisis awaiting Rome is distinct from far more banal crises – wars, famines, plagues, and the like – that have come before. For the coming crisis represents the one to end all others. Such knowledge encourages believers to remain steadfast in their faith, regardless of what they suffer. They know that the powers persecuting them ultimately will fall. By foretelling the impending destruction of Rome, John hopes to instill in his readers urgency to resist its earthly power. As John Collins explains, "[A]pocalyptic language is *commissive* in character: it commits us to a view of the world for the sake of the actions and attitudes that are entailed."[12] Revelation's prediction of crisis serves the role of spurring action.

(3) *A divine force guiding crisis*. A key element of the crisis to come, which helps guard against despair, is the promise that God will direct it. Despite the fear and chaos associated with the looming crisis, believers take hope knowing that God has control over it. When the forces of the beast "make war on the Lamb," John assures his readers that "the Lamb will conquer them, for he is Lord of lords and King of kings" (Revelation 17:14). It will be a moment of justice, in which God "judge[s] the great whore who corrupted the earth with

---

[10] New Revised Standard Version. All subsequent biblical quotes come from this version.
[11] Collins, *Crisis and Catharsis*, 84.
[12] Collins, *The Apocalyptic Imagination*, 283.

her fornication, and ... avenge[s] ... the blood of his servants" (Revelation 19:2). All eventually will recognize God's authority. Even those engaged in idolatry will cry out to the mountains: "Fall on us and hide us from the face of the one seated on the throne and from the wrath of the Lamb; for the great day of their wrath has come, and who is able to stand?" (Revelation 6:16–17). For believers in the midst of the crisis, they are assured that it will result in the fulfillment of God's ultimate plan for history and creation. This hopeful view differs from what Jürgen Moltmann calls "exterminism," which anticipates mass extermination of life due to war, economic collapse, or environmental destruction.[13] Exterminism lacks hope because it anticipates devastation without redemption. Christian apocalyptic beliefs, in contrast, embrace the hope that God will realize his perfect kingdom through crisis and upheaval. Without such intervention, society's corruption would continue indefinitely.

(4) *Lasting utopia in the form of the kingdom of God.* Crisis wipes away corruption and prepares the way for God's kingdom. Rather than a marginal improvement, God's coming kingdom embodies perfection and surpasses all others. In Revelation, this promised kingdom is the new Jerusalem, where "[d]eath will be no more; mourning and crying and pain will be no more" (Revelation 21:4). John's vision taps into deep human hopes. Death, sorrow, pain, and all that has tormented humankind will end when Christ returns to "reign forever" (Revelation 11:15). This hope motivates believers to prepare themselves for the coming kingdom, which requires sacrifice as Revelation reminds its readers: "Do not fear what you are about to suffer. Beware, the devil is about to throw some of you into prison so that you may be tested .... Be faithful until death, and I will give you the crown of life" (Revelation 2:10). Sacrifice resulting in martyrdom and apparent defeat represents, from God's perspective, victory over sin and corruption.[14] Such knowledge consoles believers facing persecution, who see God's perfect kingdom as having transcendent value and thus worthy of sacrifice.

SECULAR APOCALYPTIC THOUGHT

Even in religious form, notes J. G. A. Pocock, apocalyptic thought often operates as a "powerful instrument of secularization."[15] With this remark,

---

[13] Jürgen Moltmann, *The Coming of God: Christian Eschatology,* trans. Margaret Kohl (Minneapolis, MN: Fortress Press, 1996), 203.

[14] Richard Bauckham, *The Theology of the Book of Revelation* (New York: Cambridge University Press, 1993), 66–108.

[15] J. G. A. Pocock, *The Machiavellian Moment: Florentine Political Thought and the Atlantic Republican Tradition,* 2nd ed. (Princeton, NJ: Princeton University Press, 2003), 46.

Pocock highlights apocalyptic thought's power to heighten the importance of social and political events by infusing them with transcendent meaning. Apocalyptic thought can give the divine concrete form in the present. *This* war, *this* uprising, *this* religious revival, or *this* natural disaster, proclaims the apocalyptic prophet, is God's plan unfolding before our eyes. By interpreting change in this way, apocalyptic thought confers significance and meaning to the forces causing upheaval, while also undermining the authority of institutions resistant to change.

Established church authorities have long recognized the potentially explosive and destabilizing nature of apocalyptic thought and, not surprisingly, worked to disarm it. From a pragmatic perspective, a certain level of social stability facilitates routine church activities – weekly services, administering the sacraments, providing aid to the poor, and the like. Apocalyptic thought that fosters social upheaval and hinders these activities is cause for concern. So too are forms of apocalyptic thought that deify earthly events by proclaiming them to be God's instruments for bringing history to a close. Traditionally, church authorities have cautioned against placing one's faith in the world and its imperfections, emphasizing that it is beyond human understanding to know how sacred history may be unfolding in the present. In Christian thought, Augustine in particular played an influential role in undermining the authority of those claiming to know the hidden eschatological meaning behind world events. Notably, his monumental work the *City of God* closes by citing Acts 1:7: "It is not for you to know the dates [e.g., of Christ's return]: the Father has decided those by his own authority."[16]

The current *Catechism of the Catholic Church* takes a similar strategy and warns against "every time the claim is made to realize within history that messianic hope which can only be realized beyond history." The *Catechism* specifically emphasizes the danger posed by apocalyptic beliefs that take "intrinsically perverse" form in denying God and trusting entirely in political forces to bring about earthly perfection.[17] Beyond just its potential for disruption, apocalyptic thought worries the Catholic Church because, in deifying the political, it can jettison belief in God altogether.

This form of apocalyptic thought, which functions not only as an *instrument* of secularization but is *itself* secular, is the focus here. Apocalyptic concepts

---

[16] Augustine, *City of God*, XXII.30: 1091. See also R. A. Markus, *Saeculum: History and Society in the Theology of St Augustine* (New York: Cambridge University Press, 1970), 166–78; and J. Kevin Coyle, "Augustine and Apocalyptic: Thoughts on the Fall of Rome, the Book of Revelation, and the End of the World," *Florilegium* 9 (1987): 1–34.

[17] Catholic Church, *Catechism of the Catholic Church*, 2nd ed. (Washington, D.C.: United States Conference of Catholic Bishops, 2019), § 676.

that originated in religious thought can migrate into new ideological frameworks where they become disconnected from belief in God and his providence. In such instances, apocalyptic thought places its trust in non-divine rather than divine forces.

So when cataclysmic apocalyptic thought takes secular form, it consists of beliefs similar to those found in the Christian tradition – present corruption, impending crisis, a divine force guiding crisis, and lasting utopia – with certain modifications. In secular form, cataclysmic apocalyptic thought anticipates a crisis guided by human or natural forces that will wipe away corruption and bring about the ideal society, while denying any role for the divine. This view puts some constraints on its vision for utopia. In religious form, cataclysmic apocalyptic thought imagines a utopia free from various constraints found in the natural world, like mortality. Divine intervention throws off these constraints. By forgoing appeals to divine power to explain the transition to the ideal society, secular apocalyptic thought offers visions of utopia that are less supernatural. Still, such thought has lofty expectations for the ideal society. It envisions a transformative crisis that will eliminate the ills that have long plagued human society, such as strife, poverty, and violence. The resulting utopia will be stable, since any utopia that quickly collapses hardly counts as ideal. Both secular and religious varieties of cataclysmic apocalyptic thought foresee a lasting utopia in humanity's future.

APOCALYPTIC THOUGHT AS IDEAL THEORY

The apocalyptic worldview, both in Christian and secular forms, sets its sights on more than a mere improvement over the present. It puts forward a vision of the most perfect society. Cataclysmic apocalyptic thought specifically emphasizes crisis as the vehicle for reaching the ideal society. Through this vision, the apocalyptic tradition theorizes about the ideal society and the path to it. We thus can understand apocalyptic thought as a form of ideal theory.

Some may object to this claim and dismiss any equation between apocalyptic thought and ideal theory as an anachronistic mistake. Indeed, political philosophers today rarely if ever connect the apocalyptic tradition with ideal theory. Part of the reason why is the ahistorical nature of the debate over ideal theory in contemporary political philosophy. It sometimes gives the impression that ideal theory suddenly emerged in 1971 with the publication of *A Theory of Justice*.[18] Here John Rawls argues that "the nature and aims of

---

[18] See Laura Valentini, "Ideal vs. Non-ideal Theory: A Conceptual Map." *Philosophy Compass* 7, no. 9 (2012): 655.

a perfectly just society" play a fundamental role in a theory of justice: one must understand what justice requires under ideal conditions to understand its requirements under nonideal conditions.[19] Rawls's distinction between ideal and nonideal theory sparked a flurry of philosophical debate, but sometimes lost in this debate is Rawls's place within a broader tradition of theorizing about the ideal society.

Utopian thought has long been concerned with the nature of the ideal society and goes all the way back to Plato,[20] as Lea Ypi and Gerald Gaus note.[21] The work that coined the term utopia reminds us of that point. In *Utopia* published in 1516, Thomas More compares the ideal society that he describes to the one outlined in Plato's *Republic*, thus situating his work within a tradition of ideal theorizing that long preceded him.[22] The apocalyptic tradition shares this interest in theorizing about the ideal society, and at times has influenced utopian literature.[23] So ideal theory is not entirely distinct from utopian and apocalyptic thought, but it overlaps with these traditions in important ways.[24]

In *The Tyranny of the Ideal*, Gaus speaks of "models of utopian-ideal thought" to emphasize the continuous tradition shared by utopian thought and contemporary ideal theory.[25] "Utopian" and "ideal theory" are contested terms,[26] so it is important to be clear on their meanings here. One common

---

[19] John Rawls, *A Theory of Justice*, rev. ed. (Cambridge, MA: Harvard University Press, 1999), 8.
[20] See Plato, *The Republic*, ed. G. R. F. Ferrari and trans. Tom Griffith (New York: Cambridge University Press, 2000), 471c–73b.
[21] Lea Ypi, "On the Confusion between Ideal and Non-ideal in Recent Debates on Global Justice," *Political Studies* 58, no. 3 (2010): 537–38; and Gerald Gaus, *The Tyranny of the Ideal: Justice in a Diverse Society* (Princeton, NJ: Princeton University Press, 2016), 2–3.
[22] Thomas More, *Utopia*, trans. Paul Turner (New York, Penguin Books, 1965), 27, 33.
[23] Barbara Goodwin and Keith Taylor, *The Politics of Utopia: A Study in Theory and Practice* (London: Hutchinson, 1982), 140.
[24] Timothy Kenyon stresses the following distinction between utopian and apocalyptic thought: "From the millenarian point of view, this work [of establishing the ideal society] must be left to God, who will intervene either directly or through His agents, the Saints. From the utopian point of view, the ideal society can only be established by Man, working unaided." See Kenyon, "Utopia in Reality: 'Ideal' Societies in Social and Political Theory," *History of Political Thought* 3, no. 1 (1982): 147. Kenyon's distinction is not as sharp as he supposes, however, since it does not apply to *secular* apocalyptic thought.
[25] Gaus, *The Tyranny of the Ideal*, 3.
[26] See Goodwin and Taylor, *The Politics of Utopia*; Ruth Levitas, *The Concept of Utopia* (Syracuse, NY: Syracuse University Press, 1990); Alan Hamlin and Zofia Stemplowska, "Theory, Ideal Theory and the Theory of Ideals," *Political Studies Review* 10, no. 1 (2012): 48–62; Zofia Stemplowska and Adam Swift, "Ideal and Nonideal Theory," in *The Oxford Handbook of Political Philosophy*, ed. David Estlund (New York: Oxford University Press, 2012), 373–88; Valentini, "Ideal vs. Non-ideal Theory"; and Kwame Appiah, *As If: Idealization and Ideals* (Cambridge, MA: Harvard University Press, 2017).

understanding of ideal or utopian theory is an approach within political philosophy that aims to identify the *best, most just* society rather than merely a *better, more just* society.[27]

Sometimes utopian implies the impossible,[28] but that view is far from universal or even standard.[29] Here our focus is on utopian or ideal theory that sets forth a vision of the best, most just society with the potential of being realized at some future point – what I call *navigational ideal theory*. In many cases, ideal theory takes this form and aims to present a goal within the realm of possibility, even if a vast gulf stands between this goal and the imperfect present. Rawls captures this idea with his understanding of ideal theory as an attempt to offer a "realistic utopia" to strive for.[30] If, as is commonly assumed, ought implies can, ideal theory must present a goal that is feasible to preserve its role as a normative guide to action. By setting forth the most just society possible, ideal theory serves as a navigational guide: it provides a normative end goal to guide efforts toward greater justice.

When thinking about ideal theory's navigational role, some mistakenly assume a sharp divide between ideal and nonideal theory. Ingrid Robeyns takes this view – specifically, that ideal theory tells us what the end goal is and nonideal theory tells us how to get there or at least closer to it. For Robeyns, it makes little sense to object to ideal theory on the grounds that it fails to provide guidance on moving us closer to a far-off ideal. Such an objection fails, argues Robeyns, because it is not the ideal theorist's task to map a path from the present to the ideal. That work instead falls to nonideal theory.[31]

This neat distinction between ideal and nonideal theory proves problematic because it obscures an important point: those interested in offering a persuasive account of navigational ideal theory must also engage in *non*ideal theory. A common metaphor for ideal theory – identifying the tallest

---

[27] See Amartya Sen, "What Do We Want from a Theory of Justice?" *Journal of Philosophy* 103, no. 5 (2006): 215–38; Sen, *The Idea of Justice* (Cambridge, MA: Harvard University Press, 2009); and Gaus, *The Tyranny of the Ideal*.

[28] Robert Jubb, "Tragedies of Nonideal Theory," *European Journal of Political Theory* 11, no. 3 (2012): 231; and David Estlund, *Utopophobia: On the Limits (if any) of Political Philosophy* (Princeton, NJ: Princeton University Press, 2020), 11–12.

[29] Goodwin and Taylor, *The Politics of Utopia*, 210–14; and Gaus, *The Tyranny of the Ideal*, 2–3.

[30] John Rawls, *The Law of Peoples* (Cambridge, MA: Harvard University Press, 1999), 11–12; and *Justice as Fairness: A Restatement*, ed. Erin Kelly (Cambridge, MA: Harvard University Press, 2001), 4, 13. See also Ben Laurence, "Constructivism, Strict Compliance, and Realistic Utopianism," *Philosophy and Phenomenological Research* 97, no. 2 (2018): 433–53.

[31] Ingrid Robeyns, "Ideal Theory in Theory and Practice," *Social Theory and Practice* 34, no. 3 (2008): 345–46.

mountain[32] – helps explain why. If we think of the most just society possible as the world's tallest mountain and lower peaks as less just societies, an ideal theorist primarily errs in one of two ways: (1) identifying as the tallest mountain a peak that, though perhaps the tallest in a particular region, is not the tallest in the world (say Denali); or (2) identifying as the tallest mountain a peak that, though taller than Mount Everest, is nowhere on earth (say, a mythical peak 50,000 feet above sea level). Accusing ideal theory of one of these errors is to raise what, respectively, can be called the *utopian* and *feasibility objections*:[33]

(1) *Utopian objection*: criticizing ideal theory for being overly pessimistic and embracing an end goal that is *insufficiently ideal*.
(2) *Feasibility objection*: criticizing ideal theory for being overly optimistic and embracing an end goal that is *too ideal*.

To give a compelling defense of ideal theory, then, one must overcome both these objections. And doing so requires engaging in nonideal theory. If a critic argues for an ideal superior to that outlined by the ideal theorist, the theorist can ask the critic to explain a possible path to this superior ideal – that is, engage in nonideal theory – and then challenge this account of nonideal theory. Conversely, if a critic doubts the feasibility of an ideal theorist's vision, the theorist can defend it by engaging in nonideal theory to show a potential path to this ideal.

So when doubts arise about the path to an ideal, the ideal theorist cannot simply respond: "Not my problem! Ask someone doing nonideal theory." This response leaves ideal theory without an actual defense and gives others little reason to believe it. To avoid this pitfall, a compelling account of ideal theory also engages in nonideal theory. The ideal theorist need not do all the work of nonideal theory and specify every step from the present to the ideal. But the ideal theorist at least should work to allay skeptics' doubts by sketching potential, general paths to a particular ideal.[34]

Since considering paths to the ideal takes on such importance in ideal theory, apocalyptic thought – with its emphasis on crisis as the vehicle to

---

[32] See, e.g., Sen, "What Do We Want from a Theory of Justice?"; A. John Simmons, "Ideal and Nonideal Theory," *Philosophy and Public Affairs* 38, no. 1 (2010): 5–36; and Gaus, *The Tyranny of the Ideal*, 61–67.

[33] For a similar point, see Mark Jensen, "The Limits of Practical Possibility," *Journal of Political Philosophy* 17, no. 2 (2009): 168–84.

[34] An example of sketching general paths to an ideal, while recognizing numerous discoveries along the way that still need to be made, is Nick Bostrom's account of achieving superintelligence – that is, artificial intelligence that outperforms human intelligence across all domains of interest. See Bostrom, *Superintelligence: Paths, Dangers, Strategies* (New York: Oxford University Press, 2014).

utopia – proves relevant to such theorizing. Robeyns's characterization of ideal theory, which limits it to describing an ideal endpoint, would render many elements of apocalyptic thought irrelevant to this manner of theorizing. But a closer look at ideal theory reveals the importance of outlining both the ideal endpoint and the path to it. While some understandings of ideal theory ignore the latter, cataclysmic apocalyptic thought gives considerable attention to the path to the ideal. According to this strand of apocalyptic thought, crisis opens the way to a seemingly impossible ideal.

THE CATCH-22 OF IDEAL THEORY

To review, the ideal theorist has to guard against formulating a vision of society deemed either insufficiently ideal (the utopian objection) or too ideal (the feasibility objection). When one of these objections is valid, responding to it in isolation is straightforward. One can temper the goals of a vision that is too ideal and infeasible. And when a vision is insufficiently ideal, one can revise it to make it more utopian and appealing. But ideal theorists face a dilemma: *both* the utopian and feasibility objections loom over their projects as potential criticisms, and attempts to avoid one objection render them more vulnerable to the other.

Let's look at each horn of this dilemma. The first is the utopian objection, which demands an appealing moral goal that is worth striving for. Yet the more utopian the ideal, the more disconnected it becomes from the present and the less feasible it seems. This concern raises the second horn of the dilemma – the feasibility objection – which also is important to overcome, since an unattainable ideal cannot be realized and thus is not worth striving for. But settling on a modest, feasible ideal risks depriving it of normative force due to its insufficient moral appeal. This concern brings us back again to the utopian objection. So, together, the utopian and feasibility objections create a catch-22 for the ideal theorist: a more utopian ideal is a less feasible moral goal, which diminishes reasons to strive for it and its normative force, but a more modest and feasible ideal is a less appealing moral goal, which also diminishes the reasons to strive for it and its normative force. Regardless of whether one moves in a more or less ideal direction, one risks diminishing ideal theory's normative force (see Figure 2.1).

Some may contend that this catch-22 represents an illusory rather than real dilemma for ideal theory. Indeed, there are political philosophers who dismiss some version of either the feasibility or utopian objection against ideal theory. It is important, then, to address this skepticism and show that the catch-22 outlined here does in fact pose challenges for ideal theory.

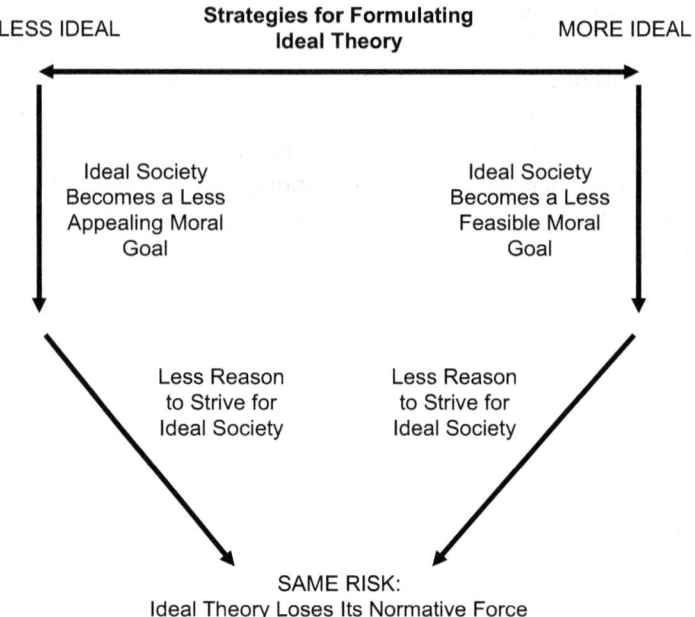

FIGURE 2.1 The catch-22 of ideal theory

Skepticism toward the feasibility objection. This view stems from two related but distinct concerns: (1) feasibility assessments are often wrong and (2) feasibility considerations are irrelevant to ideal theory. David Estlund explains the first concern:

> The great achievements in the development of human social life have typically been preceded by incredulity about their very possibility, much less their likelihood. If theoretical inquiry had limited itself to what was plausibly thought to be achievable, the achievements might never have happened. For at least this reason, we ought not to lower our gaze in a practical and realistic spirit.[35]

Sometimes a theory deemed infeasible ends up being realized. Critics of the theory err because they fail to appreciate what is truly possible. For this reason, says Estlund, philosophers should not give up on a theory whenever concerns about feasibility are raised since defenders of the theory may have better foresight than their critics.[36] This argument provides reasons to reject feasibility objections that are potentially inaccurate.

---

[35] David Estlund, "Utopophobia," *Philosophy and Public Affairs* 42, no. 2 (2014): 133.
[36] See also Eva Erman and Niklas Möller, "Three Failed Charges Against Ideal Theory," *Social Theory and Practice* 39, no. 1 (2013): 36–40.

A more fundamental critique of the catch-22 comes from a general rejection of feasibility considerations when engaging in ideal theory. G. A. Cohen takes this stronger view in defense of "fact-insensitive" principles of justice, which take conditional form: "One ought to do A if it is possible to do A."[37] His approach opens the door for ideal theory to outline an ideal based partly or entirely on conditional principles that are impossible to carry out. Without feasibility constraints on ideal theory, the most perfect and just society could be a hopeless goal. That scenario leaves ideal theory without a feasible end goal to guide action.

Such varieties of ideal theory still count as moral, according to Estlund: "[A] theory can be normative in one sense by being evaluative, whether or not evaluation itself counsels action. 'Society would be better like this' might be true whether or not there is anything it makes sense to do in light of this fact."[38] Unconstrained by feasibility concerns, ideal theory is free to explore what true justice consists of, and such inquiry has value even if it fails to guide action.[39]

One can adopt Estlund's approach and understand ideal theory as having a purely evaluative role, but it comes at a high cost. Most importantly, this approach leaves ideal theory vulnerable to the charge that it is irrelevant to promoting justice.

To illustrate this point, consider one of Amartya Sen's criticisms of ideal theory and how its defenders respond. Sen sees little value for ideal theory in a world filled with injustice, since endless debates over perfect justice distract from the more pressing task of making incremental steps toward a more just world.[40] Normally, defenders of ideal theory have a counterargument available to them in response to this criticism: because of the path-dependent nature of social change, an ideal end point is needed to guide efforts toward greater justice.[41] Without such an ideal to guide action, incremental steps toward justice could lead to a *more* just society, yet away from the *most* just society. To return to the mountain metaphor, someone in Anchorage, Alaska, trying to climb the highest peak but unfamiliar with world geography may think that traveling a few hundred miles north to Denali will accomplish this goal. Climbing Denali takes one to a higher altitude yet away from the highest peak, which is on a different continent altogether. As this analogy suggests, we

---

[37] G. A. Cohen, "Facts and Principles," *Philosophy and Public Affairs* 31, no. 3 (2003): 231.
[38] Estlund, "Utopophobia," 121.
[39] Estlund, "What Good Is It? Unrealistic Political Theory and the Value of Intellectual Work," *Analyse & Kritik* 33, no. 2 (2011): 395–416.
[40] Sen, "What Do We Want from a Theory of Justice?"; and *The Idea of Justice*.
[41] Simmons, "Ideal and Nonideal Theory."

need an ideal to guide the pursuit of justice and avoid paths that delay or block greater advances later.

This defense of ideal theory, however, loses its force when theorizing becomes disconnected from considerations of feasibility and takes on a purely evaluative role. Assuming ought implies can, an infeasible ideal fails to provide a moral end goal to guide efforts toward greater justice. In this case, ideal theory lacks the navigational value that the most powerful counterargument to Sen appeals to. Without navigational value, ideal theory could persist as an intellectual pursuit, but Sen would be right – it would be an intellectual pursuit irrelevant to advancing justice in the real world.

Uncomfortable with that conclusion, some still may try to salvage a navigational role for ideal theory that offers an unattainable ideal. Perhaps such an ideal can serve as a goal that we strive to get closer to, even if it will always be beyond our reach. But though reasonable on its face, this argument runs into a problem: there is no guarantee that moving closer to an unattainable ideal of justice will lead toward the most just society possible.

To illustrate this point, consider the following example. Some believe that future advances in artificial intelligence will lead to an ideal society that remedies a host of injustices common today. According to this view, ideal theory must set forth principles of justice to govern the development, distribution, and use of artificial intelligence. Now suppose the goal outlined by this ideal theory is impossible to achieve, both now and in the future. Perhaps human capacities cannot effectively control artificial intelligence, which if developed would exercise tyrannical power over humanity. Or, more prosaically, perhaps humans lack the capacity to develop artificial intelligence to the point where it becomes truly effective in remedying injustice.[42] Either way, investing in and pursuing artificial intelligence would hinder efforts to advance justice. Instead of leading to the most just and perfect society possible, pursuing this unattainable ideal takes society down a path that wastes valuable resources and perhaps even fosters tyranny.

It could be the case that pursuing an unattainable ideal corresponds with the path to the most just society possible, but that cannot be assumed, as this example suggests. Demonstrating the navigational value of an unattainable ideal requires identifying the most just ideal possible and explaining how the paths to these two ideals correspond. So, ultimately, we cannot escape questions of feasibility when formulating navigational ideal theory. The feasibility objection presents a real challenge and, to overcome it, ideal theory must set

---

[42] See Bostrom, *Superintelligence*.

forth an ideal that is attainable and a suitable guide to action, not a mythical goal that risks sidetracking efforts toward justice.

Skepticism toward the utopian objection. The utopian objection raises the concern that ideal theory puts forward a goal with insufficient moral appeal, and as such is not worth striving for. Some respond that whether people find an ideal appealing and strive for it says nothing about whether it is true. For example, Laura Valentini points out that individuals do not always follow moral principles, but that is a regrettable fact of life rather than an indictment of the principles themselves.[43] If no moral theory has perfect success in motivating individuals to act rightly, why should we single out ideal theory for criticism? For Valentini, ideal theory's success in motivating action is irrelevant to evaluating its truth.

Valentini is correct that even true moral principles do not always motivate action. But the utopian objection, or at least the strongest form of it, does not stem from concerns that weakness of will prevents the pursuit of ideal theory's goals. It instead levels a more serious charge against ideal theory: regardless of whether ideal theory actually motivates, there are compelling moral reasons why it *should not* motivate. According to the utopian objection, the insufficient moral appeal of ideal theory should preclude it from serving as a normative guide to action.

Importantly, the utopian objection presents challenges for both inaccurate *and* accurate accounts of ideal theory. Obviously, when ideal theory is overly pessimistic and specifies an ideal well short of the most perfect and just society possible, the utopian objection tells the ideal theorist to aim higher. But even when ideal theory identifies the most perfect and just society possible, the utopian objection can raise compelling reasons not to pursue it. On its face, this position seems odd. If ideal theory puts forward an ideal embodying the most perfect and just society possible, wouldn't we have strong normative reasons to pursue it? Not necessarily. It could be the case that the ideal, while representing the most just end goal possible, lacks sufficient moral appeal to justify the transition costs to realize it.

Juha Räikkä emphasizes this concern when discussing the "moral costs of the changeover," which come with transitioning to the ideal society.[44] If the ideal is distinct from the present in significant ways, achieving it likely will require dramatic societal changes. Such changes impose considerable

---

[43] Laura Valentini, "On the Apparent Paradox of Ideal Theory," *Journal of Political Philosophy* 17, no. 3 (2009): 340.

[44] Juha Räikkä, "The Feasibility Condition in Political Theory," *Journal of Political Philosophy* 6, no. 1 (1998): 33.

sacrifices and disruptions on society. When the transition costs are steep enough, there can be compelling moral reasons to balk at pursuing the ideal society.

Take, for instance, an ideal theory X, which gives an accurate account of the most just and perfect society possible. In a hypothetical state of nature without obstacles from the past to hinder the pursuit of X's ideal, individuals have good reason to strive for it. Yet, under actual conditions, advancing toward X's ideal involves higher costs because of the need to alter existing institutions. In fact, at this point in history, X's ideal only can be realized through a bloody conflict that wipes out society's dominant class. The substantial moral costs involved in achieving X's ideal prove too great to justify the transition, even if it would end various injustices (e.g., an entrenched wage and wealth gap between different groups). Other efforts short of wide-scale violence hold the promise of reducing injustice in society, and individuals may have compelling normative reasons to pursue those efforts. Yet that strategy always will fall short of achieving X's vision and will lead society down a different path. In sum, X's ideal has moral appeal, but not enough to justify the transition costs necessary to realize it.

If, as in this case, the utopian objection succeeds, ideal theory finds itself in the same position it does when the feasibility objection succeeds: it lacks navigational value and relevance to promoting justice. Without sufficient moral appeal to justify the transition costs needed to realize its goal, ideal theory fails to specify an ideal worth striving for. So despite the skepticism voiced by some philosophers, the utopian and feasibility objections do present real challenges for ideal theory. It is necessary to escape the catch-22 posed by these objections to ensure ideal theory's normative value in guiding action. The appeal of cataclysmic apocalyptic thought for politics, as the next section discusses, partly lies in offering motivational resources that seem to overcome this catch-22.

APOCALYPTIC THOUGHT'S APPEAL FOR POLITICS

Faced with the catch-22 posed by the feasibility and utopian objections, ideal theorists could just give up on trying to formulate an ideal with navigational value. In that case, ideal theory would merely have an evaluative role: specifying the best society in theory and abandoning any aspirations to formulate a feasible end goal to guide action. Some, like Estlund and Cohen, seem content limiting ideal theory to this role. Others, though, find this concession deeply unsatisfying – one suited for the ivory tower but not actual politics, a sphere that demands a more robust normative role for ideal theory.

According to this view, one consults ideal theory not only to know what the ideal society is, but also for guidance on how to achieve it. As Gaus puts it, ideal theory is both about "what we should think" and "what we should do. They are not ultimately separable, for to think about justice is to think about where we should *move*, and how to engage in the *quest*."[45] Especially for those who understand their theorizing as a contribution to bringing about the ideal society, it is essential for ideal theory to guide action.

But crafting ideal theory with navigational value requires overcoming the catch-22 and identifying a goal that is utopian and feasible. For those facing this challenge, the apocalyptic tradition – and cataclysmic apocalyptic thought in particular – offers a potentially appealing strategy. Cataclysmic apocalyptic thought refuses to be stymied by either horn of the catch-22 of ideal theory: it embraces a thoroughly utopian ideal while offering a narrative to explain its feasibility. Such thought brings together in a single ideal seemingly irreconcilable goals.

Let's start with the goal of crafting a utopian ideal. Despite the criticisms leveled against apocalyptic thought, few complain about its being *insufficiently* utopian. Apocalyptic narratives envision perfection at the end of history, such as the new Jerusalem described in Revelation. The vision of what's to come – a world finally free from strife, want, and suffering – stands in stark contrast to today. Without apology, the apocalyptic tradition sets forth a utopian vision as the destiny for God's elect. Since it outlines an ideal embodying perfection, apocalyptic thought proves less vulnerable to the charge that its vision lacks appeal.

Now let's turn to feasibility. Cataclysmic apocalyptic thought provides an explanation for how its utopian ideal could be feasible. Outlining a far-off ideal without any connection to the present naturally prompts the feasibility objection – how does one get there from here? Cataclysmic apocalyptic thought takes this concern seriously and attempts to address it: a coming crisis will open a path that links the present to utopia. Without such disruption, the apocalyptic ideal would be an impossible and foolish thing to strive for. Cataclysmic apocalyptic thought avoids this motivational dead end by predicting a coming crisis, unlike any before, that will wipe away corruption and bring about the ideal envisioned.

The appeal of cataclysmic apocalyptic thought makes further sense when considering the power of crisis generally in interpreting political events. Crisis often provides compelling grounds for indicting the status quo and developing an alternative vision of politics to pursue. Both the political right and left

---

[45] Gaus, *The Tyranny of the Ideal*, 61.

recognize the opportunities presented by crisis. "Only a crisis – actual or perceived – produces real change," writes the conservative economist Milton Friedman. "When that crisis occurs, the actions that are taken depend on the ideas that are lying around."[46] President Barack Obama's first chief of staff, Rahm Emanuel, makes a similar point: "You never want a serious crisis to go to waste .... [The 2008 economic] crisis provides the opportunity for us to do things that you could not do before."[47] This idea is far from new and, from the Age of Revolution to the present, appears in political tracts, such as *The Crisis* by Thomas Paine.[48] Of course, the idea stretches back even further, as apocalyptic texts and the events they inspired remind us. Across different eras, crisis has had the power to direct people's attention to societal failures and instill a sense of urgency to take political action.

Cataclysmic apocalyptic thought harnesses the potent idea that crisis represents a transformative moment. It argues that the perfect society to surpass all others awaits just on the other side of crisis. Within this framework of thought, crisis will wipe away obstacles that have long blocked the path to utopia. This knowledge creates urgency to take advantage of the unique opportunity at hand. The appeal of cataclysmic apocalyptic thought lies in reframing crisis so that it no longer is a source of paralyzing fear, but an opportunity for transformative change.

A STRATEGY NOT WITHOUT RISKS

Cataclysmic apocalyptic thought proves appealing for politics because of the promise it holds: overcoming the intractable catch-22 of ideal theory and motivating dramatic political action perhaps when it is most needed, in the midst of crisis. But political strategies that hold promise almost always come with risks, and that is true in this case. Cataclysmic apocalyptic thought as a lens for interpreting politics and stirring people to action can backfire in three ways: (1) lead to a quietist attitude toward politics; (2) prove unable to sustain hope and motivate action over time; and (3) exacerbate injustice by trying to force utopia under conditions of uncertainty.

---

[46] Milton Friedman, *Capitalism and Freedom*, 40th anniversary ed. (Chicago: University of Chicago Press, 2002), xiv.
[47] Gerald Seib, "In Crisis, Opportunity for Obama," *Wall Street Journal*, November 21, 2008, www.wsj.com/articles/SB122721278056345271.
[48] Thomas Paine, *The Crisis*, in *Thomas Paine: Collected Writings*, ed. Eric Foner, 91–176, 181–210, 222–52, 325–33, 348–54 (New York: Library of America, 1995).

To begin with the risk of quietism, this worry frequently comes up in the context of religious apocalyptic thought.[49] If it is foreordained that divine forces will wipe away corruption and establish a perfect society, what point is there for individuals to take action in pursuit of that goal? Given that divine plans are in motion, individual action seems insignificant and unable to impact the ultimate outcome. Secular apocalyptic thought faces similar concerns. If forces in history guarantee that society eventually will attain perfection, it can be tempting to conclude that one's own actions are ultimately meaningless. So apocalyptic thought can breed such confidence in the future that a quietist attitude toward politics results. But it is important not to overstate this worry. A far more common barrier to political action is *lack* of hope. As research from psychology finds, people are more likely to support and consider participating in collective action when they have hope that political change is possible.[50] Utopian hope, in particular, can motivate collective action by highlighting the gap between the present society and the ideal – and the need to bridge that gap.[51] Cataclysmic apocalyptic thought crafts a narrative that offers such hope, which highlights its potential to motivate political action.

It is sustaining hope that proves especially challenging. Instilling a particular crisis with historic importance creates, in the short term, a sense of urgency to seize the opportunity to radically improve society. This hopeful mindset, though, quickly can turn into disillusionment when crisis fails to produce redemptive change. That danger has long plagued apocalyptic thought. As Stephen O'Leary observes, "[T]he recurring fallacy of apocalyptic eschatology seems to rest in a human tendency to identify the particular with the ultimate."[52] Cataclysmic apocalyptic thought pins its hopes for renewal on a particular moment in history. If dramatic action in response to crisis never

---

[49] See, e.g., Timothy Weber, *Living in the Shadow of the Second Coming: American Premillennialism, 1875–1982* (Grand Rapids, MI: Academie Books, 1983), 93–104.

[50] See Smadar Cohen-Chen and Martijn Van Zomeren, "Yes We Can? Group Efficacy Beliefs Predict Collective Action, but only When Hope Is High," *Journal of Experimental Social Psychology* 77 (2018): 50–59; Simon Bury, Michael Wenzel, and Lydia Woodyatt, "Against the Odds: Hope as an Antecedent of Support for Climate Change Action," *British Journal of Social Psychology* 59, no. 2 (2020): 289–310; and Katharine Greenaway et al., "Feeling Hopeful Inspires Support for Social Change," *Political Psychology* 37, no. 1 (2016): 89–107.

[51] See Julian Fernando et al., "Functions of Utopia: How Utopian Thinking Motivates Societal Engagement," *Personality and Social Psychology Bulletin* 44, no. 5 (2018): 779–92; and Vivienne Badaan et al., "Imagining Better Societies: A Social Psychological Framework for the Study of Utopian Thinking and Collective Action," *Social and Personality Psychology Compass* 14, no. 4 (2020): e12525.

[52] Stephen O'Leary, *Arguing the Apocalypse: A Theory of Millennial Rhetoric* (New York: Oxford University Press, 1994), 218.

brings the desired change, discouragement often sets in – all the sacrifices people made were in vain. One finds this danger in Christianity when expectations for the imminent arrival of God's kingdom go unfulfilled. It also is found in secular ideologies like Marxism, which struggles to explain how the inevitable collapse of capitalism has yet to occur and usher in the communist ideal.[53]

Of perhaps greater concern, crisis sometimes motivates dramatic action that exacerbates rather than solves societal ills. Scholars on both the right and left note that crisis, real or perceived, often serves to justify troubling changes to state power.[54] When confronted with a crisis, people clamor for *something* to be done. This mindset can justify transition costs normally shunned, such as violence against those perceived as impeding the path to the ideal. Steep transition costs hardly guarantee utopia, especially given the world's complexity and the impossibility of predicting the full repercussions of political action. Efforts to bring the ideal into existence by brute force can unleash a host of ills without bringing utopia any closer – a danger that looms over apocalyptic thought and ideal theory more broadly.[55]

But despite these risks and its theological baggage, apocalyptic thought continues to prove appealing to a number of political theorists. For those interested in not just theorizing about the ideal society but in actually realizing it, they face the challenge of crafting an ideal worth striving for. Attempts to formulate such an ideal run into the catch-22 of ideal theory, and overcoming it requires outlining an ideal that is both utopian and feasible. Yet the immense tension between these goals seems to leave few if any options to realize them simultaneously. Instead of shrinking from this dilemma, cataclysmic apocalyptic thought proposes a solution: crisis will transform the world and finally make utopia possible. And that is perhaps why, as we'll see in Part II, some thinkers critical of Christianity still find themselves drawn to its apocalyptic doctrines. The allure of the ideal society makes apocalyptic thought attractive even to secular thinkers, for such thought helps in imagining a path to this elusive goal.

---

[53] See Nomi Claire Lazar, *Out of Joint: Power, Crisis, and the Rhetoric of Time* (New Haven, CT: Yale University Press, 2019), 166–208.

[54] See Robert Higgs, *Crisis and Leviathan: Critical Episodes in the Growth of American Government* (New York: Oxford University Press, 1987); and Colin Hay, "Narrating Crisis: The Discursive Construction of the 'Winter of Discontent,'" *Sociology* 30, no. 2 (1996): 253–77.

[55] See Burke Hendrix, "Where Should We Expect Social Change in Non-ideal Theory?" *Political Theory* 41, no. 1 (2013): 116–43; and Frances Flannery, *Understanding Apocalyptic Terrorism: Countering the Radical Mindset* (New York: Routledge, 2016). This danger is discussed in more detail in Chapter 7.

PART II

HISTORICAL CASE STUDIES

3

Apocalyptic Hope's Appeal: Machiavelli and Savonarola

By the end of 1494, Girolamo Savonarola was at the height of his powers. The Dominican friar, known for apocalyptic preaching, had established himself as a political force in Florence since arriving in 1490. His reputation had grown after he purportedly predicted the invasion of Charles VIII in 1494 and then negotiated the French king's departure from Florence without ruin coming to the city. This episode led some in Florence to believe Savonarola's claim that he was God's chosen prophet, bolstering his political influence. When the French invasion brought an end to the regime of Piero de' Medici, Savonarola used the opportunity to help usher in to Florence a brief but memorable period of republican rule. He revived republicanism and surprised many by bringing moral renewal to the city.[1] One contemporary observer, Francesco Guicciardini, explains the friar's impact in glowing terms: "The work he did in promoting decent behavior was holy and marvelous; nor had there ever been as much goodness and religion in Florence as there was in his time."[2] Savonarola's role in the political and spiritual life of Florence during the 1490s left a lasting impression.[3]

Among those impacted by Savonarola was Florence's most influential political thinker, Niccolò Machiavelli. From his early correspondence to his

---

[1] For more on Savonarola's life and influence, see Donald Weinstein, *Savonarola and Florence: Prophecy and Patriotism in the Renaissance* (Princeton, NJ: Princeton University Press, 1970); Donald Weinstein, *Savonarola: The Rise and Fall of a Renaissance Prophet* (New Haven, CT: Yale University Press, 2011); Lauro Martines, *Scourge and Fire: Savonarola and Renaissance Italy* (London: Jonathan Cape, 2006); and John Najemy, *A History of Florence, 1200–1575* (Malden, MA: Blackwell Publishing, 2006), 375–413.

[2] Francesco Guicciardini, *The History of Florence*, in *Selected Writings of Girolamo Savonarola: Religion and Politics, 1490–1498*, trans. and ed. Anne Borelli and Maria Pastore Passaro (New Haven, CT: Yale University Press, 2006), 360.

[3] For more on Savonarola's lasting impact in Florence, see Lorenzo Polizzotto, *The Elect Nation: The Savonarolan Movement in Florence, 1494–1545* (Oxford: Clarendon Press, 1994).

mature works, Machiavelli shows an enduring interest in the friar who was at the center of Florentine politics.[4] Like so many political figures Machiavelli analyzes, Savonarola's success did not last. After Pope Alexander VI excommunicated him in 1497, Savonarola's power declined and he was executed in 1498. Upon the pyre, Savonarola's brief but spectacular political career met a sad end. His failure became for Machiavelli a lesson in the opportunities and perils of political life.

But what *exactly* Machiavelli takes that lesson to be remains the subject of much debate.[5] Sometimes Machiavelli criticizes Savonarola's hypocrisy,[6] while in other places he speaks of his greatness.[7] This ambivalent evidence gives rise to sharply different interpretations. Perhaps Machiavelli dismisses Savonarola as a religious fanatic who is hopelessly naïve about politics. Or perhaps he admires Savonarola and draws on his thought. Common to this debate are interpretations of Machiavelli that try to explain away the ambivalence in his writings, making his attitude toward Savonarola seem more one-sided than it actually is. That tendency has the unfortunate effect

---

[4] See Niccolò Machiavelli, *Machiavelli and His Friends: Their Personal Correspondence*, trans. and ed. James Atkinson and David Sices (DeKalb, IL: Northern Illinois University Press, 1996), Letters 3, 222, 270; *The Prince*, 2nd ed., trans. Harvey Mansfield (Chicago: University of Chicago Press, 1998), VI: 24; *Discourses on Livy*, trans. Harvey Mansfield and Nathan Tarcov (Chicago: University of Chicago Press, 1996), I.11.5, I.45.2, III.30.1; and *First Decennale*, in *Machiavelli: The Chief Works and Others*, vol. 3, trans. Allan Gilbert (Durham, NC: Duke University Press, 1965), lines 154–65.

[5] See Maurice Cranston, "A Dialogue on the State between Savonarola and Machiavelli," in *Political Dialogues* (London: British Broadcasting Corporation, 1968), 1–21; J. H. Whitfield, *Discourses on Machiavelli* (Cambridge: W. Heffer & Sons, 1969), 87–110; Donald Weinstein, "Machiavelli and Savonarola," in *Studies on Machiavelli*, ed. Myron Gilmore (Florence: Sansoni, 1972), 251–64; Donald Weinstein, *Savonarola*, 311–15; Patricia Zupan, "Machiavelli and Savonarola Revisited: The Closing Chapter of *Il Principe*," *Machiavelli Studies* 1 (1987): 43–64; Alison Brown, "Savonarola, Machiavelli and Moses: A Changing Model," in *Florence and Italy: Renaissance Studies in Honour of Nicolai Rubinstein*, ed. Peter Denley and Caroline Elam (London: Westfield College, 1988), 57–72; Marcia Colish, "Republicanism, Religion, and Machiavelli's Savonarolan Moment," *Journal of the History of Ideas* 60, no. 4 (1999): 597–616; John Najemy, "Papirius and the Chickens, or Machiavelli on the Necessity of Interpreting Religion," *Journal of the History of Ideas* 60, no. 4 (1999): 659–81; John Geerken, "Machiavelli's Moses and Renaissance Politics," *Journal of the History of Ideas* 60, no. 4 (1999): 579–95; Alison Brown, "Philosophy and Religion in Machiavelli," in *The Cambridge Companion to Machiavelli*, ed. John Najemy (New York: Cambridge University Press, 2010), 157–72, esp. 167; Mark Jurdjevic, *A Great and Wretched City: Promise and Failure in Machiavelli's Florentine Political Thought* (Cambridge, MA: Harvard University Press, 2014), 16–52; Alison McQueen, *Political Realism in Apocalyptic Times* (New York: Cambridge University Press, 2018), 63–104; and John Scott, "The Fortune of Machiavelli's Unarmed Prophet," *Journal of Politics* 80, no. 2 (2018): 615–29.

[6] Machiavelli, *Machiavelli and His Friends*, Letter 3.

[7] Machiavelli, *Discourses*, I.11.5; and *First Decennale*, line 157.

of obscuring important insights into his political thought. In particular, recognizing Machiavelli's ambivalence toward the apocalyptic figure of Savonarola is key to understanding his ambivalence more generally toward apocalyptic thought.

This chapter explores that ambivalence and how Machiavelli wrestles with Savonarola's adroit use of apocalyptic concepts in politics. On the one hand, Savonarola harnesses religious ideals to advance earthly ends – a fruitful strategy according to Machiavelli, who stresses that religion and politics must work hand in hand.[8] Savonarola takes initially rival concepts – the Eternal City from pagan thought and new Jerusalem from Christian thought – and fuses them together to offer a hopeful vision for Florence. In this vision, Florence plays a key role in God's plan for history, which calls on the city to engage in conquest and to expand its power. Most importantly from Machiavelli's perspective, Savonarola interprets apocalyptic doctrines to encourage bold action in the political sphere, not withdrawal from it.

Yet on the other hand, Savonarola's apocalyptic vision ultimately proves too utopian for Machiavelli. Despite desperately hoping for Florence's redemption and return to power,[9] Machiavelli cannot accept Savonarola's view that political renewal takes the form of an *eternal* polity. This point becomes evident in the *Discourses* as he considers whether a "perpetual republic" (*republica perpetua*) is possible.[10] Though drawn to the idea of a republic that endures forever, Machiavelli concludes in his *Discourse on Remodeling the Government of Florence* that it is a goal that remains always out of reach, even for the great who strive for it. In particular, his understanding of the world as subject to continual change and decay prevents him from embracing hope in a perpetual republic.[11] Machiavelli's attitudes toward Savonarola and the notion of a perpetual republic show why, despite recognizing the political power of apocalyptic hope, he must reject it. Without faith

---

[8] Machiavelli, *Discourses*, I.12. For more on this idea in Machiavelli's thought, see Samuel Preus, "Machiavelli's Functional Analysis of Religion: Context and Object," *Journal of the History of Ideas* 40, no. 2 (1979): 171–90; Benedetto Fontana, "Love of Country and Love of God: The Political Uses of Religion in Machiavelli," *Journal of the History of Ideas* 60, no. 4 (1999): 639–58; Najemy, "Papirius and the Chickens, or Machiavelli on the Necessity of Interpreting Religion"; and Maurizio Viroli, *Machiavelli's God*, trans. Antony Shugaar (Princeton, NJ: Princeton University Press, 2010).

[9] Machiavelli, *The Prince*, XXVI.

[10] Machiavelli, *Discourses*, III.17.1, III.22.3. Quotes from the original Italian throughout this chapter come from Machiavelli, *Tutte le opere*, ed. Mario Martelli (Florence: Sansoni, 1971).

[11] Machiavelli, *A Discourse on Remodeling the Government of Florence*, in *Machiavelli: The Chief Works and Others*, vol. 1, trans. Allan Gilbert (Durham, NC: Duke University Press, 1965), 111–15; and *Florentine Histories*, trans. Laura Banfield and Harvey Mansfield (Princeton, NJ: Princeton University Press, 1988), V.1.

in divine intervention to wipe away the ills plaguing politics and forever keep them at bay, Machiavelli sees no path to the ideal that in his mind surpasses all others – a perpetual republic.

THE PRINCE'S FINAL CHAPTER

In our examination of how Machiavelli engages with Savonarola and apocalyptic thought, it makes sense to begin with a popular approach to this question. Many interested in Machiavelli's views on apocalyptic thought, Savonarola, or both focus on the final chapter of The Prince.[12] This chapter, entitled "Exhortation to Save Italy and Free Her from the Barbarians," features Machiavelli's plea to Lorenzo de' Medici to seize the opportunity before him, redeem Italy, and save it from foreign forces.

Curiously, this chapter has gained its status as a source of insight into Machiavelli's attitudes toward Savonarola and apocalyptic thought despite never explicitly mentioning the friar or any apocalyptic texts. What attracts scholars to the chapter is its perceived apocalyptic rhetoric and tone, which represents a marked shift from the rest of the work. Throughout The Prince, Machiavelli takes a detached and scientific approach to understanding how a prince should govern in different circumstances. In the Exhortation, however, Machiavelli casts aside dispassionate analysis and makes an urgent call for Lorenzo to take decisive action to liberate Italy. More than just a prince, Lorenzo can become a "redeemer" who drives out of Italy the "barbarian domination [that] stinks to everyone."[13] The crisis caused by foreign invasion created an opportunity for Lorenzo to effect a new political order, increase his power, and secure a lasting reputation.[14] No longer content to simply analyze politics, Machiavelli concludes The Prince by urging dramatic intervention aimed at reshaping Italy's political future.

Many see Machiavelli as employing in the Exhortation language and imagery drawn from Savonarola. Donald Weinstein is an early interpreter to suggest this connection, though he ultimately concludes that apocalyptic thinkers like Savonarola are "a foil" for Machiavelli, who places his hope in

---

[12] See Weinstein, "Machiavelli and Savonarola," 262; Felix Gilbert, "Machiavelli's 'Istorie Fiorentine': An Essay in Interpretation," in Studies on Machiavelli, ed. Myron Gilmore (Florence: Sansoni, 1972), 97; John Najemy, "Machiavelli and the Medici: The Lessons of Florentine History," Renaissance Quarterly 35, no. 4 (1982): 553; Zupan, "Machiavelli and Savonarola Revisited"; Jurdjevic, A Great and Wretched City, 16–52; McQueen, Political Realism in Apocalyptic Times, 63–104; and Scott, "The Fortune of Machiavelli's Unarmed Prophet," 626–27.

[13] Machiavelli, The Prince, XXVI: 105.

[14] Machiavelli, The Prince, XXVI: 101–02.

bold men rather than God to bring about redemption.[15] Others go further than Weinstein, arguing that the Exhortation shows Machiavelli's embrace of apocalyptic thought and Savonarola in particular. Patricia Zupan argues that Machiavelli concludes *The Prince* by abandoning his scientific approach to politics in favor of Savonarola's prophetic voice,[16] a move that "attempts resolution and closure through projecting a millenarian vision of unity and concord."[17] Taking a similar view, Alison McQueen writes: "The final chapter of *The Prince* ... is an apocalyptic exhortation that reiterates the Savonarolan message in a secular way."[18] Likewise, Mark Jurdjevic claims: "Machiavelli was thinking about the Savonarolan example when he wrote that chapter and intended his audience to see that connection."[19] So for a number of scholars, Savonarola and his apocalyptic message serve as a source of inspiration for *The Prince*'s final chapter.

Though a popular way of linking Machiavelli's thought to Savonarola, this interpretation runs into several problems. Let's start with the claim that Machiavelli specifically has Savonarola in mind and wants his audience to think of the friar's example when they read the Exhortation. It is difficult to square this view with textual evidence found in the chapter and elsewhere in *The Prince*. Machiavelli spends much of the chapter urging Lorenzo to assemble a strong army.[20] In light of that advice, Savonarola – an unarmed prophet as an earlier passage from *The Prince* describes him[21] – seems like the last person Machiavelli would want to evoke for his audience in the Exhortation. Moreover, it is far from clear why Machiavelli would think that an apocalyptic prophet who ended up executed would be a compelling example to the Medici, *The Prince*'s stated audience. At the time Machiavelli wrote the work, the Medici regime was cracking down on apocalyptic preachers and followers of Savonarola.[22] This combination of historical and textual evidence casts doubt on the theory that one goal of the Exhortation is to direct readers' attention to the example of Savonarola.

Another possibility is that *The Prince*'s final chapter appropriates elements from the preaching of Savonarola, even if it does not intend to evoke his memory. To be sure, there are some similarities between the Exhortation

---

[15] Weinstein, "Machiavelli and Savonarola," 262.
[16] Zupan, "Machiavelli and Savonarola Revisited," 45.
[17] Zupan, "Machiavelli and Savonarola Revisited," 49.
[18] McQueen, *Political Realism in Apocalyptic Times*, 63.
[19] Jurdjevic, *A Great and Wretched City*, 30.
[20] Machiavelli, *The Prince*, XXVI: 102–5.
[21] Machiavelli, *The Prince*, VI: 24.
[22] Weinstein, *Savonarola and Florence*, 346–73.

and Savonarola's thought. The latter draws on apocaltic texts and themes to craft a narrative that emphasizes crisis as a vehicle for bringing about the redemption of Florence. Likewise in the Exhortation, Machiavelli hopes for redemption as the ultimate outcome of the crisis facing Italy at the time. "[T]o know the virtue of an Italian spirit," argues Machiavelli, "it was necessary that Italy be reduced to the condition in which she is at present, which is more enslaved than the Hebrews, more servile than the Persians, more dispersed than the Athenians, without a head, without order, beaten, despoiled, torn, pillaged, and having endured ruin of every sort."[23] Similar to many authors of apocalyptic texts, Machiavelli infuses crisis with meaning by interpreting it as a path to redemption.

But despite a few similarities, the Exhortation departs in significant ways from the Christian apocalyptic tradition embraced by Savonarola. That tradition entails more than just hope for a better future following crisis. It espouses a truly utopian vision for the future – the perfect kingdom of God, which will surpass anything in human history. In contrast, Machiavelli does not anticipate such a radical break from the past. He instead frames the opportunity to redeem Italy as similar to opportunities faced by past founders. After discussing the examples of Moses, Cyrus, and Theseus, Machiavelli urges Lorenzo "to follow those excellent men who redeemed their countries" by establishing a strong army.[24] Rather than hope for something radically novel, Machiavelli wants history to repeat itself and for Lorenzo to imitate the boldness and virtue of past founders.

By overlooking this point, some interpreters exaggerate the utopian nature of the political vision outlined in the Exhortation. For instance, McQueen argues that the redemption of Italy envisioned by Machiavelli "marks an end to the variability, contingency, and contestation that define the political world," which shows his reliance on "a Savonarolan set of rhetorical maneuvers."[25] Though Savonarola certainly preached a future for Florence free from contingency and political strife (as will be discussed further), the Exhortation stops short of such utopian hope. Machiavelli never suggests in *The Prince* that the political renewal he calls for will endure forever. In making the case to Lorenzo to seize the opportunity before him, Machiavelli stresses the honor, love, and reputation that will come to him, not that his new orders will last forever.[26] Machiavelli expresses optimism that a leader will rise up and assemble an army

---

[23] Machiavelli, *The Prince*, XXVI: 102.
[24] Machiavelli, *The Prince*, XXVI: 104.
[25] McQueen, *Political Realism in Apocalyptic Times*, 87–88.
[26] Machiavelli, *The Prince*, XXVI: 105.

capable of driving foreign troops out of Italy. This optimism, however, remains distinct from the utopian prediction that a new political order founded by Lorenzo can permanently escape contingency and variability – a claim Machiavelli avoids.

For this reason, a more accurate characterization of the closing of *The Prince* is as a redemption narrative rather than an apocalyptic one. Maurizio Viroli makes this point, noting that the Exhortation "shares some features of millenarianism" but that the more apt comparison is with the story of Exodus.[27] The redemption narrative found in Exodus details how God empowers a political and spiritual leader, Moses, to lead his people out of slavery and into the Promised Land. There is strong textual evidence supporting this interpretation of the Exhortation. In it, Machiavelli specifically compares the Italians to "the people of Israel ... enslaved in Egypt" and praises Moses as an "excellent [man]" to follow.[28] He uses imagery directly from Exodus to describe the opportunity before Lorenzo: "[T]he sea has opened; the cloud has escorted you along the way; the stone has poured forth water; here manna has rained; everything has concurred in your greatness."[29] Like Moses who led the Hebrew people out of bondage, the founder hoped for by Machiavelli will lead the Italians in emancipating themselves from foreign domination. But even in these flights of optimism, Machiavelli steers clear of the utopian hope characteristic of apocalyptic beliefs – a permanent end to woe for an elect group of people. Such hope is conspicuously absent from the Exhortation.

In sum, the Exhortation's links to Savonarola and apocalyptic thought end up being more tenuous than many claim. It is necessary to look elsewhere in Machiavelli's writings to understand his attitudes toward Savonarola and apocalyptic thought. Notably, Machiavelli shares with Savonarola a deep interest in the possibility of a polity that would endure forever. Their reflections on this possibility reveal affinities between them, but also why they ultimately must part ways over whether to embrace apocalyptic hope, as we explore later.

THE ETERNAL CITY AND NEW JERUSALEM

Machiavelli brings up the concept of the perpetual republic at two separate points in the *Discourses*. The first time he concludes that it would be impossible to realize a republic that lasts forever. Five chapters later, he strikes

---

[27] Maurizio Viroli, *Redeeming* The *Prince: The Meaning of Machiavelli's Masterpiece* (Princeton, NJ: Princeton University Press, 2014), 14–15.
[28] Machiavelli, *The Prince*, XXVI: 102, 104.
[29] Machiavelli, XXVI: 103. The miracles cited by Machiavelli come from Exodus 14:21, 13:21, 17:6, 16:4.

a slightly less pessimistic tone and expresses the faint hope that a perpetual republic would be possible under certain rare conditions.[30] In these passages, Machiavelli gives voice to a hope going back to ancient Rome – the idea of the "Eternal City" (urbs aeterna). It was common for ancient writers to refer to Rome as eternal. One notable example is Livy, whose History of Rome is the focus of Machiavelli's Discourses.[31] Like the ancients he closely studies, Machiavelli entertains the notion of a polity that endures forever.

This hope for a city or kingdom that will last forever also appears in Christian apocalyptic thought. Whereas the Roman tradition places its hope in Rome as the Eternal City, the Christian tradition anticipates the coming of the kingdom of God or new Jerusalem, which will endure forever. These two concepts – the Eternal City and new Jerusalem – eventually merged together in the world that Machiavelli and Savonarola both inhabited, Renaissance Florence. The result was what Weinstein calls the "myth of Florence": the idea that Florence was chosen by God, imbued with eschatological importance, and destined to flourish like ancient Rome in wealth and power.[32]

That myth developed long after the concepts of the Eternal City and new Jerusalem first emerged. The reign of the Roman Emperor Augustus, which began in the first century B.C.E., inaugurated the Pax Romana, helped allay anxieties that Rome would be destroyed, and gave way to the hope that Rome would endure forever.[33] Formulations used to express Rome's immortality took various forms, but the term that initially came into widespread use was urbs aeterna or "Eternal City."[34] Praising Rome as the Eternal City was especially common in Roman poetry.[35] Perhaps most famously, Virgil in the Aeneid proclaims Rome to be "an empire that will know no end."[36] In the second century C.E., during the reign of Hadrian, Roma aeterna or "eternal Rome" emerged as another expression alongside urbs aeterna.[37]

Belief in Rome as the Eternal City initially existed in tension with Christian beliefs, especially its apocalyptic doctrines. Early Christians anxiously

---

[30] Machiavelli, Discourses, III.17.1, III.22.3.
[31] Livy, The Early History of Rome: Books I–V of The History of Rome from Its Foundation, trans. Aubrey de Sélincourt (Baltimore: Penguin Books, 1960), IV.4.4, V.7.10.
[32] Weinstein, Savonarola and Florence, 27–66.
[33] Mircea Eliade, The Myth of the Eternal Return: Cosmos and History, trans. Willard Trask (Princeton, NJ: Princeton University Press, 2005), 135–36.
[34] Kenneth Pratt, "Rome as Eternal," Journal of the History of Ideas 26, no. 1 (1965): 25.
[35] See, e.g., Ovid, Fasti, trans. and ed. A. J. Boyle and R. D. Woodard (New York: Penguin Books, 2000), III.72.
[36] Virgil, The Aeneid, trans. David West (New York: Penguin Books, 1991), I.279.
[37] Pratt, "Rome as Eternal," 28.

anticipated the coming of God's kingdom – the only kingdom, in their view, that would last forever. From this perspective, the notion of Rome as the Eternal City stood in direct opposition to God's divine plan for history. In the book of Revelation, one finds that the promise of God's everlasting kingdom goes hand in hand with fierce attacks on the Roman Empire's belief in its invincibility. As New Testament scholar Adela Yarbro Collins notes, Revelation's criticism of Rome's arrogance "was probably a response to Roman propaganda regarding the eternity and universality of Roman dominance."[38] The early Christian apocalyptic tradition took a hostile view toward the myth of the Eternal City because, if Rome ruled forever, that stood in the way of Christ's eternal kingdom.

John, the author of Revelation, specifically attacks the myth of the Eternal City by pointing to Rome's coming destruction. It is not a city destined to rule forever, and instead enjoys only fleeting glory. John emphasizes this point through a voice from heaven announcing Rome's fate: "As she glorified herself and lived luxuriously, so give her a like measure of torment and grief.... [H]er plagues will come in a single day – pestilence and mourning and famine – and she will be burned with fire" (Revelation 18:7–8).[39] In its vision of Rome's destruction, Revelation describes the shock of those who see that such a great city "in one hour ... has been laid waste" (Revelation 18:19). Revelation closes with the vision of the new Jerusalem coming down from heaven to earth, which marks the establishment of God's earthly rule and an end to all suffering (Revelation 21). Rome's greatness pales in comparison to the perfection of the new Jerusalem – a kingdom, unlike the Roman Empire, destined to endure forever.

So the Christian apocalyptic tradition offered its own vision of an everlasting kingdom, which competed with the idea of Rome as the Eternal City. In the words of theologian Barbara Rossing, beliefs in the Eternal City and new Jerusalem represented "dueling eschatologies."[40] Both the Roman and Christian traditions voiced hope in an eternal kingdom, but looked for it in different places.

Christianity's dim view of Rome as the Eternal City largely persisted throughout the Middle Ages.[41] Augustine in the *City of God* makes the case

---

[38] Adela Yarbro Collins, *Crisis and Catharsis: The Power of Apocalypse* (Philadelphia: Westminster Press, 1984), 122.
[39] New Revised Standard Version. All subsequent biblical quotes come from this version.
[40] Barbara Rossing, "River of Life in God's New Jerusalem: An Eschatological Vision for Earth's Future," in *Christianity and Ecology: Seeking the Well-Being of Earth and Humans*, ed. Dieter Hessel and Rosemary Radford Ruether (Cambridge, MA: Harvard University Press, 2000), 207.
[41] Pratt, "Rome as Eternal," 31.

for the superiority of the heavenly city compared to Rome. Notably, he takes Virgil's famous description of Rome in the *Aeneid* – "an empire without end" – and instead applies it to the heavenly city.[42] In this way, Christian writers subverted the intended meaning of the Eternal City so as to downplay Rome's greatness and glorify God's kingdom.

With time, though, Rome's designation as the Eternal City came back into use as it lost its blasphemous connotations. For intellectual and political leaders in Italy and the Holy Roman Empire, identifying Rome as the Eternal City was a way to express pride in their historical connection to the ancient Romans.[43] In *The Banquet*, Dante approvingly quotes Virgil's description of Rome as an "empire without end," with the added twist that the *Christian* God chose Rome as the empire that would endure with unrivalled power.[44] Rather than an affront to Christ's kingdom, the designation of Rome as the Eternal City comes from God. For Dante, the Eternal City and new Jerusalem no longer stand in conflict with one another – a marked shift away from Augustine's view that only the heavenly city could be eternal.

Dante, a native of Florence, gave voice to a view that became prevalent during the Renaissance. For many elites in Florence, republican Rome was a model for their city to follow. This view emerged in a context where apocalyptic preaching flourished and identified Florence as the new Jerusalem described in Revelation. As Weinstein explains, "The myth that celebrated Florence both as the New Jerusalem and as the New Rome in a dual mission of spiritual and political leadership was one with which Florentines of every class would have been familiar."[45] This idea helped shape Florentine political and religious thought at the time when Machiavelli became active in politics. Savonarola in particular represented this fusion of Christian and Roman thought, which sparked hopes for an eternal, expansive, and flourishing city.

SAVONAROLA'S APOCALYPTIC VISION FOR FLORENCE

Throughout his ministry in Florence, Savonarola displayed a strong interest in Christian apocalyptic doctrines and their relevance to contemporary events. After arriving in Florence in 1490 to become the lector of the monastery of San Marco, Savonarola preached a series of sermons on the book of Revelation.

---

[42] Augustine, *City of God*, trans. Henry Bettenson (New York: Penguin Books, 1984), II.29: 87.
[43] Pratt, "Rome as Eternal," 32–33.
[44] Dante Alighieri, *The Banquet*, trans. Christopher Ryan (Saratoga, CA: Anma Libri, 1989), IV.4.10–IV.4.12.
[45] Weinstein, *Savonarola and Florence*, 146–47.

These sermons emphasized that the events foretold in Revelation were imminent: a divine scourge was coming to wipe away corruption in the Church and society at large. Even before Florence's political revolution of 1494, great crowds flocked to hear Savonarola and his apocalyptic preaching.[46]

As his apocalyptic message developed, Florence took an increasingly central role in it. Weinstein describes this shift, which had major ramifications for Savonarola's political thought:

> At a certain point Savonarola's apocalyptic vision of future tribulations became millenarian and this-worldly, his ascetic piety made room for a materialistic promise of riches and power. At a certain moment his Christian universalism narrowed to a partisan civic focus, with Florence taking shape in his mind as the New Jerusalem and the future of her government and worldly fortunes becoming part of the divine plan.[47]

The idea that Florence's greatness is part of God's plan for history is largely absent from the early apocalyptic preaching of Savonarola. If he had remained wedded to an apocalyptic vision that left little role for political renewal in advancing God's plan, his religious message would have had limited significance for politics. But his message underwent a transformation, which became especially evident with the fall of the Medici regime in 1494.

At this critical juncture, Savonarola took to the pulpit to emphasize that God wanted the people of Florence to adopt republican rule. With this change, a righteous republic would emerge, flourish, and take on divine importance. On December 12, 1494, shortly after the end of Medici rule, Savonarola preached a sermon making the case that in Florence "government by the majority is better than that of a single leader."[48] Partly in response to Savonarola's preaching, the government implemented republican measures modeled after those in Venice. Savonarola proclaimed that these reforms, combined with spiritual renewal, would make Florence more glorious than ever before:

> [E]veryone go to confession and be purified of sins, and let everyone attend to the common good of the city; and if you will do this, your city will be glorious because in this way she will be reformed spiritually as well as temporally, that is, with regard to her people, and from you will issue the reform of all Italy.

---

[46] Weinstein, *Savonarola and Florence*, 75–76, 91–99.
[47] Weinstein, *Savonarola and Florence*, 77.
[48] Girolamo Savonarola, "Aggeus, Sermon XIII: 12 December 1494," in *Selected Writings of Girolamo Savonarola: Religion and Politics, 1490–1498*, trans. and ed. Anne Borelli and Maria Pastore Passaro (New Haven, CT: Yale University Press, 2006), 152.

Florence will become richer and more powerful than she has ever been, and her empire will expand into many places.[49]

Rather than simply focus on heavenly rewards, Savonarola details the earthly greatness that God has in store for Florence. In his vision for republican rule and a renewed spiritual life, Florence has the opportunity to greatly expand its earthly power.

Though it would be inaccurate to call Savonarola the author of the republican government implemented in 1494, it is important not to underestimate his role in its adoption. He persuaded many in Florence to see the new government as divinely inspired. As John Najemy puts it, "While the constitution of 1494 was not Savonarola's invention, its identification with sacred history and with divine will was indeed his, and of momentous consequence."[50] Savonarola used his religious authority to confer added significance to the political changes Florence implemented in 1494. Florence's political revolution without bloodshed was, in Savonarola's words, "a divine miracle."[51] Many in Florence, thankful for the peaceful transition, saw no reason to argue with him.

Savonarola's message and political vision bear the marks of cataclysmic apocalyptic thought. As is characteristic of this perspective, he sees pervasive corruption in the world, but has faith that God will wipe it away in a coming crisis, which will lead to a lasting utopia. Savonarola repeatedly identifies the Church as a source of corruption, which "has reached the dregs" and is in desperate need of renewal.[52] Savonarola also condemns "the haughtiness, pride, and countless hateful sins of [Italy's] princes and captains."[53] Spiritual and political corruption is leading to a crisis point, which will result in God's wrath and upheaval. "God's dagger will strike, and soon," warns Savonarola in a sermon from January 13, 1495.[54] With God's guidance, the coming crisis will remove the corrupt from power and realize his perfect kingdom.

The political significance of this vision is difficult to miss, since Savonarola singles out Florence as the city divinely chosen to fulfill it. Drawing on an end-times prophecy from the book of Matthew, Savonarola stresses that the gospel "must be preached throughout the whole world" to realize God's

---

[49] Savonarola, "Aggeus, Sermon XIII: 12 December 1494," 153.
[50] Najemy, *A History of Florence, 1200–1575*, 394.
[51] Savonarola, *The Compendium of Revelations*, in *Apocalyptic Spirituality*, trans. and ed. Bernard McGinn (New York: Paulist Press, 1979), 210.
[52] Savonarola, *The Compendium of Revelations*, 217–18.
[53] Savonarola, *The Compendium of Revelations*, 267.
[54] Savonarola, "Psalms, Sermon III: Renovation Sermon, 13 January 1495," in *Selected Writings of Girolamo Savonarola*, 74.

eternal kingdom.[55] He adds to this prophecy the twist that Florence "is loved by God more especially than other" cities, and has been chosen by him to "propagate [his divine word] throughout the world."[56] For this reason, Florence is destined to increase in wealth and power, which are necessary to spread the gospel. Savonarola places special importance on Florence's establishing itself not just as a righteous republic, but also as a wealthy and expansive one. Indeed, Savonarola goes so far as to claim that these predictions of Florence's temporal greatness come directly from the Virgin Mary. He reports a heavenly vision where Mary tells him: "May the city of Florence become more glorious, more powerful, and richer than it has ever been before. May it stretch its wings farther than it ever has done before .... May it fully recover whatever it had .... May it acquire things that till now have never come within its power."[57] In short, divine and temporal goals become unified in Savonarola's vision for Florence.

Ancient Rome also plays a significant role in this vision. In his most explicitly political work, *Treatise on the Rule and Government of the City of Florence*, Savonarola urges the citizens of Florence to perfect their government by emulating the ancient Romans. The "Romans greatly expanded their empire," he writes, "because they loved the common good of the city so much .... God gave such great power to the Romans, because they loved each other and remained at peace with each other in the beginning." Just as God rewarded the Romans for their virtue, he "will multiply both [Florence's] spiritual and temporal goods," so long as its citizens also uphold these virtues.[58] From Savonarola's perspective, the ideal embodied by ancient Rome is not in conflict with his vision for Florence. Rather, this vision incorporates Rome as an exemplary model for Florence to follow in perfecting its government.

According to Savonarola, Florence ultimately will exceed Rome's greatness because it represents the new Jerusalem, a concept that comes from the apocalyptic text of Revelation. He assures the people that, if they turn to God, "blessed will you be, Florence, for you will soon become that celestial Jerusalem (*quella Jerusalem superna*)."[59] Here Savonarola's apocalyptic hopes

---

[55] Savonarola, *A Dialogue Concerning Prophetic Truth*, in *Selected Writings of Girolamo Savonarola*, 107. See Matthew 24:14: "And this good news of the kingdom will be proclaimed throughout the world, as a testimony to all the nations; and then the end will come."
[56] Savonarola, *A Dialogue Concerning Prophetic Truth*, 116.
[57] Savonarola, *The Compendium of Revelations*, 267.
[58] Savonarola, *Treatise on the Rule and Government of the City of Florence*, in *Selected Writings of Girolamo Savonarola*, 201.
[59] Savonarola, *Prediche sopra Aggeo*, ed. Luigi Firpo (Rome: Angelo Belardetti, 1965), 151. Quoted in Weinstein, *Savonarola and Florence*, 142.

for Florence come through most explicitly. By identifying Florence with the celestial Jerusalem described in Revelation that comes down to earth, Savonarola sets forth his vision of Florence as God's perfect kingdom. Given these divine plans for Florence, the only true king for the city could be Christ. "Take Christ as your King," urges Savonarola, "and place yourself under His law."[60] God has a special relationship with Florence and will bless it unlike any other city, as his eschatological promises are fulfilled.

As the new Jerusalem, Florence will embody perfection and endure forever. For Savonarola, the upheaval plaguing Italy is a necessary but temporary step in God's plan. From these difficulties, God's kingdom will emerge in Florence. Savonarola outlines this utopian future near the end of his *Treatise on the Rule and Government of the City of Florence*:

> [I]n a very short time, the city shall return to such devotion that it will be like a terrestrial paradise, and will live in jubilation and in songs and psalms; boys and girls will be like angels, and they will be brought up to live both as Christians and as good citizens. In time, through these practices, the government of the city will become more heavenly than earthly, and the happiness of the good will be so great that they will enjoy a kind of spiritual felicity even in this world.[61]

This hope pervades Savonarola's writings and sermons during the turbulent years following the return to republican rule in 1494. In the midst of turmoil, he assures the people of Florence that unparalleled greatness lies ahead – spiritual righteousness, territorial expansion, wealth, and happiness. His message found a sympathetic audience among many in Florence, who came to believe his apocalyptic vision for their city. As one of his followers put it, when Savonarola led the city, "Florence was happy and blessed and seemed a new Jerusalem."[62]

The vision for Florence embraced by Savonarola and his followers is thoroughly utopian. He embraces a utopian ideal from the Christian apocalyptic tradition, the new Jerusalem, and claims that God has chosen Florence to embody it. But despite the utopian nature of Savonarola's message, it is not merely otherworldly and unconcerned with politics. To fulfill its destiny as the new Jerusalem, Florence must become great by expanding in wealth and

---

[60] Savonarola, "Aggeus, Sermon XXIII: 28 December 1494," in *Selected Writings of Girolamo Savonarola*, 171.
[61] Savonarola, *Treatise on the Rule and Government of the City of Florence*, 203.
[62] Timoteo Bottonio, *La vita del Beato Ieronimo Savonarola*, in *Selected Writings of Girolamo Savonarola: Religion and Politics, 1490–1498*, trans. and ed. Anne Borelli and Maria Pastore Passaro (New Haven, CT: Yale University Press, 2006), 243.

power like ancient Rome. Savonarola thus fashions an apocalyptic vision for Florence uniquely suited to advance political goals because it infuses them with divine meaning.

REASSESSING MACHIAVELLI'S VIEW OF SAVONAROLA

The general consensus among scholars, notes Jurdjevic, is that Machiavelli "had a rather dim view of Savonarola."[63] As an apocalyptic preacher who met political ruin, Savonarola is not a figure that many would expect Machiavelli to admire. In his discussions of politics, Machiavelli is brutally honest. It seems that he would have little patience for someone who relies on Christian eschatology to make far-fetched claims about politics. Well after Savonarola's death, Machiavelli does express exasperation with prophets in his city who preach doom and destruction, calling Florence "a magnet for all the world's pitchmen."[64] So when scholars argue that Machiavelli finds aspects of Savonarola's thought appealing, it is not surprising that they rarely point to the friar's apocalyptic message as the reason why.[65] The few who do focus on the last chapter of *The Prince* as evidence,[66] but that interpretation runs into problems because this chapter never embraces Savonarola's apocalyptic message and its utopian hope, as discussed earlier. Since that line of interpretation fails, it is tempting to jump to the conclusion that Machiavelli "loathed" Savonarola's apocalyptic message.[67]

There are reasons, though, to resist this conclusion. The various remarks regarding Savonarola in Machiavelli's writings prove far more ambivalent than how many interpreters characterize them. At some places Machiavelli criticizes the friar, yet at others he praises him. When viewed together, this evidence reveals an important point: Machiavelli's criticisms of Savonarola do not stem from concerns over his apocalyptic vision for Florence but from other concerns. A likely reason why is that Savonarola avoids a message entirely filled with doom, which treats politics as futile and something to retreat from. Instead, he crafts an apocalyptic message full of hope for

---

[63] Jurdjevic, *A Great and Wretched City*, 16. For a similar assessment, see also Colish, "Republicanism, Religion, and Machiavelli's Savonarolan Moment," 612.
[64] Machiavelli, *Machiavelli and His Friends*, Letter 225: 267.
[65] See Weinstein, "Machiavelli and Savonarola"; Weinstein, *Savonarola: The Rise and Fall of a Renaissance Prophet*, 311–15; Brown, "Savonarola, Machiavelli and Moses"; Whitfield, *Discourses on Machiavelli*, 87–110; and Jurdjevic, *A Great and Wretched City*, 16–52.
[66] See Zupan, "Machiavelli and Savonarola Revisited"; and McQueen, *Political Realism in Apocalyptic Times*, 63–104.
[67] Colish, "Republicanism, Religion, and Machiavelli's Savonarolan Moment," 600.

Florence's future – one that encourages political action and, for that reason, proves far harder for Machiavelli to dismiss.

Machiavelli's first remarks on Savonarola come in a letter to Ricciardo Becchi on March 9, 1498.[68] Becchi was an ambassador for Florence stationed in Rome. This role put Becchi in a tough spot: Florence still officially supported Savonarola, but at a time when Rome was increasingly frustrated with him, due to the friar's return to preaching after Pope Alexander VI had excommunicated him in 1497.[69] In response to a request by Becchi, Machiavelli provides in his letter a summary and analysis of Savonarola's sermons during February and March 1498.[70]

At times in the letter, Machiavelli takes a critical tone toward Savonarola. Because of Savonarola's shifting criticisms of the pope and Florentine government, Machiavelli writes that, "in my judgment, he acts in accordance with the times and colors his lies accordingly."[71] Here Machiavelli's attitude toward Savonarola is the most dismissive that one finds in his writings.[72] In his analysis, Machiavelli ultimately concludes that Savonarola's sermons reveal his hypocrisy, as well as his increasingly tenuous political position.

It makes sense why Machiavelli came to this conclusion at the time. In 1498 when Machiavelli wrote to Becchi, Savonarola's political power was in sharp decline, and his maneuverings to regain his grip on it only made the situation worse. The first major event precipitating this decline was the pope's excommunication of Savonarola in 1497. Though not the death knell of his political career, it certainly hurt his support in Florence. His support took another hit in 1497 when he failed to speak in favor of the law of appeal in the case of Medici conspirators, who were sentenced to death for trying to overthrow the republic. The law of appeal empowered the most democratic element of Florence's government, the Great Council, to make the final decision on severe sentences like death.[73] Previously, Savonarola had championed adoption of the law and praised it as a key reform that provided stability

---

[68] Machiavelli, *Machiavelli and His Friends*, Letter 3.
[69] See "Letters 1497–1498," in Machiavelli, *Machiavelli and His Friends*, 4.
[70] Machiavelli, *Machiavelli and His Friends*, Letter 3: 8.
[71] Machiavelli, Letter 3: 10.
[72] The closest competitor is probably a letter from 1521 to Guicciardini, where Machiavelli briefly mentions Savonarola and calls him "wily." See Machiavelli, *Machiavelli and His Friends*, Letter 270: 336. It is not clear, though, that this remark counts as criticism, since elsewhere Machiavelli suggests that rulers should be wily. See Machiavelli, *The Prince*, XVIII: 69–70. For more on this point, see Jurdjevic, *A Great and Wretched City*, 38.
[73] Lauro Martines, *Lawyers and Statecraft in Renaissance Florence* (Princeton, NJ: Princeton University Press, 1968), 441–48.

to Florence and helped restore its glory.[74] By not wanting to apply the law when it proved inconvenient, Savonarola looked hypocritical and alienated some of his own supporters with Medici sympathies – a point Machiavelli makes in the *Discourses*.[75] Savonarola's fortunes continued to wane in March 1498 with the arrival of new members to the Signoria, Florence's ruling body, which resulted in a government more hostile to him.[76]

The opposition Savonarola faced was starting to overwhelm him. During the couple of months after Machiavelli's letter, Savonarola would be imprisoned, tortured, hanged, and burned. It is important to keep this context in mind when drawing conclusions from Machiavelli's letter. Its dismissive comments toward Savonarola in 1498 – right before his downfall – reflect his weakness at the time, but need not imply that Machiavelli consistently held this view without ever revising it.

Over time, Machiavelli's assessment of Savonarola became more nuanced and even reverential in tone, as he reflected on the friar's career with the benefit of time.[77] In numerous places, Machiavelli uses terms of respect for Savonarola – so frequently, in fact, that it is difficult to chalk his comments up to irony. When first mentioning him in the *Discourses*, Machiavelli refrains from judging Savonarola's claim that he spoke with God and adds: "one should speak with reverence of such a man."[78] Later, Machiavelli praises Savonarola's writings, which "show the learning, the prudence, and the virtue of his spirit."[79] And in his poem the *First Decennale* on Florentine history, he speaks of the "great Savonarola."[80]

This reverential language shares much in common with that used by Machiavelli's friend Guicciardini. Like Machiavelli, he refuses to say whether Savonarola "was a true prophet." Either way, Savonarola was an impressive figure from Guicciardini's perspective: "[I]f he was good, we have seen a great prophet in our time; if he was bad, we have seen a great man." Guicciardini continues by noting that, "if he was able to fool the public for so many years on so important a matter without ever being caught in a lie, he must have had great judgment, talent, and power of invention."[81] In line with Guicciardini's

---

[74] Savonarola, *The Compendium of Revelations*, 207.
[75] Machiavelli, *Discourses*, I.45.2.
[76] For more on the events in 1497 and 1498 leading to Savonarola's downfall, see Weinstein, *Savonarola and Florence*, 280–88; and Najemy, *A History of Florence*, 397–400.
[77] Weinstein and Martines also suggest that Machiavelli's view toward Savonarola changed with time. See Weinstein, "Machiavelli and Savonarola," 255; and Martines, *Scourge and Fire*, 244.
[78] Machiavelli, *Discourses*, I.11.5.
[79] Machiavelli, *Discourses*, I.45.2.
[80] Machiavelli, *First Decennale*, line 157.
[81] Guicciardini, *The History of Florence*, 362.

judgment, Machiavelli also describes Savonarola as a great man from Florence's recent past.

Admittedly, Machiavelli's praise of Savonarola often comes with caveats, as he points out failures and constraints that ultimately forced the friar from power. Unfortunately, interpreters too often restrict their focus to these caveats while failing to take seriously remarks praising Savonarola.[82] That approach hinders an honest assessment of Machiavelli's views of Savonarola, in all their nuance and complexity. It thus is important to consider *both* Machiavelli's praise and criticism of Savonarola, with the goal of understanding how they fit together in his political thought.

Chapter 6 of *The Prince* proves key for understanding the tensions in Machiavelli's reflections on Savonarola. The chapter focuses on "new princes" who acquire principalities through their "own arms and virtue." Machiavelli begins it by explaining that he will "bring up the greatest examples" of new princes.[83] He proceeds to examine an impressive list of founders: Moses who founded Israel, Cyrus who founded Persia, Romulus who founded Rome, and Theseus who founded Athens. In the context of discussing these great men, Machiavelli includes the example of Savonarola. He makes clear that Savonarola fell short of achieving the greatness of founders like Moses. For unlike Moses, Savonarola was an unarmed prophet, which led to his ruin and prevented him from maintaining the principality he had acquired.[84]

Despite Savonarola's ultimate failure in politics, Machiavelli still sees him as a founder of new orders. For this reason, Savonarola counts as a great man in the eyes of Machiavelli, and one who had the potential to achieve even more. Indeed, throughout his writings, Machiavelli exhibits a deep admiration for founders. The most famous example is his plea at the end of *The Prince* for Lorenzo to seize the opportunity to found new political orders. Such action, stresses Machiavelli, will establish for him a reputation of lasting greatness.[85] In a less well-known passage from *A Discourse on Remodeling the Government of Florence*, Machiavelli makes clear that no human achievement can rival the act of founding new orders:

> [N]o man is so exalted by any act of his as are those men who have with laws and with institutions remodeled republics and kingdoms; these are, after those who have been gods, the first to be praised. And because they have

---

[82] See, e.g., Colish, "Republicanism, Religion, and Machiavelli's Savonarolan Moment."
[83] Machiavelli, *The Prince*, VI: 21–22.
[84] Machiavelli, *The Prince*, VI: 24.
[85] Machiavelli, *The Prince*, XXVI: 105.

been few who have had opportunity to do it, and very few those who have understood how to do it, small is the number who have done it. And so much has this glory been esteemed by men seeking for nothing other than glory that when unable to form a republic in reality, they have done it in writing, as Aristotle, Plato, and many others, who have wished to show the world that if they have not founded a free government, as did Solon and Lycurgus, they have failed not through their ignorance but through their impotence for putting it into practice.[86]

This passage illustrates Machiavelli's profound respect for founders, who according to him are second only to gods. No glory compares with that of founding a government. In fact, Machiavelli identifies this desire for glory as the motivation behind philosophers who outline new orders for the ideal government, but whose impotence in politics prevents them from realizing their visions.

In conjunction with Chapter 6 of *The Prince*, Machiavelli's praise of founders in *A Discourse on Remodeling the Government of Florence* brings into sharper focus why he sees greatness in Savonarola. Like Plato, Aristotle, and other philosophers, Savonarola wrote about new orders in works such as his *Treatise on the Rule and Government of the City of Florence*. But Savonarola went beyond just writing about new orders: he worked to realize them by using his pulpit to call for republican rule in Florence. By *taking action* to put new orders in place, Savonarola surpassed in greatness philosophers who only *contemplated* new orders. When the opportunity presented itself, Savonarola aimed for great things – in fact, the greatest achievement possible. And his bold action succeeded in establishing new orders, at least for a period of time. Understanding the immense challenges that face anyone attempting to found new orders, Machiavelli treats Savonarola's achievement as no small feat and cannot help but admire him.

This admiration, of course, comes with important qualifications since Savonarola represents a failed founder. The republican form of government that he championed did not endure, nor did Savonarola, who met his demise four short years after rising to power. Machiavelli studies Savonarola's example to pinpoint the causes behind why some founders fail.

He consistently identifies two shortcomings that doomed Savonarola. First, the friar lacked arms to guarantee continued support for the measures he helped introduce in Florence. Machiavelli makes this point both in *The Prince* and the *Discourses*.[87] Second, Savonarola exhibited political hypocrisy,

---

[86] Machiavelli, *A Discourse on Remodeling the Government of Florence*, 114.
[87] Machiavelli, *The Prince*, VI: 24; and *Discourses*, III.30.1.

which undermined his authority as a religious leader committed to the common good, making him instead look like a political partisan.[88] His political duplicity is a target of Machiavelli's criticism in the letter to Becchi, as well as in a passage from the *Discourses* that discusses Savonarola's shifting support for the law of appeal. By championing the law of appeal but then not calling for its observance in the case of the Medici conspirators, Savonarola irreparably damaged his reputation. "This exposure of his ambitious and partisan spirit," writes Machiavelli, "took away reputation from him and brought him very much disapproval."[89] Wary of those pursuing partisan ends, Machiavelli is quick to criticize this tendency in Savonarola, which undermined his ability to unite Florence behind the republican government established in 1494.

Interestingly, none of Machiavelli's criticisms of Savonarola focus on his religious views – contrary to what one expects from reading the secondary literature on Machiavelli. After all, a common view among scholars is that Machiavelli finds little value in Savonarola's religious message. But in fact, the textual evidence suggests that Machiavelli admires Savonarola's approach to religion, most notably his ability to harness its power to advance political ends. This point comes out even in Machiavelli's earliest remarks on Savonarola, the 1498 letter to Becchi. In addition to criticizing him, Machiavelli notes Savonarola's prediction that Florence would "prosper and be dominant in Italy."[90] From an early time, Machiavelli recognized the political vision at the heart of Savonarola's religious message: God's plan for Florence to flourish and expand in wealth and power.[91]

By no means, then, does Savonarola's Christianity represent those forms that Machiavelli criticizes – namely, a weak Christianity counseling retreat from politics. In the *Discourses*, Machiavelli famously attacks Christianity for glorifying "humble and contemplative more than active men" and asking them "to be capable more of suffering than of doing something strong."[92] Some commentators believe that Machiavelli has figures like Savonarola in mind when making these remarks. John Geerken, for instance, writes that Savonarola "represented the effort to replace vigor with delicacy. In place of

---

[88] Similarly, Guicciardini singles out "simulation" as Savonarola's lone vice. See Guicciardini, *The History of Florence*, 360.

[89] Machiavelli, *Discourses*, I.45.2.

[90] Machiavelli, *Machiavelli and His Friends*, Letter 3: 9.

[91] Similarly, Guicciardini describes Savonarola as "continually preaching of the great felicity and expansion of power destined for the Florentine Republic after many travails." See Francesco Guicciardini, *The History of Italy*, trans. and ed. Sidney Alexander (Princeton, NJ: Princeton University Press, 1984), 116.

[92] Machiavelli, *Discourses*, II.2.2.

glory-seeking *virtù*, physical action, and vengeance, Savonarola sought humility, contemplation, suffering, and patience."[93] This characterization of Savonarola deeply misreads him.

It is true that Savonarola urged the people of Florence to practice traditional Christian virtues, such as doing penance and accepting suffering as a way to purify themselves.[94] At the same time, though, his apocalyptic worldview never counseled retreat from the world. Savonarola believed that Florence must expand its power and engage in conquest to fulfill God's plans for the end times. His sermons assure Florence that it will retake Pisa as one of its territories and take control of other possessions it had never had before.[95] Florence had to expand in wealth and power so that it could spread the Christian faith across the world and bring about the kingdom of God. This apocalyptic vision championed by Savonarola, which sanctifies conquest and expansion, hardly sounds like the type of Christianity that comes under withering criticism from Machiavelli.

Furthermore, Machiavelli's suggestions for religious reforms share much in common with views embraced by Savonarola. In the *Discourses* and the *Art of War*, Machiavelli explains that religion is essential for political life. Once people lose respect for religion, they soon will lack unity, military valor, and a strong state.[96] When discussing how to foster strong religious commitments in society, Machiavelli notes the central role of belief in miracles: "[T]he prudent enlarge upon [miracles] from whatever beginning they arise, and their authority then gives them credit with anyone whatever."[97] It is doubtful that all miracles are true, implies Machiavelli, but the prudent know how to interpret events as miracles so as to bolster their authority. No one in Florence embodied this strategy better than Savonarola, who constantly reminded the city of predicting the arrival of the French King Charles VIII to Italy – one of his many prophecies that purportedly were fulfilled.[98]

---

[93] Geerken, "Machiavelli's Moses and Renaissance Politics," 592.
[94] See, e.g., Savonarola, "Sermons on the Book of Haggai, Sermon No. 1 (1 Nov. 1494): 'Do Penance,'" in *Girolamo Savonarola: A Guide to Righteous Living and Other Works*, trans. and ed. Konrad Eisenbichler (Toronto: Centre for Reformation and Renaissance Studies, 2003), 81–97; and "Ten Rules to Observe in Times of Tribulation," in *Girolamo Savonarola: A Guide to Righteous Living and Other Works*, 177–79.
[95] Savonarola, *Prediche sopra i Salmi*, vol. 1, ed. Vincenzo Romano (Rome: Angelo Belardetti, 1969), 203–4. Cited in Weinstein, *Savonarola and Florence*, 146.
[96] Machiavelli, *Discourses*, I.12.1; and *Art of War*, trans. and ed. Christopher Lynch (Chicago: University of Chicago Press, 2003), VI.125.
[97] Machiavelli, *Discourses*, I.12.1.
[98] Savonarola, *The Compendium of Revelations*, 201–06; and "Psalms, Sermon III," 68–71.

Machiavelli notes Savonarola's effectiveness in making sure that all of Florence knew that his prophecies came true. "[E]veryone," he writes, "knows how much had been foretold by Friar Girolamo Savonarola before the coming of King Charles VIII of France into Italy."[99] Machiavelli is not prepared to say that God actually told Savonarola of the coming French invasion, but he credits Savonarola with persuading the people of Florence "that he spoke with God."[100] Founders must cultivate such myths to establish their authority. Savonarola did exactly that in becoming known as a prophet and using that reputation to found new orders. In this way, he exemplified Machiavelli's recommendation on how to use religion to advance political ends.

In addition, Machiavelli makes specific recommendations for Christianity that echo themes found in Savonarola's sermons and writings. Like Savonarola, he bemoans the corruption plaguing the Catholic Church. Though some believe that the Church promotes Italy's well-being, Machiavelli disagrees. He draws attention to "the wicked examples of that court" in Rome, which have caused Italy to lose "all devotion and all religion – which brings with it infinite inconveniences and infinite disorders."[101] Savonarola levels similar criticisms against the Church, calling it an institution "full of simony and wickedness."[102] One of the consistent themes throughout his ministry was calling for and predicting the renewal of the Church, which would soon arrive and eliminate entrenched corruption.[103]

There is further evidence of Machiavelli's sympathies with Savonarola in his emphasis on the importance of religious renewal. Machiavelli specifically cites Saint Francis and Saint Dominic as figures who strengthened religion by fostering such renewal. Their Christ-like examples "brought back into the minds of men what had already been eliminated there." That is, they reversed the erosion of faith caused by "the dishonesty of the prelates and of the heads of religion."[104] Similarly, Machiavelli identifies "Savonarola's life" as one of the factors that strengthened people's faith in his religious message, suggesting that his exemplary nature bolstered the friar's influence.[105]

This view of Savonarola as a virtuous figure, whose godly life contributed to his religious and political authority, was common in Florence and appears in

---

[99] Machiavelli, *Discourses*, I.56.1.
[100] Machiavelli, *Discourses*, I.11.5.
[101] Machiavelli, *Discourses*, I.12.2.
[102] Savonarola, "Psalms, Sermon III," 68.
[103] See, e.g., Savonarola, "Psalms, Sermon III," 59; and *The Compendium of Revelations*, 196.
[104] Machiavelli, *Discourses*, III.1.4.
[105] Machiavelli, *Discourses*, I.11.5.

other accounts. Guicciardini describes Savonarola's virtue in the following terms: "Those who observed his life and habits for a long time found not the slightest trace of avarice, lust, or of any other form of cupidity or frailty. On the contrary, they found evidence of a most devout life, full of charity, full of prayers, full of observances not of the externals but of the very heart of the divine cult."[106] For Machiavelli, this reputation for piety was an asset for Savonarola, since it enabled him to promote the sort of religious renewal needed for political renewal.

So when Machiavelli discusses Savonarola, he consistently avoids criticizing the friar's religious message and instead expresses admiration for it. The one passage that stands as a potential exception is Chapter 6 of *The Prince*. Here Machiavelli notes that Savonarola "was ruined in his new orders as soon as the multitude began not to believe them."[107] Savonarola's apocalyptic message, which merged religion and politics together, proved persuasive when republican institutions were founded in 1494, but eventually the people of Florence began to doubt it. In making this point, does Machiavelli intend to criticize Savonarola's religious message as ill-suited for commanding durable belief, which politics demands?

If one looks at the context of this passage, it quickly becomes clear that Machiavelli is not criticizing Savonarola's approach to religion. The people did not grow skeptical of Savonarola because his religious message was defective. Rather, Machiavelli explains, doubts *always* arise in response to new orders introduced by founders, even those most revered:

> Moses, Cyrus, Theseus, and Romulus would not have been able to make their peoples observe their constitutions for long if they had been unarmed, as happened in our times to Brother Girolamo Savonarola .... Men such as these ... find great difficulty in conducting their affairs; all their dangers are along the path, and they must overcome them with virtue. But once they have overcome them and they begin to be held in veneration, having eliminated those who had envied them for their quality, they remain powerful, secure, honored, and happy.[108]

Great founders all run into the same problem Savonarola did: inevitably, at some point, challengers arise who try to cast doubt on the new religious and political orders introduced. When such doubt gains strength, only coercion through arms can combat and prevent it from overturning new orders. What separates Savonarola from successful founders, according to Machiavelli, is

---

[106] Guicciardini, *The History of Florence*, 360.
[107] Machiavelli, *The Prince*, VI: 24.
[108] Machiavelli, *The Prince*, VI: 24–25.

his lack of arms. Importantly, it is *not* his apocalyptic message that made him ill-suited for politics. Far from it – his apocalyptic preaching and prophecies helped establish his authority among the people of Florence and found new orders. But without arms, these orders could not endure.

Even in identifying this shortcoming in Savonarola, Machiavelli is careful to avoid characterizing him as politically naïve and unaware of his need for arms. His analysis of Savonarola's downfall in the *Discourses* begins by citing the slaughter of 3,000 Israelites carried out by Moses and his men against those who worshipped the golden calf (Exodus 32:19–28). In Machiavelli's interpretation of this story, "Moses was forced to kill infinite men ... opposed to his plans" to ensure that "his laws and his orders" went forward. Machiavelli then adds: "Friar Girolamo Savonarola knew this necessity very well." Unfortunately, Savonarola was unable to use arms against his opponents, as did Moses, "because he did not have the authority to enable him to do it ... and because he was not understood well by those who followed him, who would have had the authority."[109] According to Machiavelli, Savonarola understood that he needed arms to preserve the new orders he founded. Since his position as a friar prevented him from directly taking up arms, he had to encourage his supporters to do so.

When making this observation, Machiavelli may have had in mind some of the bellicose language common to Savonarola's sermons. In a 1513 letter to Francesco Vettori, Machiavelli says that he agrees "with the friar [Savonarola] who said, 'Peace, peace, there will never be peace!'"[110] A similar remark appears in one of Savonarola's sermons discussed by Machiavelli in his 1498 letter to Becchi. In the sermon, Savonarola proclaims: "I do not ask for peace, my Lord, but I call out 'War! War!'"[111] His followers, though, failed to heed his calls to take up arms. So despite his shrewd use of religion to found new orders, Savonarola fell victim to constraints that doomed hopes for these orders to continue.

To summarize, Machiavelli's attitude toward Savonarola turns out to be more complex than is often assumed. Rather than portray this apocalyptic figure as an object of scorn, Machiavelli casts him in a different light: Savonarola possesses many of the qualities he admires in leaders who found new orders through religious renewal. Machiavelli does criticize Savonarola – specifically, for his lack of arms and political duplicity – but not for his

---

[109] Machiavelli, *Discourses*, III.30.1.
[110] Machiavelli, *Machiavelli and His Friends*, Letter 222: 257.
[111] Savonarola, "Sermon No. 1 on the Book of Exodus, 11 Feb. 1498: 'Renovation Sermon,'" in *A Guide to Righteous Living and Other Works*, 168.

religious message and apocalyptic vision for Florence. In fact, Savonarola uses religion in just the ways Machiavelli recommends for politics. After criticizing Savonarola in his early correspondence, Machiavelli with time sees the friar as an example of religion's power to persuade people to embrace new orders. If Savonarola had had the benefit of arms to preserve his new orders, he may have joined Machiavelli's pantheon of great founders. Still, Savonarola remains a "great man" – what should be read as a sincere compliment by Machiavelli – because he used his religious authority to aim at the greatest achievement possible, the founding of new orders.

MACHIAVELLI'S AMBIVALENCE TOWARD APOCALYPTIC THOUGHT

Given Machiavelli's appreciation for the power of Savonarola's religious message, how should we understand his view of apocalyptic thought? At the very least, the seriousness with which Machiavelli treats Savonarola shows that he does not dismiss apocalyptic thought as bizarre and wholly unsuited for politics. Machiavelli recognizes the power of apocalyptic thought to shape politics, sometimes in positive ways. More than anyone, Savonarola made that point clear in the context of Florence.

Beyond this implicit respect for apocalyptic thought, Machiavelli develops his political philosophy in ways that bear some resemblance to it. Drawing on apocalyptic texts like the book of Revelation, Savonarola preached that there was pervasive corruption in the world, especially within the Church, and that this corruption had reached a crisis point. Out of this crisis, Florence would establish its greatness and usher in the new Jerusalem. Likewise, Machiavelli in his analysis of politics sees crisis as creating conditions from which greatness can emerge. He most famously makes this case at the end of *The Prince*. A similar argument appears in the *Florentine Histories* when discussing how conditions within states evolve: "once they have descended and through their disorders arrived at the ultimate depth, since they cannot descend further, of necessity they must arise."[112] As is often the case in apocalyptic narratives, Machiavelli identifies crisis as a vehicle for renewal.

It is important, though, to recognize what distinguishes Machiavelli's political thought from Savonarola's vision for politics. Because of his faith in Christian apocalyptic doctrines, Savonarola proclaimed the coming of a perfect and eternal government to Florence. God would assure this outcome. Machiavelli does not allow himself the luxury of such faith. In contrast

---

[112] Machiavelli, *Florentine Histories*, V.I.

to Savonarola, Machiavelli sees a limited role for divine intervention in establishing new orders – that task ultimately falls to human beings. At the end of *The Prince*, Machiavelli tells Lorenzo that God has made conditions favorable for founding new orders and redeeming Italy, but the "remainder you must do yourself. God does not want to do everything, so as not to take free will from us and that part of the glory that falls to us."[113]

Machiavelli lacks Savonarola's faith that divine intervention will take care of the difficult task of establishing and preserving new orders. Nevertheless, the utopian ideal of an eternal polity, which occupies a central role in Savonarola's apocalyptic vision, clearly tempts Machiavelli. His interest in an eternal polity is closely linked with his interest in founders, who hope that their new orders will last forever. This point comes out in the *Discourse on Remodeling the Government of Florence*, where Machiavelli urges Pope Leo X to institute new orders. Machiavelli explains the challenge facing Leo: "to give the city [Florence] institutions that can by themselves stand firm."[114] Achieving this goal, according to Machiavelli, would be Leo's greatest achievement and make him "immortal."[115] If new orders preserve a polity long after the founder is gone, they serve as an enduring sign of the founder's greatness. The most lasting institutions imaginable, of course, are those that continue without end. So the greatest act a founder could achieve is crafting institutions that preserve a state and its people forever. It is this daunting goal that founders aim for.

When Machiavelli considers the possibility of an eternal polity, he faces the challenge of reconciling his strong desire for this ideal with its implausibility. In Book III of the *Discourses*, he addresses the prospect of achieving a perpetual republic. At first he makes clear his doubts about ever achieving this ideal: "[I]t is impossible to order a perpetual republic, because its ruin is caused through a thousand unexpected ways."[116] Five chapters later he returns to the subject, and here he allows himself to speculate about the possibility of a perpetual republic. He writes: "[I]f a republic were so happy that it often had one who with his example might renew the laws, and not only restrain it from running to ruin but pull it back, it would be perpetual."[117] So after first rejecting any hope for a perpetual republic, Machiavelli later finds himself looking for *some* scenario to keep that hope alive. Perhaps if a republic benefitted from a long series of wise founders – an unlikely scenario, given

---

[113] Machiavelli, *The Prince*, XXVI: 103.
[114] Machiavelli, *A Discourse on Remodeling the Government of Florence*, 115.
[115] Machiavelli, *A Discourse on Remodeling the Government of Florence*, 114.
[116] Machiavelli, *Discourses*, III.17.1.
[117] Machiavelli, *Discourses*, III.22.3.

their rarity – they could preserve and keep strong a republic's institutions forever.

In *A Discourse on Remodeling the Government of Florence*, similar considerations emerge in Machiavelli's discussion of what is necessary to found firm orders. Using language reminiscent of the *Discourses*, Machiavelli argues that, under its current government, Florence faces the risk of "a thousand dangers."[118] New orders are necessary to eliminate these dangers. Machiavelli outlines an initial set of reforms that Leo should implement in Florence, and expresses confidence that these reforms will benefit and sustain the city. He tempers this confidence, though, with a caveat: these new orders' effectiveness may wane after the founder (Leo) dies. The new orders could persist indefinitely if Leo "were going to live forever," but as Machiavelli bluntly points out, at some point he "must cease to be."[119] In response to this unavoidable challenge, Machiavelli outlines additional reforms, with the hope that a slightly altered set of new orders will continue even after Leo's death. Throughout this discussion, Machiavelli is acutely aware of the dangers that government institutions face after a founder dies and tries to offer solutions in response. Notably, Machiavelli avoids the claim that the new orders he recommends can last forever. Leo's reputation could become immortal if he successfully implements new orders, but Machiavelli never uses this language for the orders themselves, even as he tries to think of ways to prolong them.

These discussions in the *Discourses* and *A Discourse on Remodeling the Government of Florence* reveal Machiavelli's desire for a perpetual republic, but also his resistance to embracing this hope. This reluctance stems from his cyclical view of history and time, which precludes human institutions from ever achieving a permanent state of perfection. Rather than embrace a linear conception of time in which history moves inexorably toward perfection, as found in Christian eschatology, Machiavelli sees history as confined to a pattern that continually alternates between degeneration and progress. Good governments inevitably degenerate into bad ones until they reach a low point from which they must improve, and the cycle starts anew.[120]

Machiavelli expresses this general principle in his play *The Golden Ass* where he writes: "[I]t is and always has been and always will be, that evil follows after good, good after evil."[121] Such constant flux means that

---

[118] Machiavelli, *A Discourse on Remodeling the Government of Florence*, 114.
[119] Machiavelli, *A Discourse on Remodeling the Government of Florence*, 111.
[120] Machiavelli, *Discourses*, I.2.
[121] Machiavelli, *The [Golden] Ass*, in *Machiavelli: The Chief Works and Others*, vol. 2, trans. Allan Gilbert (Durham, NC: Duke University Press, 1965), Ch. 5, lines 103–5. I thank an anonymous reviewer for bringing my attention to this passage.

perfection, if ever achieved, can only be fleeting. As Machiavelli emphasizes in the *Florentine Histories*, "worldly things are not allowed by nature to stand still. As soon as they reach their ultimate perfection, having no further to rise, they must descend."[122] Machiavelli makes a similar comment about "worldly things" (*cose del mondo*) at the start of Book III of the *Discourses*: "It is a very true thing that all worldly things have a limit to their life."[123] So throughout his writings, a basic tenet of Machiavelli's thought is that nothing on earth is immune to decay, especially those things that have achieved perfection. When he applies this rule to republics, Machiavelli finds himself unable to embrace Savonarola's utopian hope in one that would last forever.

Machiavelli's explicit use of the phrase "worldly things" brings attention to the limits of his secular vision for political renewal – that is, secular in the sense that it does not rely on divine intervention to achieve it. Savonarola places his faith in God to ensure the apocalyptic vision for Florence detailed in his preaching. Machiavelli, on the other hand, lacks this apocalyptic faith. He recognizes the power of apocalyptic thought in establishing new orders, and for this reason respects Savonarola. But he cannot fully embrace Savonarola's apocalyptic vision because political renewal occurs entirely within the realm of worldly things for Machiavelli. New orders will always be mortal, subject to decay. This foundational principle in Machiavelli's political philosophy stands in tension with his desire for a perpetual republic – the ultimate achievement for any founder. Given this tension for Machiavelli, perhaps part of Savonarola's appeal lies in the friar's ability to wholeheartedly place his faith in the ideal of a perpetual polity – something Machiavelli desires but cannot expect because of his realism. Machiavelli shares Savonarola's hope for renewal in the midst of crisis, but not the totality of his apocalyptic vision, which culminates in an eternal and perfect kingdom. Such a tantalizing ideal ultimately has no place in Machiavelli's political universe. Here human founders are the creators of new orders, which, like the founders themselves, at some point must cease to be.

THE PYRE OF SAVONAROLA

In his earliest writings, Machiavelli takes a mostly negative view of Savonarola. His 1498 letter to Becchi notes the power of Savonarola's preaching but criticizes his hypocrisy at a time when his power was in rapid decline. With the benefit of time and distance to assess Savonarola's impact on Florence,

---

[122] Machiavelli, *Florentine Histories*, V.I.
[123] Machiavelli, *Discourses*, III.1.1.

Machiavelli comes to have a greater respect for him. From his perspective, Savonarola stands out as that rare contemporary figure who used religion's power to found new orders. Savonarola specifically achieved this goal through preaching an apocalyptic vision for Florence, which merged heavenly and earthly hopes together. Machiavelli's writings on religion suggest his recognition of the power that Savonarola's apocalyptic message had in advancing political ends. Still, Machiavelli cannot fully accept Savonarola's vision – specifically, its utopian belief in a perfect and enduring polity to come.

As Machiavelli's views evolved, one wonders whether the image of Savonarola's fiery execution came to mind. It is unknown whether Machiavelli witnessed Savonarola's death, though it would not have been surprising if he did. Savonarola's execution was a spectacle: officials built a scaffold and pyre in the middle of the bustling Piazza della Signoria, where many came to watch the execution (see Figure 3.1). Machiavelli was curious enough about Savonarola to attend his sermons – he very well may have made his way to the Piazza della Signoria on May 23, 1498, to watch his

FIGURE 3.1 Execution of Savonarola
Painting by Filippo Dolciati at the Museum of San Marco in Florence[124]

---

[124] This image is in the public domain and available on Wikimedia Commons at the following link: https://commons.wikimedia.org/wiki/File:Filippo_Dolciati_(1443_-_1519)_Execution_of_Girolamo_Savonarola._1498,_Florence,_Museo_di_San_Marco.jpg.

final moments. Even if he did not, he at least would have read some of the vivid accounts of the execution. Luca Landucci, a follower of Savonarola, paints the scene:

> When all three were hung, Fra Girolamo [Savonarola] being in the middle ... a fire was made on the circular platform round the cross, upon which gunpowder was put and set alight, so that the said fire burst out with a noise of rockets and cracking. In a few hours they were burnt, their legs and arms gradually dropping off; part of their bodies remaining hanging to the chains, a quantity of stones were thrown to make them fall, as there was a fear of the people getting hold of them; and then the hangman and those whose business it was, hacked down the post and burnt it on the ground, bringing a lot of brushwood, and stirring the fire up over the dead bodies, so that the very least piece was consumed.[125]

It was a pitiful end to a short life that left its mark on Florentine politics.

This image of Savonarola on the pyre may not have evoked much sympathy from Machiavelli as a young man, if his 1498 letter to Becchi shortly before the execution is any indication. At the time, Machiavelli described a political figure who was losing his grip on power and resorting to ineffective tactics that only worsened the situation. But later on, Machiavelli came to express a deeper appreciation for the challenges faced by those who fail while attempting great things in politics. His direct experience with political failure may have contributed to this shift. When a new regime came to power in Florence in 1512, Machiavelli found himself tortured, imprisoned, and stripped of his political post.[126] He knew all too well the vicissitudes of politics and that no one is immune to their dangers.

So though Savonarola failed in politics, Machiavelli's later writings treat him with greater sympathy, as someone who endeavored to bring political renewal to Florence despite the perils involved. In the same chapter of *The Prince* that identifies Savonarola as a founder, Machiavelli emphasizes the incredible dangers founders face: "[N]othing is more difficult to handle, more doubtful of success, nor more dangerous to manage, than to put oneself at the head of introducing new orders."[127] The image of Savonarola upon the pyre illustrates in dramatic fashion the dangers that always loom for those who take on the task of founding new orders. Despite these risks, Savonarola took action to advance republican rule and his apocalyptic vision for Florence.

---

[125] Luca Landucci, *A Florentine Diary*, in *Selected Writings of Girolamo Savonarola*, 352.
[126] Maurizio Viroli, *Niccolò's Smile: A Biography of Machiavelli*, trans. Antony Shugaar (New York: Hill and Wang, 2002), 131–40.
[127] Machiavelli, *The Prince*, VI: 23.

For this reason, the image of Savonarola likely became more for Machiavelli than just a symbol of failure. Yes, Savonarola's burnt corpse hung for all to see as an example of a failed founder. But at the same time, the scene represented the perils that great individuals are willing to accept in pursuit of glorious ends. By using his religious authority and apocalyptic message to found new orders – at great risk to himself – Savonarola represents for Machiavelli a figure who merits respect.

4

Tempering Apocalyptic Ideals: Hobbes and Pretenders to God's Kingdom

Throughout his writings, Thomas Hobbes makes clear his disdain for apocalyptic prophecy, especially when used to further rebellion. His early work *The Elements of Law* criticizes "learned madmen" who "determine ... the time of the world's end."[1] Later in *Behemoth*, Hobbes calls the Fifth Monarchy Men – the most explicitly apocalyptic sect of the English Civil War – "fanatics."[2] In his view, they and other religious sects were among the diverse "seducers" whose agitation plunged England into civil war.[3] Similarly, in *Historia Ecclesiastica*, Hobbes lists the Fifth Monarchy Men as one of several sects that "sated savage Mars with much blood."[4]

Quentin Skinner perhaps best sums up Hobbes's attitude toward these sects and those who reaped political benefits from them during the English Civil War. He describes Hobbes as understanding the period between 1640 and 1660 as "an era of collective insanity."[5] Though this reaction by Hobbes occurred within a specific historical context, it is recognizable to anyone who has ever been skeptical of apocalyptic claims. The notion that the English Civil War signaled the imminent arrival of Christ's kingdom on earth, as some of his contemporaries claimed, struck Hobbes as sheer madness.

Beyond its far-fetched claims, what troubles Hobbes about apocalyptic thought is its potential to spur continuous political upheaval. Apocalyptic thought anticipates nothing short of perfection – a divine kingdom breaking

---

[1] Thomas Hobbes, *The Elements of Law*, ed. Ferdinand Tönnies (Cambridge: Cambridge University Press, 1928), I.10.9.

[2] Hobbes, *Behemoth, or The Long Parliament*, ed. Ferdinand Tönnies (Chicago: Chicago University Press, 1990), 136.

[3] Hobbes, *Behemoth*, 2.

[4] Hobbes, *Historia Ecclesiastica*, ed. and trans. Patricia Springborg, Patricia Stablein, and Paul Wilson (Paris: Honoré Champion 2008), lines 1557–62.

[5] Quentin Skinner, *Reason and Rhetoric in the Philosophy of Hobbes* (New York: Cambridge University Press, 1996), 436.

into the present to wipe away corruption. Political movements motivated by such utopian goals have difficulty living up to them, and almost invariably end in disappointment. Even if new rulers come to power, they like their predecessors fall short of achieving the perfection promised. The failure to realize utopia breeds an endless cycle of dissatisfaction, disruption, and instability that plagues politics.

Hobbes is keenly aware of the destabilizing effects that utopian visions – like those found in apocalyptic thought – can have on politics. To counter this danger, he opts against the most straightforward option: making the case to abandon the pursuit of apocalyptic ideals altogether. Sensitive to the power that apocalyptic ideals have in politics, he co-opts them instead – most notably, the concept of the kingdom of God from Christian eschatology.

This strategy is on display in *Leviathan*, where Hobbes singles out subversive interpretations of the kingdom of God as "the greatest, and main abuse of Scripture."[6] Religious sects claim to represent God's kingdom, and in turn believe that this status gives them authority over civil matters. This interpretation of the kingdom of God creates continual conflict with the civil sovereign. Hobbes responds by dedicating numerous passages in *Leviathan* to reinterpreting the doctrine of the kingdom of God so that it is safe for politics. He arrives at an interpretation that denies, at present, all claims to represent God's kingdom made by prophets and sects challenging the sovereign's authority. For now, the kingdom of God can only take one form – what Hobbes calls the natural kingdom of God. Importantly, the Leviathan state is a manifestation of the natural kingdom of God, where God rules through principles of reason rather than his prophetic word. By identifying God's kingdom with the Leviathan state, Hobbes transforms a Christian doctrine used to justify rebellion into one that bolsters the sovereign's authority.

So apocalyptic ideals have a place in Hobbes's political philosophy, but only after he tempers their utopian hopes. Hobbes advises those looking for God's kingdom to stop chasing after utopia and instead look for it in the civil commonwealth already before them. Far from perfect, commonwealths sometimes command idolatry and kill the innocent. Hobbes frankly admits these shortcomings. To equate God's perfect kingdom with such imperfection strikes some as deeply unsatisfying and even downright blasphemous. But wary of attempts to achieve perfection in politics, Hobbes sees value in an ideal emptied of its utopian content. When outlining his vision for politics, he concedes that "life shall never be without Inconveniences."[7] Efforts to

---

[6] Hobbes, *Leviathan*, ed. Noel Malcolm (New York: Oxford University Press, 2012), XLIV: 960.
[7] Hobbes, *Leviathan*, XX: 320.

eliminate *all* inconveniences end up leading to far greater ones: political upheaval when perfect rulers and institutions never come, followed by dissolution of the commonwealth and the perilous existence found outside of it. Worried about these dangers, Hobbes uses the concept of the kingdom of God to defend the Leviathan state and all its imperfections, as well as discredit the utopian aspirations of the prophets and revolutionaries of his day.

THE APOCALYPTIC CONTEXT IN WHICH HOBBES WROTE

The widespread nature of apocalyptic thought in seventeenth-century England is well documented.[8] What stands out about apocalyptic thought in this context is the extent to which it motivated those in political power. There is a tendency to characterize apocalyptic belief as primarily taking hold among the outcasts and marginalized in society.[9] Yet in seventeenth-century England, apocalyptic hopes captured the imagination of soldiers, scholars, members of Parliament, and even kings.[10]

Many in England began to see their king as a "godly prince" divinely chosen to defeat the Antichrist, understood as the papacy. James I embraced this role

---

[8] See Bryan Ball, *A Great Expectation: Eschatological Thought in English Protestantism to 1660* (Leiden: Brill, 1975); Andrew Bradstock, "Millenarianism in the Reformation and the English Revolution," in *Christian Millenarianism: From the Early Church to Waco*, ed. Stephen Hunt (Bloomington, IN: Indiana University Press, 2001), 77–87; B. S. Capp, *The Fifth Monarchy Men: A Study in Seventeenth-Century English Millenarianism* (London: Faber & Faber, 1972); B. S. Capp, "The Political Dimension of Apocalyptic Thought," in *The Apocalypse in English Renaissance Thought and Literature*, ed. C. A. Patrides and Joseph Wittreich (Ithaca, NY: Cornell University Press, 1984), 93–125; Paul Christianson, *Reformers and Babylon: English Apocalyptic Visions from the Reformation to the Eve of the Civil War* (Toronto: University of Toronto Press, 1978); Katharine Firth, *The Apocalyptic Tradition in Reformation Britain, 1530–1645* (New York: Oxford University Press, 1979); Crawford Gribben, *The Puritan Millennium: Literature & Theology, 1550–1682* (Dublin: Four Courts Press, 2000); Christopher Hill, *Antichrist in Seventeenth-Century England* (New York: Oxford University Press, 1971); Christopher Hill, *The World Turned Upside Down: Radical Ideas during the English Revolution* (New York: Penguin Books, 1991); William Lamont, *Godly Rule: Politics and Religion, 1603–60* (New York: St. Martin's Press, 1969); Richard Popkin, "Seventeenth-Century Millenarianism," in *Apocalypse Theory and the Ends of the World*, ed. Malcolm Bull (Oxford: Blackwell Publishers, 1995), 112–34; Michael Walzer, *The Revolution of the Saints: A Study in the Origins of Radical Politics* (Cambridge, MA: Harvard University Press, 1965); Arthur Williamson, *Apocalypse Then: Prophecy and the Making of the Modern World* (Westport, CT: Praeger, 2008), 135–66; and John Wilson, *The Pulpit in Parliament: Puritanism during the English Civil Wars, 1640–1648* (Princeton, NJ: Princeton University Press, 1969).

[9] See, e.g., Norman Cohn, *The Pursuit of the Millennium: Revolutionary Millenarians and Mystical Anarchists of the Middle Ages*, rev. ed. (New York: Oxford University Press, 1970).

[10] Capp, "The Political Dimension of Apocalyptic Thought," 109–18.

to a certain extent, writing in 1609 that he had established from Revelation that the pope was the Antichrist. James ultimately would disappoint Puritan hopes of destroying the Antichrist, as would his successor Charles I. In fact, under Charles there was growing concern that the Church of England *was* the Antichrist.[11] The monarchy's transformation from God's instrument for furthering his kingdom into the Antichrist shows how quickly political allegiances influenced by apocalyptic belief could shift.

Scholarly study of Revelation and Christ's return helped legitimize and spur interest in apocalyptic thought. Joseph Mede, a Cambridge theologian, in 1627 published *Clavis Apocalyptica*, one of the most influential apocalyptic works at the time. As one of the "learned madmen" (to use Hobbes's words) advancing apocalyptic prophecies, Mede provided an intellectual framework to interpret contemporary events. Like James, he understood the papacy as the Antichrist and believed it was destined to fall. A member of Parliament translated *Clavis Apocalyptica* into English in 1643, and its publication received official government approval.[12]

When pastors in the 1640s came before Parliament to preach, apocalyptic themes often were prominent in their sermons.[13] For many clergy, the upheaval of the civil war was clear evidence that they were living in the end times foretold by Revelation. Thomas Goodwin notes in his 1646 sermon before Parliament that "as the *shorter time* Satan hath, the more is his *rage*; so the shorter time Christ hath, and the nearer he is to the possession of his Kingdome."[14] He cites Revelation 17:14 – "*These [kingdoms] shall make war with the Lambe, and the Lambe shall overcome them*" – to emphasize that "it is certaine, we are in the last times of these kingdoms."[15] In John Maynard's sermon before Parliament, he argues that England is living in the time of the seventh trumpet discussed in Revelation 11:15, when "*[t]he kingdoms of this world are become the kingdoms of our Lord, and of His Christ, and He shall reign for ever and ever.*"[16] Another minister, Henry Wilkinson, uses vivid apocalyptic imagery to describe the task facing members of Parliament:

> [S]ince your businesse lies professedly against the *Apocalypticall beast*, and all his complices; you must expect that the *militia* of Hell and the trayned bands of Satan, *(i.e.)* those that have received the mark of the beast, shall be put into a posture of warre, furnished with all their traines of Artillery, and the whole

---

[11] Capp, "The Political Dimension of Apocalyptic Thought," 102–9.
[12] Capp, "The Political Dimension of Apocalyptic Thought," 108, 111.
[13] Wilson, *The Pulpit in Parliament*, 197–235.
[14] Thomas Goodwin, *The Great Interest of States & Kingdomes* (London, 1646), 46.
[15] Goodwin, *The Great Interest of States & Kingdomes*, 47.
[16] John Maynard, *A Shadow of the Victory of Christ* (London: F. Neile, 1646), 10.

Magazine of Satan, to put in execution their black *Commission*, which breathes forth nothing but blood, and slaughter, and ruine of our persons and our Religion.[17]

According to this view, Parliament's work had eschatological significance because it furthered God's plan for the end times. As these sermons highlight, the 1640s was a time when clergy and political leaders alike embraced an apocalyptic vision to interpret their world and the turmoil within it.

Apocalyptic ideas reached the height of their political influence during the English Civil War with the rise of the Fifth Monarchy Men. This movement began in the late 1640s, shortly before the publication of *Leviathan*. In his later work *Behemoth*, Hobbes describes the Fifth Monarchy Men as a sect whose central tenet was "that there ought none to be sovereign but King Jesus, nor any to govern under him but the saints."[18] The movement took its name from Daniel 7, which outlines four different monarchies that rise and fall before a final *fifth* monarchy establishes its everlasting rule over all. The Fifth Monarchy Men viewed events of their day through the lens of cataclysmic apocalyptic thought. That is, they interpreted the upheaval of the English Civil War as evidence that God was intervening to wipe away corruption and set up Christ's perfect kingdom on earth, where his saints would rule.

So according to the Fifth Monarchy Men, the chaos surrounding Charles I's downfall was no reason to fear. It rather served as a sign that the fifth monarchy, Christ's kingdom, was near. This view comes out in a Fifth Monarchist petition from 1649: "[T]he great design of God in the falls and overthrows of worldly powers, that have opposed the kingdom of His Son, is . . . to lift up Him on high, far above all principality, and powers, and might, and dominion, and every name that is named in this world, that He may be PRINCE of the kings of the earth."[19]

William Aspinwall's *Brief Description of the Fifth Monarchy*, though published in 1653 after *Leviathan*, provides insight into this movement that emerged while Hobbes wrote his masterpiece.[20] Aspinwall celebrates the execution of Charles – "a fierce & arrogant Tyrant & persecuter of the Saints"[21] – as the fulfillment of the apocalyptic prophecies of Daniel and

---

[17] Henry Wilkinson, *Babylons Ruine, Jerusalems Rising* (London, 1643), introductory letter.
[18] Hobbes, *Behemoth*, 182.
[19] Fifth Monarchist Petitioners, "King Jesus," in *The English Civil War and Revolution: A Sourcebook*, ed. Keith Lindley (New York: Routledge, 1998), 175.
[20] Hobbes likely began writing *Leviathan* in mid-1649. See Noel Malcolm, *Leviathan: Introduction* (London:Oxford University Press. 2012), 1–12.
[21] William Aspinwall, *A Brief Description of the Fifth Monarchy Men* (London: M. Simmons, 1653), 1.

a sign that the fifth monarchy would soon rise.[22] Whereas it horrified Hobbes that the English people executed their own king, the Fifth Monarchy Men saw the event as reason to believe that God's kingdom was near (see Figure 4.1).

Though the Fifth Monarchy Men's views struck Hobbes and others as bizarre, this sect exerted no small influence over politics during the early 1650s. Disgusted by the Rump Parliament's perceived inability to realize apocalyptic hopes, Major-General Thomas Harrison led the Fifth Monarchy Men in pressuring Oliver Cromwell to dissolve the Rump and establish in its place what became known as the Barebones Parliament. Eventually Cromwell would dissolve Barebones to set up the Protectorate, at which point the Fifth Monarchy Men's influence declined.[23] Their sway lasted for only a short time, yet they demonstrated apocalyptic thought's power to impact politics.

Hobbes clearly took notice of the apocalyptic beliefs that pervaded religious and political life during the civil war period. As Kinch Hoekstra notes, "[A]fter 1640 it became obvious that the learned madness of eschatology was not an

FIGURE 4.1 Execution of King Charles I
Etching by an unknown artist from 1649[24]

---

[22] Aspinwall, *A Brief Description of the Fifth Monarchy Men*, 14.
[23] Capp, "The Political Dimension of Apocalyptic Thought," 114–16.
[24] This image is reprinted with permission of the National Portrait Gallery and available at the following link: www.npg.org.uk/collections/search/portrait/mw35443/The-execution-of-King-Charles-I.

easily dismissed fringe phenomenon. Together, these reasons explain why Hobbes strove to discredit eschatological excess from the commonly accepted basis of scripture."[25] One finds throughout Hobbes's works enduring concerns over the misinterpretation of Christian eschatology and its ramifications for politics. In *The Elements of Law*, he expresses disdain for "madmen" who try to predict the world's end.[26] Then in *Leviathan* he warns against subversive understandings of a key concept from Christian eschatology – the kingdom of God – and condemns "Authors ... of this Darknesse in Religion" for encouraging political strife.[27] Concerns over the abuse of Christian eschatology persist in Hobbes's posthumously published works, evident in his criticism of the Fifth Monarchy Men in *Behemoth* and *Historia Ecclesiastica*.[28] Confronted with the disruptive effects of apocalyptic thought on English politics, Hobbes repeatedly returns to the subject, determined to neutralize its dangers.

THE DANGER OF LOOKING FOR GOD'S KINGDOM

Christian eschatology takes diverse forms, yet one feature is universal to almost all of them: faith that the kingdom of God will be realized. History, according to the Christian view, is moving inexorably toward its ultimate goal – God's perfect kingdom. Hobbes does not deny the coming of God's kingdom, but has grave worries about churches and sects claiming to represent this kingdom *now*. In fact, of all the theological doctrines that Hobbes finds fault with in *Leviathan*, he singles out misinterpretations of the kingdom of God as the most dangerous. "The greatest, and main abuse of Scripture," he writes, "and to which almost all the rest are either consequent, or subservient, is the wresting of it, to prove that the Kingdome of God, mentioned so often in the Scripture, is the present Church, or multitude of Christian men now living, or that being dead, are to rise again at the last day."[29] As believers anticipate God's kingdom, they often look for some form of it in the present. For Hobbes, such speculation takes a subversive turn when it equates God's current kingdom with any entity distinct from the civil sovereign.

A letter from 1662 provides further evidence that this worry was at the forefront of Hobbes's mind when he wrote *Leviathan*. After the Civil War

---

[25] Kinch Hoekstra, "Disarming the Prophets: Thomas Hobbes and Predictive Power," *Rivista di storia della filosofia*, 59, no. 1 (2004): 107.
[26] Hobbes, *The Elements of Law*, I.10.9.
[27] Hobbes, *Leviathan*, XLVII: 1106.
[28] Hobbes, *Behemoth*, 136; and *Historia Ecclesiastica*, lines 1557–62.
[29] Hobbes, *Leviathan*, XLIV: 960.

had ended and the monarchy had been restored, Hobbes explained to England's new king his motivations for writing *Leviathan*. His letter assures Charles II that, despite the controversy sparked by the theological views expressed in the book, his motives for writing it were blameless:

> It was written in a time when the pretence to Christ's kingdom was made use of for the most horrid actions that can be imagined; and it was in just indignation of that, that I desired to see the bottom of that doctrine of the kingdom of Christ, which divers ministers then preached for a pretence to their rebellion: which may reasonably extenuate, though not excuse the writing of it.[30]

So Hobbes understood *Leviathan* as an attempt to correct subversive understandings of the kingdom of God. Today, that motivation for Hobbes's masterpiece is often overlooked. With *Leviathan*, he hoped to wrest the kingdom of God away from those using it as a pretext for "the most horrid actions that can be imagined," and show that this doctrine – when properly understood – never justifies rebellion.

Who in Hobbes's view were distorting the doctrine of the kingdom of God to encourage rebellion? *Leviathan* identifies the primary culprits as "the Romane, and the Presbyterian Clergy."[31] For Hobbes, belief that the church represents God's kingdom began with the Catholic Church, before then spreading to the Presbyterians and other Protestant sects. Since Catholic theology is the root source of this error, Hobbes gives special attention to addressing it, evident from his extensive critique of this and other Catholic doctrines in Chapter 42 of *Leviathan*.

It is easy to see why Hobbes has such problems with the Catholic view of God's kingdom. In Catholic thought, the pope is understood as the head of Christ's spiritual kingdom on earth. From this belief stems the concept of the pope's "indirect power" (*potestas indirecta*), which refers to his authority to intervene in temporal matters when they have ramifications for Christ's spiritual kingdom.

This idea is most closely associated with the Catholic theologian Robert Bellarmine, whom Hobbes directly addresses and critiques in *Leviathan*.[32]

---

[30] Hobbes, *Seven Philosophical Problems*, in *The English Works of Thomas Hobbes of Malmesbury*, vol. 7, ed. William Molesworth (London: Longman, Brown, Green, and Longmans, 1845), 5.

[31] Hobbes, *Leviathan*, XLVII: 1106.

[32] Part of this critique includes singling out the problems with Bellarmine's conception of the kingdom of God. See Hobbes, *Leviathan*, XLIV: 976. For more on Hobbes's engagement with Bellarmine, see Patricia Springborg, "Thomas Hobbes and Cardinal Bellarmine: Leviathan and 'The Ghost of the Roman Empire,'" *History of Political Thought* 16, no. 4 (1995): 503–31.

Though Bellarmine denies that the pope has supreme temporal authority, attributing that instead to civil sovereigns, he does argue that the pope's responsibility to safeguard souls as the head of Christ's kingdom sometimes requires intervention in politics. Christ's spiritual kingdom takes precedence over any civil kingdom, especially since it offers eternal life, the supreme end that all individuals should strive for. So if civil sovereigns lead souls astray by, say, commanding heretical practices, the pope has the authority to depose them in the interest of protecting Christ's spiritual kingdom. Bellarmine's understanding of the kingdom of God leads him to the view that "the temporal authority of the princes is subject and subordinate to the spiritual authority of the Popes."[33] This claim challenges the authority of civil sovereigns, and for Hobbes poses grave dangers to political life.

Unfortunately from Hobbes's perspective, Catholic beliefs about the kingdom of God made their way into Protestant thought, particularly Presbyterian theology. The Presbyterians prided themselves on rejecting "popish" practices and doctrines. But with regard to the kingdom of God, Hobbes notes, they conveniently chose to hold on to Catholic doctrine: "[I]n those places where the Presbytery took that Office, though many other Doctrines of the Church of Rome were forbidden to be taught; yet this Doctrine, that the Kingdome of Christ is already come, and that it began at the Resurrection of our Savior, was still retained."[34] This doctrine provided a basis for claiming spiritual authority, which in turn led to claims of political authority.

As a case in point, during the English Civil War Presbyterians played a lead role in calling the Westminster Assembly in defiance of Charles I. This move was part of an effort to reform the Church of England, abolish episcopacy, and bring it in line with their model of church government.[35] Notably, the Westminster Confession that came out of this assembly of clergy explicitly identifies the church as "the kingdom of the Lord Jesus Christ."[36] To ensure Christ's kingdom on earth, the Presbyterians intervened in politics and asserted their authority over religious matters. In this way, Hobbes warns,

---

[33] Robert Bellarmine, *On the Temporal Power of the Pope. Against William Barclay*, in *On Temporal and Spiritual Authority*, ed. and trans. Stefania Tutino (Indianapolis, IN: Liberty Fund, 2012), 161. See also Stefania Tutino, *Empire of Souls: Robert Bellarmine and the Christian Commonwealth* (New York: Oxford University Press, 2010), 9–47.

[34] Hobbes, *Leviathan*, XLVII: 1106.

[35] For more on the Westminster Assembly, see Robert Paul, *The Assembly of the Lord: Politics and Religion in the Westminster Assembly and the "Grand Debate"* (Edinburgh: T. & T. Clark, 1985).

[36] Westminster Assembly, *The Westminster Confession of Faith*, in *Creeds and Confessions of Faith in the Christian Tradition*, vol. 2, ed. Jaroslav Pelikan and Valerie Hotchkiss (New Haven, CT: Yale University Press, 2003), 25.2.

Presbyterians embraced an understanding of God's kingdom that fostered rebellion and political upheaval during the civil war.[37]

Subversive understandings of God's kingdom eventually found their way into apocalyptic sects like the Fifth Monarchy Men, which only exacerbated the turmoil plaguing England. Hobbes sees the Fifth Monarchy Men as partly a consequence of Presbyterian theology, calling them a "brood of their [the Presbyterians'] own hatching."[38] Not content with Presbyterian attempts at religious and political reform, other sects took more extreme positions. The Fifth Monarchy Men also believed that they represented the kingdom of God, with the twist that "Christ's kingdom was at this time to begin upon earth."[39] Belief in the imminent arrival of Christ's literal kingdom on earth helped justify what for Hobbes was the greatest crime of the English Civil War, executing the king. For the Fifth Monarchy Men, such action was necessary to eliminate a corrupt ruler and make way for God's kingdom.

In short, the civil war period made clear to Hobbes the explosive and disruptive effects of claiming to represent God's kingdom. As he emphasizes in *Leviathan*, "points of doctrine concerning the Kingdome of God, have so great influence on the Kingdome of Man" that they must be determined "by them, that under God have the Soveraign Power."[40] The civil sovereign needs to exercise tight control over this doctrine because of the immense power associated with claiming to represent God's kingdom – namely, the power to block or grant access to a kingdom that promises eternal life. According to Hobbes, Christ placed the keys of his kingdom in the hands of his "Supreme Pastors" – namely, "Christian Civill Soveraignes."[41] So in this vision for Christian commonwealths, civil sovereigns have ultimate say over the doctrine of the kingdom of God, as they are God's appointed officials for overseeing this kingdom.

If, though, a church opposed to the sovereign comes to represent the kingdom of God, political allegiances can shift and throw a commonwealth into turmoil. Once the church is perceived as God's kingdom, it acquires a power exceeding any power possessed by the civil authority, since it becomes in the people's eyes the body that determines entrance into God's kingdom. Consequently, people fear the church more than the civil authority – a disastrous development in Hobbes's view. He writes: "[M]en that are once

---

[37] Indeed, Hobbes blames "Presbyterian ministers" for the "incitement" of the civil war. See Hobbes, *Behemoth*, 95.
[38] Hobbes, *Behemoth*, 136.
[39] Hobbes, *Behemoth*, 3.
[40] Hobbes, *Leviathan*, XXXVIII: 708.
[41] Hobbes, *Leviathan*, XLII: 872.

possessed of an opinion, that their obedience to the Soveraign Power, will bee more hurtfull to them, than their disobedience, will disobey the Laws, and thereby overthrow the Common-wealth, and introduce confusion, and Civill war."[42] Ultimately, for Hobbes, claims about representing God's kingdom are attempts by ministers to exercise "Soveraign Power over the People."[43]

Not surprisingly, Hobbes directs harsh language against those who pervert Christian teaching in an effort to augment their power, calling them a "Kingdome of Darknesse" and *"Confederacy of Deceivers."* These enemies of peace advance *"dark, and erroneous Doctrines"* so as to *"obtain dominion over men in this present world."*[44] What results is confusion among the people regarding their political obligations. Misinterpretations of the kingdom of God have just this effect, says Hobbes: "[T]his Errour, that the present Church is Christs Kingdome ... causeth so great a Darknesse in mens understanding, that they see not who it is to whom they have engaged their obedience."[45] By sowing such confusion, this teaching erodes the sovereign's authority and poses grave risks to the commonwealth.

Subversive teachings concerning the kingdom of God create perceived conflicts between God's commands and the civil sovereign's. For Hobbes, such conflicts are the "most frequent praetext of Sedition, and Civill Warre, in Christian Common-wealths."[46] Challenges to sovereign authority can plunge society into the horrors of war, while undermining efforts to establish peace well into the future. For whenever sovereignty dissolves due to an act of rebellion, it becomes more difficult for subsequent sovereigns to hold on to their authority and exercise it effectively. If a faction gains sovereignty through rebellion, cautions Hobbes, "others are taught to gain the same in like manner."[47] In other words, rebellion encourages further rebellion and perpetual instability. Hobbes thus sees grave dangers in challenging the sovereign's religious authority, which is why he singles out understandings of God's kingdom for criticism. Use of this doctrine to challenge the sovereign's authority opens up a Pandora's box, resulting in a continuous cycle of regimes rising to and falling from power.

This account of continuous instability is reminiscent of the English Civil War, a period when religion played a prominent role in bringing down the king and various manifestations of Parliament. No one coming to power could

---

[42] Hobbes, *Leviathan*, XLII: 850.
[43] Hobbes, *Leviathan*, XLVII: 1106.
[44] Hobbes, *Leviathan*, XLIV: 956.
[45] Hobbes, *Leviathan*, XLIV: 960.
[46] Hobbes, *Leviathan*, XLIII: 928.
[47] Hobbes, *Leviathan*, XV: 224.

fulfill apocalyptic hopes. Such disappointment quickly transformed rulers from servants chosen by God into agents of the Antichrist.[48] Religiously motivated attacks against the sovereign released a cannibalizing force adept at destruction, but ill-suited to establish anything of permanence. Hobbes brings attention to this aspect of the civil war in *Behemoth*: "[F]rom the beginning of the rebellion, the method of ambition was constantly this: first to destroy, and then to consider what they should set up."[49] The leaders of the rebellion acted like "fools which pull down anything which does them good, before they have set up something better in its place."[50] The havoc they inflicted fell far short of achieving perfection, and instead brought long-lasting harm to the commonwealth.

So in many ways, the English Civil War embodied the dangers of looking for God's perfect kingdom. Fervent religious hopes never ushered in this kingdom, but rather weakened existing political institutions. As new sovereigns came to power, they failed to meet the lofty expectations preceding them, which bred dissatisfaction as a result. Writing in the midst of these failed expectations, Hobbes understood all too well the close connection between apocalyptic hope and political instability.

DISCREDITING DIVINE REVELATION

In response to the problems that stem from misinterpreting the doctrine of the kingdom of God, Hobbes offers a two-part solution: (1) discredit the legitimacy of those who claim to represent God's kingdom and (2) offer his own interpretation of the kingdom of God as an alternative. This section focuses on the first part of Hobbes's solution, while the following section focuses on its second part.

Throughout his political writings and especially *Leviathan*, Hobbes radically severs the link between God and humanity in the present time. This move has the effect of "disarming the prophets," as Hoekstra puts it.[51] Hobbes casts so much doubt on divine revelation in the present that he leaves no room for purported revelation to guide politics. It is important to remember that he took aim at prophecy's authority at a time when *apocalyptic* prophecy in particular was widespread and leaving its mark on English politics. When Hobbes sought to discredit the prophets of his day, the target of his attacks clearly included

---

[48] See Hill, *Antichrist in Seventeenth-Century England*.
[49] Hobbes, *Behemoth*, 192.
[50] Hobbes, *Behemoth*, 155.
[51] Hoekstra, "Disarming the Prophets."

those madmen boldly proclaiming the world's end and using such claims to acquire political power.

In his case against such imposters, Hobbes avoids denying that God *can* communicate directly to his servants, since that would contradict much of scripture. For instance, Hobbes describes Moses as a prophet "in the sense of speaking from God to the People."[52] Moses had a unique relationship with God, in which God directly communicated to him commands for the Israelites.[53] But God's practice of speaking with Moses stands out as a rare exception because it took place at a time when God ruled directly over his people through a chosen representative. Today, Hobbes stresses, it is impossible to decipher true from false prophecy, and therefore we should not expect God to convey his commands through means plagued by such uncertainty.

Hobbes's view that we no longer can distinguish true from false prophecy ultimately rests on his claim that, in the present, God no longer empowers individuals to perform miracles. Referencing Deuteronomy 13:1–5, Hobbes says that scripture sets forth two requirements to establish someone as a true prophet: performance of miracles and only teaching religious doctrines that are established by God and avoid encouraging revolt against the sovereign. Neither condition by itself is sufficient to show that a prophecy is from God. Miracles are insufficient since false prophets can perform them, like the Egyptian sorcerers described in Exodus 7 and 8. Likewise, someone who teaches the established religion but fails to perform miracles provides no credible evidence for their prophecy, since we cannot be expected to trust prophetic predictions that lie far in the future and cannot be verified now.[54] After establishing these points, Hobbes asserts that "Miracles now cease," which allows him to conclude: "we have no sign left, whereby to acknowledge the pretended Revelations, or Inspirations of any private man; nor obligation to give ear to any Doctrine, farther than it is conformable to the Holy Scriptures." In a world without miracles, we lack grounds for believing prophetic claims. Hobbes assures his readers that this aspect of the current world is no reason for concern, since scripture provides all the revelation necessary to guide Christians in their "duty both to God and man."[55]

This argument establishes for Hobbes that individuals have no obligation to accept revelation merely on the grounds that someone claims to be divinely inspired. Hobbes is skeptical of purported prophecy, which is clear from his

---

[52] Hobbes, *Leviathan*, XXXVI: 658.
[53] Hobbes, *Leviathan*, XXXII: 582.
[54] Hobbes, *Leviathan*, XXXII: 582–84.
[55] Hobbes, *Leviathan*, XXXII: 584.

dismissive comment that the best prophet is simply the "best guesser."⁵⁶ Nevertheless, Hobbes avoids characterizing all present revelation as *necessarily* false. His point is more modest: prophecy in the present is possible – nothing could prevent God from communicating directly to someone now if he chooses – but it is impossible to verify its validity. Given this uncertainty, an authority is needed to determine which revelations and religious doctrines are true and which are false. For Hobbes, a Christian sovereign makes these determinations and is the only one deserving of the title "Gods Prophet."⁵⁷ If Hobbes were to claim that *no* prophecy in the present could be valid, he would deprive the sovereign of its authority to determine which religious doctrines, including purported revelation, are true – a conclusion he wishes to avoid.

Hobbes's case against the legitimacy of revelation, at least when it lacks the civil sovereign's approval, applies equally to the doctrine of the kingdom of God. Whenever a sect claims to embody the kingdom of God, it purports to have a unique covenant with God. Such a covenant, says Hobbes, "is impossible, but by Mediation of such as God speaketh to, either by Revelation supernaturall, or by his Lieutenants that govern under him."⁵⁸ In other words, covenants with God only come via direct communication with him. Though in the past God communicated with Abraham and established a covenant with the Jewish people, Hobbes emphasizes that now it is impossible to verify anyone's claims that God spoke to them. As a result, any claims about representing God's kingdom on the basis of a divine covenant are necessarily beyond verification.

During the civil war period, some did appeal to a purported covenant with God to justify defying the civil sovereign. A key event in the lead-up to the war was the National Covenant of 1638 signed by the Scottish Covenanters. These Presbyterians joined the covenant to declare their opposition to religious practices introduced in Scotland by the Anglican Archbishop William Laud and backed by Charles I. They grounded their opposition in the belief that the Church of Scotland had a covenant with God, and the obligations of this covenant required them to oppose religious practices in conflict with the true church.⁵⁹ Beyond just rejecting this idea, Hobbes attacks it as a ruse for wresting authority away from the civil sovereign. He writes: "[S]ome men

---

⁵⁶ Hobbes, *Leviathan*, III: 44.
⁵⁷ Hobbes, *Leviathan*, XXXVI: 680.
⁵⁸ Hobbes, *Leviathan*, XIV: 210.
⁵⁹ For more on the religious and political thought of the Scottish Covenanters, see Ian Smart, "The Political Ideas of the Scottish Covenanters. 1638–88," *History of Political Thought* 1, no. 2 (1980): 167–93.

have pretended for their disobedience to their Sovereign, a new Covenant, made, not with men, but with God .... [T]his pretence of Covenant with God, is so evident a lye, even in the pretenders own consciences, that it is not onely an act of an unjust, but also of a vile, and unmanly disposition."[60] For Hobbes, there is nothing redeeming in the motivations of those challenging the sovereign on the grounds that they have a special covenant with God.

Hobbes further undermines such claims by relegating all manifestations of God's kingdom founded on a pact or covenant to the distant past or end of time. In his view, the kingdom of God takes two forms:

(1) the prophetic kingdom of God or kingdom of God by pact, covenant, or agreement (terms he uses interchangeably)
(2) the natural kingdom of God or kingdom of God by nature (also terms he uses interchangeably)[61]

Hobbes believes that only the natural kingdom of God exists today. In this form of God's kingdom, the law of nature – accessible to all through reason – governs God's subjects. In contrast, God communicates law much differently in his prophetic kingdom. Here God uses his prophetic word to establish a covenant with a chosen people and communicate his laws to them. Unlike the natural kingdom of God, which exists today, the prophetic kingdom of God existed only once in history according to Hobbes – the nation of Israel until it elected Saul as king.[62] Besides ancient Israel, the only other prophetic kingdom of God lies in the future and will be realized upon Christ's return.[63] By limiting the prophetic kingdom of God to these two instances, Hobbes adopts an understanding of sacred history that rejects any current claims to represent God's kingdom that appeal to a revealed covenant.

In line with Hobbes's materialism, both the historic and future prophetic kingdoms of God are earthly kingdoms. For "the Nation of the Jews," writes Hobbes, the kingdom of God "properly meant a Common-wealth, instituted ... for their Civill Government ... which properly was a Kingdome, wherein God was King, and the High priest was to be (after the death of Moses) his sole Viceroy, or Lieutenant."[64] Similarly, Christ's

---

[60] Hobbes, *Leviathan*, XVIII: 266.
[61] Hobbes, *On the Citizen*, ed. and trans. Richard Tuck and Michael Silverthorne (New York: Cambridge University Press, 1998), XV–XVII; and *Leviathan*, XXXI: 556, 572, XXXV: 634–36, XLI: 764.
[62] Hobbes, *Leviathan*, XXXI: 556, XXXV: 644.
[63] Hobbes, *Leviathan*, XXXV: 634–44.
[64] Hobbes, *Leviathan*, XXXV: 640.

kingdom "is a reall, not a metaphoricall Kingdome."⁶⁵ Citing Revelation's account of the new Jerusalem descending from heaven to earth, Hobbes argues that "the Paradise of God, at the coming again of Christ, should come down to Gods people from Heaven" rather than "they goe up to it from Earth."⁶⁶ That Christ's kingdom is still to come strikes Hobbes as obvious, and he points to language from the Lord's Prayer – *"Thy Kingdome come"* – to back up this view.⁶⁷

Hobbes admits that interpreting the kingdom of God as a literal earthly kingdom existing at two distinct points in time goes against how many understand it. Clergy often interpret the kingdom of God as existing "in the Highest Heaven" and never as an actual monarchy where God has sovereign power over his subjects "acquired by their own consent, which is the proper signification of Kingdome."⁶⁸ According to Hobbes, many opt for a metaphorical understanding of God's kingdom instead of his because the latter gives Christian kings too much power over "Ecclesiasticall Government."⁶⁹

Hobbes's interpretation of the kingdom of God grants kings so much power because of the role they play in its current manifestation. For Hobbes, there is no prophetic kingdom of God at present. But despite being cut off from this kingdom, people still can join the *natural* kingdom of God. Here the principles of reason dictate that the civil sovereign has absolute authority, including over religion. By denying the possibility of God's prophetic kingdom and identifying his natural kingdom as the only option now, Hobbes advances a view that leaves little room to challenge the sovereign's authority in religious matters, as the next section explains.

THE LEVIATHAN AS GOD'S KINGDOM

Discussion of the natural kingdom of God comes at a significant juncture in *Leviathan* – the final chapter of Part II. The argument in *Leviathan* moves in a systematic fashion: Part I outlines the nature of man and principles of reason; Part II draws on Part I to set forth the principles to govern the ideal commonwealth; Part III applies these principles to Christian commonwealths; and Part IV examines perverse understandings of Christian commonwealths. Within this schema, Chapter 31, "Of the Kingdome of God by Nature," represents the culmination of Parts I and II. If individuals follow the dictates of reason as

---

[65] Hobbes, *Leviathan*, XXXV: 642.
[66] Hobbes, *Leviathan*, XXXVIII: 702.
[67] Hobbes, *Leviathan*, XXXV: 642.
[68] Hobbes, *Leviathan*, XXXV: 634.
[69] Hobbes, *Leviathan*, XXXV: 642.

outlined by Hobbes, without reliance on divine revelation, they will cede authority to a sovereign and enter a manifestation of the natural kingdom of God – the Leviathan state.

In making this argument, Hobbes refashions the concept of the kingdom of God so that it is no longer a source of political disruption. By giving a prominent place in his political philosophy to the concept of the kingdom of God, Hobbes directly draws on Christian eschatology. But while maintaining a connection to this tradition, his concept of the natural kingdom of God also departs from it in important ways.

First off, Hobbes chooses a term – the kingdom of God by nature – that never appears in scripture and was not in wide use. Though rare, the term does appear prior to Hobbes in Catholic thought. The *Catechism of the Council of Trent* from 1566 uses the term, and Bellarmine also uses it when discussing the teachings of the Catechism.[70] These Catholic texts outline a threefold understanding of God's kingdom: the kingdom of nature, the kingdom of grace, and the kingdom of glory.[71] Hobbes likely was familiar with this typology since he read Bellarmine, evident from his extensive critique of him in Chapter 42 of *Leviathan*. But in Hobbes's hands, the natural kingdom of God ends up looking much different from the Catholic understanding of it.[72]

According to the Catholic view, the kingdom of nature refers to God's rule over all creation.[73] Hobbes explicitly rejects this view when describing the natural kingdom of God in *Leviathan*:

> [T]o call this Power of God, which extendeth it selfe not onely to Man, but also to Beasts, and Plants, and Bodies inanimate, by the name of Kingdome, is but a metaphoricall use of the word. For he onely is properly said to Raigne, that governs his Subjects, by his Word, and by promise of Rewards to those that obey it, and by threatning them with Punishment that obey it not. Subjects therefore in the Kingdome of God, are not Bodies Inanimate, nor creatures Irrationall; because they understand no Precepts as his.[74]

---

[70] Catholic Church, *Catechism of the Council of Trent*, trans. John McHugh and Charles Callan (New York: Joseph F. Wagner, 1934), 522–23; Bellarmine, *Disputationes de controversiis Christianae fidei*, in *Opera omnia*, vol. 6, ed. Justinus Fèvre (Paris: Vivès, 1873), 402; and Bellarmine, *Dichiarazione piu copiosa della dottrina cristiana*, in *Opera omnia*, vol. 12, ed. Justinus Fèvre (Paris: Vivès, 1874), 298.
[71] Catholic Church, *Catechism of the Council of Trent*, 522–25.
[72] For more on the intellectual history of Hobbes's concept of the natural kingdom of God, see my article, "The Natural Kingdom of God in Hobbes's Political Thought," *History of European Ideas* 45, no. 3 (2019): 436–53.
[73] Catholic Church, *Catechism of the Council of Trent*, 522.
[74] Hobbes, *Leviathan*, XXXI: 554.

For Hobbes, the natural kingdom of God does not refer to his reign over all creation – the dominant view at the time – but rather to his reign over human beings who understand his commands, as well as the rewards and punishments tied to them.

Hobbes calls this form of God's kingdom the *natural* kingdom of God because of the type of law governing it. God rules subjects in his natural kingdom through the "naturall Dictates of Right Reason," by which Hobbes means the law of nature.[75] That feature distinguishes God's natural kingdom from his prophetic kingdom, where he instead communicates law in the form of prophecy. Such divine revelation is unnecessary in the natural kingdom of God, since individuals should be able to comprehend the law of nature through reason alone.[76]

Hobbes worries, though, that self-interested interpretations of the law of nature cause confusion over its meaning and render it "of all Laws the most obscure."[77] Such confusion poses a threat to the natural kingdom of God, especially given the importance Hobbes places on commands' being "manifestly made known" in order to count as laws. Otherwise, he writes, "they are no Lawes: For to the nature of Lawes belongeth a sufficient and clear Promulgation, such as may take away the excuse of Ignorance."[78] If uncertainty plagues the law of nature, the natural kingdom of God rests on shaky ground and is potentially in jeopardy.

What is needed, says Hobbes, is someone to clearly interpret the law of nature and ensure its status as law. In *De Cive*'s chapter on the natural kingdom of God, he points to the civil sovereign as the one chosen by God to carry out this role:

> [T]he *interpretation* of *natural laws*, both *sacred* and *secular*, where God reigns through nature alone, depends on the authority of the commonwealth, i.e. of the man or council which has been granted sovereign power in the commonwealth; and whatever God commands, he commands through its voice. And, conversely, whatever commonwealths command both about the manner of worshipping God and about secular matters, is commanded by God.[79]

This passage makes clear the critical function that the civil commonwealth serves in the natural kingdom of God. It is the entity responsible for

---

[75] Hobbes, *Leviathan*, XXXI: 556.
[76] Hobbes, *Leviathan*, XXVII: 454.
[77] Hobbes, *Leviathan*, XXVI: 430.
[78] Hobbes, *Leviathan*, XXXI: 556.
[79] Hobbes, *On the Citizen*, XV.17.

communicating to individuals God's law in his natural kingdom. When most people come in contact with the natural kingdom of God, it is through their civil commonwealth. So for Hobbes, the Leviathan state is a manifestation of God's kingdom – specifically, the natural kingdom of God.[80]

Since the laws governing this kingdom are based on reason rather than divine revelation, it is not necessarily a Christian kingdom. As Hobbes explains in the opening to Part III of *Leviathan*, when turning to the principles of a Christian Commonwealth, God's word never contradicts reason but aspects of it are "above Reason."[81] Since reason does not conflict with Christian beliefs, the natural kingdom of God can take the form of a Christian commonwealth, but that is not guaranteed. Many Christian beliefs, including the one most fundamental for Hobbes – "*Jesus is the Christ*"[82] – come from a source beyond reason: revelation preserved by the Christian tradition. Hobbes dedicates Part III to explaining how to interpret revelation recorded in scripture when determining the responsibilities of Christian sovereigns and subjects. For most of Hobbes's readers, the only commonwealth imaginable is a Christian commonwealth, and for that reason he singles it out for analysis. But despite Hobbes's focus on Christian commonwealths, he sees reason as insufficient to establish the doctrines of Christianity, and therefore the principles of reason do not lead inevitably to a Christian commonwealth.

The dictates of reason do exclude, in Hobbes's view, atheists as potential subjects in the natural kingdom of God. Hobbes sees belief in God as grounded in reason, since it explains "a First, and an Eternall cause of all things."[83] In the natural kingdom of God, individuals recognize God's

---

[80] Some argue that, for Hobbes, the natural kingdom of God exists and its law (i.e., natural law) obligates prior to the establishment of a civil commonwealth. See Howard Warrender, *The Political Philosophy of Hobbes: His Theory of Obligation* (Oxford: Clarendon Press, 1957); A. P. Martinich, *The Two Gods of* Leviathan: *Thomas Hobbes on Religion and Politics* (New York: Cambridge University Press, 1992); and Michael Byron, *Submission and Subjection in* Leviathan: *Good Subjects in the Hobbesian Commonwealth* (London: Palgrave Macmillan, 2015). Others reject this view. See Gregory Kavka, *Hobbesian Moral and Political Theory* (Princeton, NJ: Princeton University Press, 1986); Perez Zagorin, *Hobbes and the Law of Nature* (Princeton, NJ: Princeton University Press, 2009); and John Deigh, "Political Obligation," in *The Oxford Handbook of Hobbes*, ed. Al Martinich and Kinch Hoekstra (New York: Oxford University Press, 2016), 293–314. Here I avoid taking a position in that debate. Even if we assume that Hobbes's natural kingdom of God exists before a commonwealth, that view is compatible with my interpretation of Hobbes: the Leviathan state – where it exists – is the present manifestation of God's kingdom. For Hobbes, the Leviathan state functions as the entity that communicates law and directs worship in the natural kingdom of God, and thus helps to more fully realize it.

[81] Hobbes, *Leviathan*, XXXII: 576.
[82] Hobbes, *Leviathan*, XLIII: 948.
[83] Hobbes, *Leviathan*, XII: 166.

authority and honor him due to his "*Irresistible Power.*"[84] It is in line with reason to fear God and submit to him given his omnipotence – opposing him is futile. Atheists are enemies of the natural kingdom of God because they fail to acknowledge God's power.[85] There are limits, then, to how much Hobbes departs from the biblical concept of the kingdom of God. Though Christian faith is not a requirement in the natural kingdom of God, belief in God is.

Yet what ultimately stands out about Hobbes's natural kingdom of God is how it diverges from traditional understandings of God's kingdom. When opening *Leviathan*'s chapter on the natural kingdom of God, Hobbes frames it as a guide to navigating one's obligations to obey both the civil and divine law. By properly understanding these obligations and their relation to each other, individuals can "avoyd both these Rocks" of either offending God through "too much civill obedience" or transgressing "the commandements of the Common-wealth" through "feare of offending God."[86] Hobbes proceeds to present a description of the natural kingdom of God in which obeying God almost never requires disobeying the sovereign and the civil law. In fact, he references Acts 5:29 – "*It is better to obey God than man*" – to point out that this precept "hath place in the kingdome of God by Pact, and not by Nature."[87] In the natural kingdom of God, subjects obey God by obeying the civil sovereign, the authoritative interpreter of God's natural law. That authority extends to matters of worship. Since a commonwealth is to worship God as "one Person," according to Hobbes, public worship in the natural kingdom of God is to be uniform and determined by the sovereign.[88] The sovereign can command non-Christian forms of worship – after all, reason does not require the natural kingdom of God to be Christian – and subjects would have an obligation to participate in such worship.

Hobbes emphasizes this point when addressing how Christians should respond to civil authorities who command subjects to confess doctrines contrary to Christianity. Such outward professions of faith should not cause concern, reassures Hobbes, "because Beleef, and Unbeleef never follow mens Commands. Faith is a gift of God, which Man can neither give, nor take away by promise of rewards, or menaces of torture." Regardless of the command or threat, the sovereign cannot rob individuals of their internal beliefs. Hobbes backs up his point by citing the Old Testament story of Naaman, whom God

---

[84] Hobbes, *Leviathan*, XXXI: 558.
[85] Hobbes, *Leviathan*, XXXI: 554–56.
[86] Hobbes, *Leviathan*, XXXI: 554.
[87] Hobbes, *Leviathan*, XXXI: 572.
[88] Hobbes, *Leviathan*, XXXI: 570.

pardons for bowing before an idol (2 Kings 5:17–18).[89] Like Naaman, Christians must be willing to publicly confess other gods if authorities demand it, while maintaining their inner faith. For Hobbes, the only exception is missionaries called to convert nonbelievers. Even in this case, missionaries should not violently oppose the ruling authority but instead accept martyrdom as a witness to Christ.[90]

Hobbes's transformation of the ideal of the kingdom of God thus leads to a possibility radically different than how it is described in scripture. The natural kingdom of God as outlined by Hobbes could consist of a people worshipping non-Christian gods. Christians in such a kingdom would have to hide their faith and participate in the public worship of these gods.[91] This scenario creates a jarring juxtaposition: the worship of false gods in the kingdom of God, or at least Hobbes's modified version of it. His attempt to downplay the sin of worshipping false gods exists in tension with the standard Christian view, which condemns worship of anything but the one true God (e.g., Exodus 20:1–6).[92]

The position staked out by Hobbes also stands in sharp contrast to how the ideal of the kingdom of God is imagined in Christian eschatology. The book of Revelation urges Christians to resist the worship of false gods as they await God's ideal kingdom. The arrival of this kingdom will decisively put an end to such sinful practices, replacing them with the continual, public, and exclusive worship of the Lamb.[93] In *Leviathan*, Hobbes does affirm the coming prophetic kingdom of God where Christ will rule on earth.[94] But in conjunction with this orthodox belief, Hobbes adopts the more controversial view that the precursor to the coming prophetic kingdom – or, put another way, the current embodiment of God's kingdom – is the natural kingdom of God. Hobbes's description of this kingdom makes room for the worship of non-Christian gods, a view directly at odds with the biblical ideal of God's kingdom.

---

[89] Hobbes, *Leviathan*, XLII: 784.

[90] Hobbes, *Leviathan*, XLII: 788.

[91] This position drew criticism from Hobbes's contemporaries. See, e.g., John Bramhall, *The Catching of Leviathan*, in *The Collected Works of John Bramhall*, vol. 4 (Oxford: John Henry Parker, 1844), 587.

[92] Hobbes does suggest that idolatry is contrary to the laws of nature, since reason tells us that God is infinite and "to attribute *Figure* to him" is to dishonor him. See Hobbes, *Leviathan*, XXXI: 564. Nonetheless, Hobbes clearly sees the law of nature's command to obey the sovereign as trumping its prohibition against idolatry.

[93] For more on Revelation's emphasis on the dangers of idolatry, see Richard Bauckham, *The Theology of the Book of Revelation* (New York: Cambridge University Press, 1993).

[94] Hobbes, *Leviathan*, XXXV: 642.

Regardless of what religious practices it commands, the natural kingdom of God plays a key role in God's plan for history according to Hobbes. The natural kingdom of God manifests itself as civil commonwealths, which protect individuals until Christ returns to establish the final prophetic kingdom of God. Unlike others who call for dramatic political action to help realize Christ's kingdom, Hobbes does not believe that subjects of the natural kingdom of God can hasten the arrival of Christ's kingdom. Cataclysm will visit the earth upon Christ's return when a "Conflagration" consumes the wicked and refines the elect.[95] But Hobbes never indicates that God's people will war against the godless as a prelude to Christ's return. It is God alone who will bring about his kingdom on earth.[96]

In line with this view, Hobbes uses the phrase "quiet waiting" in *Behemoth* to describe the period before Christ's return[97] – an apt description for the Leviathan state given its role as the natural kingdom of God. With authority unified, the natural kingdom of God quietly safeguards individuals until Christ's return. This arrangement represents the full manifestation of God's kingdom in the present, in contrast to societies plagued by divided authority, instability, and civil war. Hobbes makes the hopeful point that the promise of peace is not delayed until Christ's prophetic kingdom arrives, but is possible now through the natural kingdom of God.

With his concept of the natural kingdom of God, Hobbes seeks to transform and rehabilitate a Christian ideal long associated with political instability. In his view, those who claim that God's kingdom will come through war and violence not only err in their prediction, but also set themselves up as enemies against God's current kingdom. In response to those anxiously expecting, predicting, and trying to realize God's kingdom, Hobbes says that it *already* exists in a real way on earth. It is standing right before them in the form of the civil commonwealth. The Leviathan is thus more than a vehicle for overcoming conflict between individuals: it takes on eschatological significance as a manifestation of God's current kingdom.

---

[95] Hobbes, *Leviathan*, XLIII: 946, XLIV: 1002.
[96] Hobbes, *Leviathan*, XLIV: 978–80. This view by Hobbes, where God alone determines the timing of his coming kingdom, goes against Wolfgang Palaver's interpretation of the Leviathan state as a secular force holding back God's kingdom. See Palaver, "Hobbes and the *Katéchon*: The Secularization of Sacrificial Christianity," *Contagion: Journal of Violence, Mimesis and Culture* 2, no.1 (1995): 57–74.
[97] Hobbes, *Behemoth*, 58.

IDEALISM WITHOUT PERFECTION

The ideal of the kingdom of God plays a prominent role in *Leviathan*, which raises questions about idealism's role in Hobbes's thought. The kingdom of God represents the ultimate ideal that history is moving toward. By equating the Leviathan to God's kingdom, Hobbes transports a divine ideal into the realm of human politics. Such language suggests a hope and idealism for politics that, at least on its surface, goes against the standard interpretation of Hobbes as the consummate realist.

Hobbes's idealism has captured the interest of a number of scholars.[98] They include Richard Tuck, who goes so far as to argue that there is a utopian element in *Leviathan*.[99] In his view, Hobbes sets forth a political philosophy and theology designed to free individuals from fear's paralyzing effects, and in this sense the work is utopian. Tuck is partly correct. Hobbes does cast doubt on sources of fear with destabilizing effects and seeks to ease readers' concerns at various points in *Leviathan*. For instance, the laws of nature do not require great sacrifices but are easy to observe;[100] people need not live in constant threat of death but can find security within the Leviathan state;[101] those damned will not face everlasting torment but the milder penalty of destruction;[102] salvation does not demand mastering theology's finer points but simply faith in Christ and obedience to the civil law;[103] and God rarely demands heroic acts of martyrdom but rather a quiet inner faith.[104] Through such principles, Hobbes aims to make the world less frightening.

It is important, though, to distinguish between how Hobbes embraces *and* rejects idealism. Often an imprecise term, idealism can mean "pursuit of an

---

[98] See Bryan Garsten, "Religion and Representation in Hobbes," in *Thomas Hobbes, Leviathan*, ed. Ian Shapiro (New Haven, CT: Yale University Press, 2010), 519–46; and S. A. Lloyd, *Ideals as Interests in Hobbes's* Leviathan: *The Power of Mind over Matter* (New York: Cambridge University Press, 1992).

[99] Richard Tuck, "The Utopianism of *Leviathan*," in Leviathan *after 350 Years*, ed. Tom Sorrell and Luc Foisneau (New York: Oxford University Press, 2004), 125–38. See also Sarah Mortimer and David Scott, "*Leviathan* and the Wars of the Three Kingdoms," *Journal of the History of Ideas*, 76, no. 2 (2015): 269–70; David Runciman, "What Is Realistic Political Philosophy?" *Metaphilosophy* 43, nos. 1–2 (2012): 68; and Leo Strauss, *The Political Philosophy of Hobbes: Its Basis and Its Genesis*, trans. Elsa Sinclair (Chicago: University of Chicago Press, 1952), 138.

[100] Hobbes, *Leviathan*, XV: 240.

[101] Hobbes, *Leviathan*, XIV: 200.

[102] Hobbes, *Leviathan*, XXXVIII: 716–18, XLIV: 972–74, 992–94. See also Christopher McClure, "Hell and Anxiety in Hobbes's *Leviathan*," *Review of Politics* 73, no. 1 (2011): 1–27; and *Hobbes and the Artifice of Eternity* (New York: Cambridge University Press, 2016).

[103] Hobbes, *Leviathan*, XLIII: 930.

[104] Hobbes, *Leviathan*, XLII: 784–88.

ideal."[105] When the ideal pursued is a perfect polity, idealism has a meaning synonymous with utopianism. But utopian is the wrong term for *Leviathan*'s political philosophy, for it implies a level of perfection in politics that Hobbes rejects. In fact, at the end of Chapter 31 in the Latin edition, he dismisses utopian works like Plato's *Republic*, Thomas More's *Utopia*, and Francis Bacon's *New Atlantis*, implying that it would be a mistake to associate *Leviathan* with such works.[106] This remark highlights Hobbes's unease with utopian thought. Its political ambitions prompt concern because the relentless striving after utopia can lead to discontentment, instability, and even rebellion, which Hobbes observed on full display during the English Civil War.

So a more plausible reading of *Leviathan* is that it reveals Hobbes's wariness toward utopian ideals that risk going unrealized and breeding dissatisfaction. Far from utopian, his idealism consists of adopting ideals that undermine political aspirations aimed at perfection. Rather than dismiss people's ideals and utopian hopes as foolish or irrelevant to politics, Hobbes recognizes their power. As Sharon Lloyd points out, Hobbes formulates his political philosophy with the conviction that, to be successful, it must take seriously people's ideals – especially religious ones – and find a place for them.[107] Hobbes accomplishes this goal by recognizing the ideals that motivate people, transforming them, and incorporating them into his political philosophy.

His concept of the natural kingdom of God reflects this strategy. Many hope for God's perfect kingdom yet differ on what form it will take and how to achieve it. Competing visions of perfection lead to conflict, which Hobbes seeks to prevent by pointing to a more modest goal – the Leviathan state, understood as a form of God's kingdom. Hobbes co-opts this biblical ideal in an effort to redirect utopian aspirations toward a more feasible vision of politics.

When describing the Leviathan state, Hobbes indicates in numerous places that his political ideal falls well short of perfection. One example comes from his explanation for choosing the term Leviathan to describe the sovereign. For Hobbes, the Old Testament beast known as leviathan symbolizes unparalleled greatness on earth, but also vulnerability. Quoting the description of the leviathan from Job 41:33, he writes, *"There is nothing ... on earth, to be compared with him. He is made so as not to be afraid."* Hobbes, however, adds that the leviathan "is mortall, and subject to decay, as all other Earthly creatures are."[108] Though it aims for immortality, the sovereign faces

---

[105] *Oxford English Dictionary*.
[106] Hobbes, *Leviathan*, XXXI: 574–75.
[107] Lloyd, *Ideals as Interests in Hobbes's* Leviathan.
[108] Hobbes, *Leviathan*, XXVIII: 496.

numerous threats that render it mortal.[109] Even at his most hopeful, when suggesting that the principles of reason could make a commonwealth's constitution "everlasting," Hobbes concedes that external violence can frustrate this hope.[110] In politics, individuals hope to construct a commonwealth that provides lasting security, and some commonwealths do endure for long periods. But on earth, at least at this point in history, no structures prove immortal.

The Leviathan's imperfections go beyond its mortality. It also risks errors in governance, which can manifest themselves in egregious ways. Because of Hobbes's understanding of sovereignty, it is impossible for the sovereign to break the civil law. The sovereign has absolute authority over the law and cannot be bound it. This idea comes with troubling implications for Hobbes's political philosophy. The sovereign on a whim could put an innocent subject to death, robbing them of the very thing the sovereign is entrusted to protect – their life.

Hobbes does not try to explain away this possibility but admits it as a potential consequence of his concept of sovereignty. He writes: "[N]othing the Soveraign Representative can doe to a Subject, on what pretence soever, can properly be called Injustice, or Injury; because every Subject is Author of every act the Soveraign doth ... . [T]he same holdeth ... in a Soveraign Prince, that putteth to death an Innocent Subject." To illustrate this point, he references the Old Testament story of Uriah, whom King David had killed in battle so as to take Uriah's beautiful wife Bathsheba as his own (2 Samuel 11). In Hobbes's view, when David killed Uriah, he committed no injury against Uriah but did commit an injury against God, since David was still God's subject.[111] There is no guaranteed remedy in the Leviathan state to protect innocent subjects who find themselves under threat of death from their sovereign. In *De Cive*, Hobbes brings up figures far more reviled than David – Caligula and Nero – and similarly maintains their authority to kill subjects without cause.[112]

That danger casts a shadow over the Leviathan and its purported promise of peace. Hobbes attempts to allay concerns about arbitrary executions by arguing that vicious sovereigns usually only target those involved in political intrigue. If subjects avoid political agitation and live a quiet life, they usually escape persecution.[113] That advice is somewhat ironic coming from Hobbes,

[109] Hobbes, *Leviathan*, XXIX: 498–518.
[110] Hobbes, *Leviathan*, XXX: 522.
[111] Hobbes, *Leviathan*, XXI: 330.
[112] Hobbes, *On the Citizen*, X.7.
[113] Hobbes, *On the Citizen*, X.7.

given the controversy sparked by his writings and his need to cross the English Channel on multiple occasions to flee persecution.[114] Moreover, such assurances ring somewhat hollow in light of the Uriah example. Uriah dutifully obeyed his sovereign to the point of risking his life in battle. In return, the sovereign stole Uriah's wife and killed him. As Hobbes implicitly admits with this example, sovereigns can be petty and cruel, and sometimes there is little that obedient subjects can do to protect themselves.

Hobbes does allow subjects to resist the sovereign when their life is threatened, for they can never be obligated to willingly cede their right to life.[115] But this point by Hobbes hardly implies that resistance is likely to succeed. With power unified in Hobbes's ideal state, resistance has little chance of attracting others' support and succeeding.[116] The permission to resist when the sovereign threatens a subject's life is a logical consequence of Hobbes's political psychology, which treats self-preservation as the most fundamental motivation. But this concession should not be understood as a fail-safe mechanism to protect subjects from vicious sovereigns.

Ultimately, Hobbes permits a great deal of imperfection in his "ideal" state. He avoids whitewashing over all the Leviathan's possible problems and instead sets forth an ideal with its fair share of warts. A more perfect ideal would be unattainable, and thus would encourage instability and a political situation far worse than the occasional evils plaguing the Leviathan. Rather than striving for heaven in the political sphere, Hobbes is more interested in an ideal that keeps hell at bay. Indeed, he rejects that there is any *summum bonum* (greatest good) that individuals can obtain, and treats it as a foolish goal to chase after.[117] While philosophers and theologians endlessly debate the greatest good, Hobbes sees greater potential for agreement on the worst possible evil – anarchy, war, and violent death. People readily recognize this evil and its gravity, which makes it more promising as a starting point for political

---

[114] Richard Tuck, *Hobbes* (New York: Oxford University Press, 1989), 24–39.
[115] Hobbes, *Leviathan*, XXI: 336–40.
[116] Hobbes recognizes one case where subjects are justified in joining together to resist the sovereign's power to execute: collaborators who all face execution and whose shared interest in self-preservation gives them reason to cooperate. Otherwise, a subject is not to interfere with punishment ordered by the sovereign, even on the innocent. See Hobbes, *Leviathan*, XXI: 340. This point, along with Hobbes's preference for unified sovereignty with unlimited power, highlights that conditions within the Leviathan state are ill-suited for resistance. See Hobbes, *Leviathan*, XXIX: 498–500, 506, 512. A few disagree and attribute a theory of rebellion to Hobbes. See Susanne Sreedhar, *Hobbes on Resistance: Defying the Leviathan* (New York: Cambridge University Press, 2010); and Peter Steinberger, "Hobbesian Resistance," *American Journal of Political Science* 46, no. 4 (2002): 856–65.
[117] Hobbes, *Leviathan*, XI: 150. I thank an anonymous reviewer for suggesting this passage and noting its relevance.

action.[118] Hobbes therefore grounds his political philosophy in identifying the state of nature's violence and insecurity as the worst possible evil that must be avoided above all else.

This mindset helps explain the enduring concern with apocalyptic thought in Hobbes's writings. He condemns such thought, with its constant pursuit of perfection, for its destabilizing effects on politics. There is no better illustration for this point than the English Civil War. Recognizing the danger and power of apocalyptic ideals, Hobbes chooses to transform the ideal of the kingdom of God and incorporate it into his political philosophy. His concept of the natural kingdom of God links the Leviathan state with the apocalyptic ideal of God's perfect kingdom.

What results is incongruence between the reality of the Leviathan and the biblical ideal it represents. Hobbes's decision to identify the Leviathan state with the kingdom of God evokes the virtues of divine governance: permanence, unassailable authority, and perfect justice. Yet what Hobbes actually offers is a far more modest political arrangement: one that does not last forever and whose justice is imperfect. Worried about the disruptive consequences of chasing after utopia, he co-opts apocalyptic ideals to instill reverence for political structures that fall well short of perfection. It is only by tempering our visions of perfection, argues Hobbes, that politics has a chance to deliver on its promise of security.

---

[118] This idea has links to an ancient one formulated by the Roman historian Sallust. He argues that fear of enemies (*metus hostilis*) unified and strengthened Rome, and that once there was no longer fear of Carthage as a common enemy to unite the people, the state fell into strife and decay. See Neal Wood, "Sallust's Theorem: A Comment on 'Fear' in Western Political Thought," *History of Political Thought* 16, no. 2 (1995): 174–89. Hobbes transforms this idea by identifying the state of nature as a more general common enemy, which always lurks and is available as a source of fear to mobilize collective action. See Ioannis Evrigenis, *Fear of Enemies and Collective Action* (New York: Cambridge University Press, 2008), 94–130.

5

Reimagining God's Kingdom: Engels and Müntzer

It is a curious development that Thomas Müntzer came to occupy such a place of honor in Marxist thought.[1] Müntzer strikes a somewhat sad figure as a historical hero. He led a revolt that ended in disaster and the deaths of thousands of German peasants. In 1525, Müntzer managed to escape the bloody Battle of Frankenhausen with his life, but survived for only a short period thereafter. Following his defeat, the authorities tracked down Müntzer, coerced a confession from him through torture, beheaded him, and put his body on display as a warning to anyone else contemplating rebellion.[2] Müntzer met this fate while fighting for greater equality in the distribution of property, which is the primary reason for his appeal in the Marxist tradition. During his short revolutionary life, he relentlessly attacked those with wealth and power. Yet intermingled with this rhetoric was a deep religiosity at odds with Marxism's avowed atheism. Still, a no less canonical figure than Friedrich Engels lauds Müntzer as a forerunner to Marxism, whose one fatal flaw was leading a revolution far ahead of its time.

Engels easily could have dismissed Müntzer as a religious fanatic. Hope in the imminent arrival of Christ's kingdom pervades Müntzer's writings and helped motivate his revolutionary actions. When he took up arms, he did so

---

[1] For more on Müntzer's role in the history of Marxism, see Abraham Friesen, "Thomas Müntzer in Marxist Thought," *Church History* 34, no. 3 (1965): 306–27; and *Reformation and Utopia: The Marxist Interpretation of the Reformation and Its Antecedents* (Wiesbaden: F. Steiner, 1974).

[2] For more on Müntzer's life, see Michael Baylor, "Introduction," in *Revelation and Revolution: Basic Writings of Thomas Müntzer*, trans. and ed. Michael Baylor (Bethlehem, PA: Lehigh University Press, 1993), 13–46; Abraham Friesen, *Thomas Muentzer, a Destroyer of the Godless: The Making of a Sixteenth-Century Religious Revolutionary* (Berkeley, CA: University of California Press, 1990); and Hans-Jürgen Goertz, *Thomas Müntzer: Apocalyptic Mystic and Revolutionary*, trans. Jocelyn Jaquiery and ed. Peter Matheseon (Edinburgh: T. & T. Clark, 1993).

with the conviction that God would lead the peasants to victory over the corrupt ruling authorities and, in the process, realize his kingdom on earth. Such religious baggage fails to deter Engels from taking a keen interest in Müntzer, most notably in his 1850 work *The Peasant War in Germany*.[3]

Müntzer's transformation into a Marxist hero, largely spurred by Engels's praise of him, offers an example of how Christian apocalyptic thought becomes secularized. Here a secular thinker directly engages with a figure in the Christian apocalyptic tradition, as well as texts from that tradition like the book of Revelation.[4] Engels's study of apocalyptic thought leads him to conclude that aspects of it prove valuable for interpreting politics. His writings thus provide fertile ground for exploring apocalyptic thought's appeal for politics, even to thinkers without strong religious commitments.

Toward that end, the first step is to understand Müntzer's vision for apocalyptic change and its parallels to Marxism. In his writings, Müntzer espouses a cataclysmic understanding of apocalyptic thought, in which God uses crisis to wipe away earthly corruption and usher in his perfect kingdom. Related beliefs are found in Marxist thought, with the twist that economic rather than divine forces guide crisis to the ideal society where the proletariat will rule. Through his interpretation of Müntzer, Engels strengthens the parallels between Marxism and Christian apocalyptic thought. According to Engels, when Müntzer seeks after the kingdom of God, he is actually pursuing a communist ideal that emphasizes economic rather than spiritual renewal.

It is important to exercise caution when identifying links between Marxism and Christian apocalyptic thought. Some try to undermine Marxism's credibility by dismissing it as a secularized version of Christian eschatology.[5] Such criticisms often lack textual evidence and resort to extraordinary interpretive leaps to make their case. In response, some argue that we would be better off abandoning the premise behind the criticism – that Marxism is indebted to apocalyptic thought for its theory.[6]

Ultimately, that view proves less than satisfying. It is true that interpretations motivated by ideology sometimes use the concept of secular apocalyptic thought as a weapon to undermine Marxism rather than as a tool to better

---

[3] Friedrich Engels, *The Peasant War in Germany*, in *Marx and Engels: Collected Works*, vol. 10 (London: Lawrence & Wishart, 1978), 397–482.

[4] Engels, "The Book of Revelation," in *Marx and Engels: Collected Works*, vol. 26 (London: Lawrence & Wishart, 1990), 112–17; and "On the History of Early Christianity," in *Marx and Engels: Collected Works*, vol. 27 (London: Lawrence & Wishart, 1990), 445–69.

[5] See, e.g., Murray Rothbard, "Karl Marx: Communist as Religious Eschatologist," *Review of Austrian Economics* 4, no. 1 (1990): 123–79.

[6] See Roland Boer, "Marxism and Eschatology Reconsidered," *Mediations* 25, no. 1 (2010): 39–59.

understand it. But denying *any* meaningful connection between Marxism and Christian apocalyptic thought also has drawbacks. That interpretation fails to make sense of why thinkers like Engels repeatedly return to Christian apocalyptic thought as an interpretive lens for understanding politics.

Here the goal is to stake out a more compelling approach. Though Karl Marx and Engels do not draw directly on Christian apocalyptic belief to develop Marxism, these two systems of thought share key features with each other. Specifically, the concept of crisis plays a key role in resolving a tension inherent in Marxism: its dual commitment to offering a theory that is both utopian and feasible. In Marxism and the Christian apocalyptic tradition, crisis brings utopia within reach. That shared feature helps explain why Engels finds elements of Christian apocalyptic thought appealing, and why such thought interests secular thinkers engaged in the task of imagining a path to the ideal state.

MÜNTZER'S VISION FOR APOCALYPTIC CHANGE

When writing about Müntzer, Engels stresses that much of his thought was at odds with Christian orthodoxy. He certainly has good reason to see many aspects of Müntzer's thought as radical. But, as we will see, Engels goes beyond just arguing that Müntzer pushes the bounds of orthodoxy. He claims that Müntzer may have left Christianity behind altogether. Müntzer's own writings fail to back up this interpretation, however, and make clear that his apocalyptic vision remains thoroughly Christian in its assumptions.

Within the context of the Reformation, Müntzer is part of what is called the Radical Reformation. This movement believed that initial reformers, like Martin Luther, did not go far enough in their calls for religious and political change. The Radical Reformation was incredibly diverse, consisting of figures who often disagreed with each other.[7] This diversity has led to confusion over Müntzer's thought, with the labels applied to him ranging from atheist to Anabaptist.[8]

Müntzer's ties to the Anabaptists are tenuous. It is true that he rejects the practice of infant baptism, thus embracing a core tenet of Anabaptism.[9] But

---

[7] For more on the Radical Reformation, see the anthology by Michael Baylor, ed., *The Radical Reformation* (New York: Cambridge University Press, 1991).

[8] For a survey of Marxist interpretations of Müntzer, especially as he relates to the Anabaptists, see Abraham Friesen, "The Marxist Interpretation of Anabaptism," *Sixteenth Century Essays and Studies* 1 (1970): 17–34.

[9] Thomas Müntzer, *Protestation or Proposition*, in *The Collected Works of Thomas Müntzer*, trans. and ed. Peter Matheson (Edinburgh: T. & T. Clark, 1988), 191.

there is no evidence that Müntzer participated in the practice of believers' baptism – the most distinctive feature of the Anabaptist movement – where one would be baptized as an adult in a public profession of faith and sign of joining the church.[10] A 1524 letter to Müntzer from Conrad Grebel and the Swiss Brethren, who initiated the practice of believers' baptism, reveals the differences between them. Though Grebel and his companions praise some of Müntzer's teachings, like his rejection of infant baptism and condemnation of church corruption, they find fault with his endorsement of violence and other aspects of his theology.[11] The Swiss Brethren certainly had an interest in Müntzer, but some of his beliefs – most notably his reliance on the sword to advance God's kingdom – differ in important respects from those of the mostly pacifist Anabaptists.

The historian William Estep uses the term "inspirationist" to describe Müntzer, which provides some clarity in distinguishing him from the Anabaptists.[12] Müntzer does not reject the Bible's authority, but does emphasize the Holy Spirit as a source of inspiration and revelation that continues to speak to God's elect. For inspirationists like Müntzer, relying solely on the Bible proves insufficient for learning God's truth in all its fullness.

This feature of Müntzer's thought comes under harsh criticism from Luther and other contemporaries. Luther scoffs at the idea that a heavenly spirit inspires Müntzer's teachings, calling any spirit in him "evil," whose fruits are "the destruction of churches and cloisters."[13] Despite this criticism, it is important to keep in mind that Müntzer understands his belief in inspiration as wholly compatible with scripture. Indeed, his writings are littered with scriptural references offered as evidence for his claims. Scripture from his perspective shows that God's spirit, not theologians, must be the source of truth for believers. In his *Manifest Exposé of False Faith*, Müntzer writes: "Everyone must receive the knowledge of God, the true Christian faith, not from the stinking breath of the devilish biblical scholars, but from the eternal, powerful word of the father in the son as explained by the holy spirit ... Eph[esians] 3."[14] By carefully listening to and sharing the message of God's

---

[10] William Estep, *The Anabaptist Story: An Introduction to Sixteenth-Century Anabaptism*, 3rd ed. (Grand Rapids, MI: Eerdmans, 1996), 21.

[11] Conrad Grebel et al., "Letter 69," in *The Collected Works of Thomas Müntzer*, trans. and ed. Peter Matheson (Edinburgh: T. & T. Clark, 1988), 121–30.

[12] Estep, *The Anabaptist Story*, 22–23.

[13] Martin Luther, *Letter to the Princes of Saxony Concerning the Rebellious Spirit*, trans. Conrad Bergendoff, in *Luther's Works*, vol. 40, ed. Conrad Bergendoff (Philadelphia, PA: Muhlenberg Press, 1958), 52.

[14] Müntzer, *A Manifest Exposé of False Faith*, in *The Collected Works of Thomas Müntzer*, 298.

spirit, Müntzer believes that he is one of the faithful few following the Lord and not deaf to his voice.

For Müntzer, it is clear that God's spirit is communicating to him an apocalyptic vision for society. This idea pervades both his early and late writings. In Müntzer's view, he is among God's elect living at a critical juncture in history. Soon God will no longer tolerate earthly corruption and will intervene to cast down the wicked to establish his kingdom. This basic insight appears in the *Prague Manifesto* from 1521, Müntzer's first major work. There he writes: "[E]rrors [in the church] had to take place so that all men's deeds, those of the elect and those of the damned, could flourish freely until our time when God will separate out the tares from the wheat."[15] Müntzer infuses this parable from Matthew 13:24–30 with added urgency by proclaiming that it will be realized in "our time." He also believes that he has a special role to play in the upcoming harvest: "The time of harvest has come! That is why he [God] himself has hired me for his harvest. I have sharpened my sickle, for my thoughts yearn for the truth and with my lips, skin, hands, hair, soul, body and life I call down curses on the unbelievers."[16]

So Müntzer sees himself as God's chosen agent to advance his kingdom, whose violent arrival is imminent. In fact, his vision for societal transformation embodies all the elements of cataclysmic apocalyptic thought – beliefs in present corruption, impending crisis, a divine force guiding crisis, and finally utopia in the form of the kingdom of God.[17]

Müntzer's writings make clear that he views society as plagued by deep and entrenched corruption. A letter from 1521 proclaims that the "time of the Antichrist is upon us."[18] For Müntzer, the world has entered a period of corruption foretold by scripture, where the godless rule both inside and outside the church. People find themselves living under "unintelligent rulers who offend against all equity and do not accept the word of God."[19] False priests exude an air of learning, but in fact are "lacking in judgment," as they lead many astray with their sham authority to teach scripture.[20] Given its pervasiveness among those in authority, the corruption of Müntzer's day puts enormous pressure on people to turn away from God.

In his bleak account of society, Müntzer sees a silver lining. Present corruption provides an opportunity for the elect to sharpen their faith and

---

[15] Müntzer, *Prague Manifesto*, in *The Collected Works of Thomas Müntzer*, 370.
[16] Müntzer, *Prague Manifesto*, 371.
[17] For more on cataclysmic apocalyptic thought, see Chapter 2.
[18] Müntzer, "Letter 25," in *The Collected Works of Thomas Müntzer*, 35.
[19] Müntzer, *A Manifest Exposé of False Faith*, 286.
[20] Müntzer, *A Manifest Exposé of False Faith*, 292.

prove their commitment to God. Indeed, in Müntzer's view, true faith only comes through enduring severe trials and persecution. As he puts it in *On Counterfeit Faith*, "Hell has to be endured, before one can take due precautions against its engulfing gates, with all their wiles."[21] Similarly, in a letter from 1524, he writes: "One has to walk in the mortification of the flesh every single moment; in particular our reputation has to stink in the nostrils of the godless. Then the person who has been tested can preach."[22] This vivid imagery emphasizes to the elect that they must leave behind creature comforts and dreams of gaining respect from society's ruling powers. God uses evil in the world to break the faithful until they wholly submit to him. He "makes the tyrants rage more," stresses Müntzer, "so that the countenance of his elect is covered in shame and vice and they are driven to seek the name and glory and honour of God alone."[23] In the midst of such corruption, the elect ultimately reach a point where nothing – from "tyrants" to a "sack of gunpowder" – can stop them from venturing their "body, goods and honour for the sake of God."[24]

This conflict between the elect and the godless gives birth to crisis and violence. The coming crisis will be bloody and plunge society into great upheaval, but is necessary according to Müntzer. Corrupt rulers currently in place lack legitimacy, and God will not allow them stay in power forever. "A true Christianity for our days," writes Müntzer, "will soon be in full swing despite all the previous corruption."[25] Before true Christianity arrives, the authority of corrupt rulers will crumble – a prediction Müntzer makes by drawing on the apocalyptic book of Daniel. The demise of the final corrupt empire foretold in Daniel "is now in full swing."[26] The event that deprives the wicked of authority once and for all has already begun in Müntzer's view.

His enthusiasm for societal upheaval elicits the rebuke of his contemporaries. The reformer Johann Agricola condemns him for breathing out "nothing but slaughter and blood."[27] Luther, never shy in his criticism of Müntzer, calls him the "archdevil who rules at Mühlhausen, and does nothing except stir up robbery, murder, and bloodshed."[28] In Müntzer's defense, there are instances

---

[21] Müntzer, *On Counterfeit Faith*, in *The Collected Works of Thomas Müntzer*, 223.
[22] Müntzer, "Letter 49," in *The Collected Works of Thomas Müntzer*, 76–77.
[23] Müntzer, "Letter 41B," in *The Collected Works of Thomas Müntzer*, 62.
[24] Müntzer, "Letter 53," in *The Collected Works of Thomas Müntzer*, 84.
[25] Müntzer, *A Manifest Exposé of False Faith*, 312.
[26] Müntzer, *Sermon to the Princes*, in *The Collected Works of Thomas Müntzer*, 244.
[27] Johann Agricola, "Letter 21," in *The Collected Works of Thomas Müntzer*, trans. and ed. Peter Matheson (Edinburgh: T. & T. Clark, 1988), 30.
[28] Luther, *Against the Robbing and Murdering Hordes of Peasants*, trans. Charles Jacobs, in *Luther's Works*, vol. 46, ed. Robert Schultz (Philadelphia, PA: Fortress Press, 1967), 49.

where he counsels restraint. For example, in a 1523 letter to followers at Stolberg, he urges them to refrain from rebellion.[29] Nevertheless, despite the occasional calls for peace, violent language runs throughout Müntzer's writings. In a 1524 letter he proclaims: "[T]he time has come when a bloodbath will befall this obstinate world because of its unbelief."[30] His celebration of violence alarms rulers fearful that the Reformation will turn into widespread rebellion. Müntzer, though, sees no reason to fear the violent crisis beginning to engulf society, for he is assured that it will bring the elect to power.

His optimism about the coming crisis stems from his conviction that it is part of a divine plan. The violence and upheaval starting to break out during his lifetime are not without purpose, but signs that God is intervening to make way for his kingdom. In this final stage of history, Müntzer emphasizes that the elect will be active participants in making God's kingdom on earth a reality. Initially, he believes that a few righteous rulers will rise up to defend the elect, dispatch the wicked, and help bring about God's kingdom. Yet if the princes fail to seize this opportunity, God will find others to do his work.

Müntzer communicates this warning to Frederick III, Elector of Saxony: "[T]he people ... should love princes rather than fear them: Romans 13. Princes hold no terrors for the pious. But should that change, then the sword will be taken from them and will be given to the people who burn with zeal so that the godless can be defeated, Daniel 7; and then that noble jewel, peace, will be in abeyance on earth. Revelation 6."[31] Whereas Luther cites Romans 13 – "Let every person be subject to the governing authorities ... [which] have been instituted by God" – as a general command for subjects to obey their rulers,[32] Müntzer focuses on what he sees as the conditional nature of this command.[33] The people should obey *only if* their rulers act as God's servants and, in Paul's words, "are not a terror to good conduct, but to bad" (Romans 13:3).[34] Princes are called as God's servants to implement his plan for the end times, yet if they fail to, God will empower others to carry it out.

Müntzer expresses this point most forcefully in his *Sermon to the Princes*, preached to Duke John of Saxony and his son John Frederick in 1524. The sermon makes an urgent plea for the princes to delay no longer in taking

---

[29] Müntzer, "Letter 41B," 61–64.
[30] Müntzer, "Letter 55," in *The Collected Works of Thomas Müntzer*, 90.
[31] Müntzer, "Letter 45," in *The Collected Works of Thomas Müntzer*, 69.
[32] Luther, *Admonition to Peace: A Reply to the Twelve Articles of the Peasants in Swabia*, trans. Charles Jacobs and Robert Schultz, in *Luther's Works*, vol. 46, 25.
[33] Michael Baylor makes this point. See Baylor, "Introduction," in *Revelation and Revolution*, 32.
[34] New Revised Standard Version.

action. The time has come for them to "sweep aside those evil men who obstruct the gospel" and to take "them out of circulation!"[35] Violent imagery runs throughout the sermon, as Müntzer argues that it is the duty of godly princes to slaughter corrupt religious authorities.[36] He offers himself to the princes as a "new Daniel" who will help them "grasp the plight of the Christian people" persecuted by false clergy and criminals.[37] If the princes truly comprehend the depths of current corruption, they will embrace their role as God's chosen instruments to drive "his enemies away from the elect."[38] Godly princes are best positioned to carry out "in a fair and orderly manner" this important task. But if they fail to do so, cautions Müntzer, "the sword will be taken from them."[39]

This attempt to rally the princes to action ultimately fails. As a result, Müntzer loses all hope that they will lead the way in fulfilling God's plan for apocalyptic change. The princes become part of the corruption he sees all around him: "they do violence to everyone, flay and fleece the poor farm worker, tradesman and everything that breathes," while hanging the poor who "commit the pettiest crime."[40] One of his later letters uses vivid imagery from Ezekiel 39 to describe the fate awaiting corrupt rulers: "God instructs all the birds of the heavens to consume the flesh of the princes."[41] Such disillusionment leads Müntzer to place his hope in the people and conclude it is God's plan "that power should be given to the common man."[42] But the people must seize the opportunity before them, and not let the "sword grow cold" in dispatching the godless.[43]

On the other side of all this bloodshed lies utopia, God's perfect kingdom. This aspect of Müntzer's apocalyptic vision is the one least developed in his writings. He dedicates most of his energy to urging the elect to take dramatic action to topple corrupt rulers and bring about God's kingdom. Assured of the kingdom of God's imminent arrival and its worthiness as an object of sacrifice, Müntzer feels little need to speculate at great length on what it will look like.

---

[35] Müntzer, *Sermon to the Princes*, 246.
[36] For more on the role of violent language in Müntzer's *Sermon to the Princes*, see Matthias Riedl, "Apocalyptic Violence and Revolutionary Action: Thomas Müntzer's *Sermon to the Princes*," in *A Companion to the Premodern Apocalypse*, ed. Michael Ryan (Leiden: Brill, 2016), 260–96.
[37] Müntzer, *Sermon to the Princes*, 246.
[38] Müntzer, *Sermon to the Princes*, 247.
[39] Müntzer, *Sermon to the Princes*, 250.
[40] Müntzer, *Vindication and Refutation*, in *The Collected Works of Thomas Müntzer*, 335.
[41] Müntzer, "Letter 89," in *The Collected Works of Thomas Müntzer*, 157.
[42] Müntzer, "Letter 91," in *The Collected Works of Thomas Müntzer*, 159.
[43] Müntzer, "Letter 75," in *The Collected Works of Thomas Müntzer*, 142.

He does predict that, when the elect sacrifice and suffer for God's sake, they will "lay hold on the whole wide world, which will acquire a Christian government that no sack of gunpowder can ever topple."[44]

ENGELS ON RELIGION AND APOCALYPTIC THOUGHT

So despite his radicalism, Müntzer remains thoroughly Christian in his worldview and vision for the future – his writings leave little doubt on this point. Shortly we will turn to how Engels interprets and transforms Müntzer. But before doing so, it is important to examine Engels's own views on religion and apocalyptic thought, for they serve as the interpretative lens through which he studies Müntzer.

It comes as little surprise that, as an atheist, Engels is often dismissive toward religion. Nonetheless, his articles "The Book of Revelation" and "On the History of Early Christianity" show a genuine interest in apocalyptic belief. These different currents in Engels's thought result in a perspective that rejects religion's truth while recognizing its power, especially when it takes apocalyptic form.

Historical materialism provides the foundation for how Engels understands religion. This perspective sees economic relations as producing moral and religious beliefs that usually legitimize existing political and economic structures.[45] In the hands of the oppressed classes, morality and religion can become an outlet to express discontent with existing power relations. These beliefs, however, lack a feasible program to transform power relations so that they benefit the poor.[46]

As the capitalist system comes under increased strain and history marches toward a world embodying Marxist ideals, Engels is confident that religion eventually will become a vestige of the past. Religion, he argues, "will be no lasting safeguard to capitalist society. If our juridical, philosophical, and religious ideas are the more or less remote offshoots of the economical relations prevailing in a given society, such ideas cannot, in the long run, withstand the effects of a complete change in these relations."[47] This position

[44] Müntzer, "Letter 41B," 63.
[45] See, e.g., Karl Marx and Friedrich Engels, *The German Ideology*, in *Marx and Engels: Collected Works*, vol. 5 (London: Lawrence & Wishart, 1975), 36; and Engels, "Engels to Joseph Bloch," in *Marx and Engels: Collected Works*, vol. 49 (London: Lawrence & Wishart, 2001), 35.
[46] Engels, *Anti-Dühring*, in *Marx and Engels: Collected Works*, vol. 25 (London: Lawrence & Wishart, 1987), 86–88.
[47] Engels, "Introduction to the English Edition (1892) of *Socialism: Utopian and Scientific*," in *Marx and Engels: Collected Works*, vol. 27, 300–1.

aligns with an idea advanced by Marx early in his writings: "To abolish religion as the *illusory* happiness of the people is to demand their *real* happiness."[48] In short, the realization of Marxist principles will render religion obsolete by meeting people's real needs, which religion has repeatedly failed to do.

Though Marx and Engels fundamentally agree in their views on religion, the latter's writings reveal greater engagement with and curiosity in the subject. Notably, Engels exhibits an enduring interest in apocalyptic thought. Beyond just his study of Müntzer, he repeatedly returns to apocalyptic texts like the book of Revelation.

Based on the research available to him at the time (later discredited),[49] Engels takes Revelation to be the earliest Christian literature to survive.[50] To him, Revelation represents "with the most naïve fidelity" the ideas at the core of early Christianity.[51] He sees much in Revelation to commend, which is lost in later forms of Christianity. As he argues in "On the History of Early Christianity," Revelation is gritty and combative, a feature it shares with modern socialists:

> Here we have neither the dogma nor the morals of later Christianity, but instead a feeling that one is struggling against the whole world and that the struggle will be a victorious one; an eagerness for struggle and a certainty of victory which are totally lacking in the Christians of today and which are to be found in our time only at the other pole of society, among the socialists.[52]

Engels also conveys this idea in "The Book of Revelation," where he notes that early Christianity and modern socialism both captivate the attention of the masses through a message "opposed to the ruling system, to 'the powers that be.'"[53]

So Engels's affinity for Revelation is evident from the parallels he draws between early Christianity and modern socialism. Both appeal to the oppressed and persecuted by offering a path to salvation that previously seemed beyond reach. Engels strikes a hopeful tone when noting that socialism looks destined to follow and surpass Christianity in its ability to spread throughout the world:

---

[48] Marx, "Introduction to *Contribution to the Critique of Hegel's* Philosophy of Law," in *Marx and Engels: Collected Works*, vol. 3 (London: Lawrence & Wishart, 1975), 176.

[49] Most biblical scholars today believe that Revelation was written decades after Paul's letters and Mark, the New Testament's earliest gospel. See Michael Coogan, ed., *The New Oxford Annotated Bible*, 3rd ed. (New York: Oxford University Press, 2001), NT 240, 420.

[50] Engels, "On the History of Early Christianity," 468–69.

[51] Engels, "On the History of Early Christianity," 454.

[52] Engels, "On the History of Early Christianity," 457.

[53] Engels, "The Book of Revelation," 113.

[I]n spite of all persecution, nay, even spurred on by it, [Christians and socialists] forge victoriously, irresistibly ahead. Three hundred years after its appearance Christianity was the recognised state religion in the Roman World Empire, and in barely sixty years socialism has won itself a position which makes its victory absolutely certain.[54]

Engels recognizes in early Christianity, especially in its apocalyptic beliefs, the power to spur a worldwide movement. This appeal resembles what drives people to join the growing socialist movement, even in the face of persecution.

It is important not to overstate Engels's appreciation for and interest in Christian apocalyptic thought. Engels never implies that the claims in Revelation are valid. In fact, he takes a dismissive attitude toward much of the book. He scoffs at commentators who "expect [Revelation's] prophecies are still to come off, after more than 1,800 years," given that its author thought the realization of his predictions were "at hand."[55] Engels also argues that biblical criticism has revealed the origin of all John's images and signs, showing his "great poverty of mind" and "that he never experienced even in the imagination the alleged ecstasies and visions he describes."[56] While noting some redeeming aspects of Revelation and early Christianity, Engels never deviates from his underlying skepticism toward religion.

The greatest limitation that Engels identifies in Christian apocalyptic thought is not its bizarre imagery and prophecies, but its failure to prioritize the transformation of *this* world. Practices resembling socialism did appear in early Christianity, notes Engels. Yet these practices remained limited because early Christianity focused not on accomplishing "social transformation in this world, but in the hereafter, in heaven, in eternal life after death, in the impending 'millennium.'"[57] From Engels's perspective, any ideology that downplays the importance of addressing injustice in the present is impoverished and should be rejected.

In sum, Engels does find value in Christian apocalyptic thought – specifically, in its power to inspire challenges to those in power. But this tradition of thought, like other forms of religious thought, ultimately falls short in specifying a concrete program to remedy the ills that prompt people to turn to religion in the first place.

---

[54] Engels, "On the History of Early Christianity," 447.
[55] Engels, "The Book of Revelation," 115.
[56] Engels, "On the History of Early Christianity," 462.
[57] Engels, "On the History of Early Christianity," 448.

REINTERPRETING THE KINGDOM OF GOD

Given Engels's view that Christian apocalyptic thought fails to provide meaningful guidance in the present, it seems that he would find little value in its ideal of the kingdom of God – the ultimate end toward which history is moving according to the Christian perspective. Yet when Engels turns his attention to Müntzer, he comes across a conception of the kingdom of God that intrigues him. As Engels interprets him, Müntzer reimagines the kingdom of God as a communist ideal that inspires societal transformation. By using apocalyptic thought to fight economic exploitation, Müntzer overcomes a common concern with such thought – its purported lack of concern for addressing injustices here on earth. Engels thus finds in Müntzer's thought an apocalyptic vision that earns his respect.

In his work *The Peasant War in Germany*, Engels opts for an understanding of Müntzer that heightens his appeal within Marxism. According to this view, Müntzer largely abandons Christianity and comes close to embracing atheism. Engels paints a portrait of Müntzer no longer bound by Christianity and the Bible, but guided by reason alone:

> His philosophico-theological doctrine attacked all the main points not only of Catholicism, but of Christianity generally. In the form of Christianity he preached a kind of pantheism, which curiously resembled modern speculative contemplation and at times even approached atheism. He repudiated the Bible both as the only and as the infallible revelation. The real and living revelation, he said, was reason, a revelation that has existed at all times and still exists among all peoples. To hold up the Bible against reason, he maintained, was to kill the spirit with the letter, for the Holy Spirit of which the Bible speaks is not something that exists outside us – the Holy Spirit is our reason.[58]

This convenient interpretation makes it easier for communists to identify with Müntzer. Engels himself makes this connection: "As Münzer's religious philosophy approached atheism, so his political programme approached communism."[59] The more atheist Müntzer appears, the more appealing his thought becomes from a Marxist perspective. And toward that end, Engels transforms Müntzer from a religious zealot confident he was fulfilling biblical prophecies into a Marxist hero guided by reason in his fight against irrationality and economic exploitation.

---

[58] Engels, *The Peasant War in Germany*, 421–22.
[59] Engels, *The Peasant War in Germany*, 422.

With this carefully crafted interpretation, Engels portrays Müntzer as a visionary, one of the few Reformation figures who pinpointed the real sources of the conflict. According to Engels, the religious wars of the sixteenth century were in reality "class struggles ... clothed in religious shibboleths."[60] In the midst of this struggle, Müntzer represents for Engels the first to give voice to those factions in society without property. Whereas his contemporaries were concerned with protecting the status quo or pursuing apocalyptic fantasies, only in Müntzer's teachings does one find "communist notions" calling for radically altered property relations.[61]

When emphasizing Müntzer's egalitarian commitments, Engels does bring attention to a real element of his thought. In his writings, Müntzer passionately condemns existing property relations and their immense harms on the peasant class, which explains why Engels is drawn to him. According to Müntzer, princes fall into the same category as robbers and thieves because they steal from the poor and claim all creatures on earth to be their property.[62] Such views elicited the ire of authorities, evident from the charges against him. These included starting a revolt "with the aim of making all Christians equal" and creating a community where all "things are to be held in common and distribution should be to each according to his need."[63] Engels may exaggerate in places, but he is correct in stressing Müntzer's concerns with the oppressive nature of existing property relations.

These concerns lead Engels to conclude that Müntzer understands the kingdom of God differently from his predecessors. It is here that Engels takes the most liberties in his interpretation of Müntzer. Engels starts from the assumption that Müntzer equates faith and reason. He then proceeds to argue that, for Müntzer, reason makes individuals "godlike and blessed. Heaven is, therefore, nothing of another world and is to be sought in this life. It is the mission of believers to establish this Heaven, the kingdom of God, here on earth. Just as there is no Heaven in the beyond, there is also no Hell and no damnation."[64] Müntzer, as construed by Engels, sweeps away Christianity's otherworldly distractions to focus on the heart of the matter: creating a radically new society that realizes heaven in the here and now.

In addition to locating Müntzer's vision for God's kingdom on earth, Engels claims that this kingdom embodies communist ideals. Müntzer's political program, writes Engels, is "a brilliant anticipation of the conditions for the

---

[60] Engels, *The Peasant War in Germany*, 412.
[61] Engels, *The Peasant War in Germany*, 415.
[62] Müntzer, *Vindication and Refutation*, 335.
[63] Müntzer, "Interrogation and 'Recantation' of Müntzer," in *The Collected Works of Thomas Müntzer*, 436–37.
[64] Engels, *The Peasant War in Germany*, 422.

emancipation of the proletarian element that had scarcely begun" during his life. This program specifically takes the form of a call for "the immediate establishment of the kingdom of God on Earth, of the prophesied millennium." By kingdom of God, continues Engels, Müntzer "meant a society with no class differences, no private property and no state authority independent of, and foreign to, the members of society. All existing authorities, insofar as they refused to submit and join the revolution, were to be overthrown, all work and all property shared in common, and complete equality introduced." Müntzer is not content just to pray and hope for this ideal, but commits to "overthrow or kill" all who stand in its way.[65] For Engels, Müntzer transforms the kingdom of God into an ideal that promotes revolution on earth.

For Engels, Müntzer's ideas were ahead of his time – in fact, *too far* ahead of his time. During the Reformation, property relations had not developed and reached a point of crisis where a figure like Müntzer could successfully launch a revolution in line with Marxist principles. As Engels puts it, "Not only the movement of his time, but also the age, were not ripe for the ideas of which [Müntzer] himself had only a faint notion. The class which he represented was still in its birth throes. It was far from developed enough to assume leadership over, and to transform, society."[66] Müntzer stands as an early harbinger of the modern proletarian movement.[67] Yet the "chasm between his theories and the surrounding realities" proved too great for Müntzer, which is why his revolutionary program ultimately failed.[68]

Engels's interpretation of Müntzer has proven incredibly influential, ensuring the German reformer a place of honor in the communist tradition. Statues, stamps, and other imagery from the communist era in East Germany, for instance, celebrate Müntzer as a hero and patriot (see Figure 5.1). Though successful in bringing greater attention to Müntzer, Engels's account has the weakness of putting forward a portrait of Müntzer at odds with the reformer's own writings. Engels asserts that the dominant culture at the time forced Müntzer to conceal his doctrines in "Christian phraseology."[69] But he offers no evidence for this claim, and it is difficult to square with Müntzer's heavy reliance on scripture and claims to be God's chosen servant. If Müntzer's faith is an act, it certainly is an elaborate one, for he never shows any hints of deviating from it in his public life or private writings.

---

[65] Engels, *The Peasant War in Germany*, 422.
[66] Engels, *The Peasant War in Germany*, 470.
[67] Engels, *Socialism: Utopian and Scientific*, in *Marx and Engels: Collected Works*, vol. 24 (London: Lawrence & Wishart, 1989), 287; and *Dialectics of Nature*, in *Marx and Engels: Collected Works*, vol. 25, 318.
[68] Engels, *The Peasant War in Germany*, 471.
[69] Engels, *The Peasant War in Germany*, 422.

FIGURE 5.1 East German stamp of Thomas Müntzer
This stamp from the communist era portrays Müntzer as a "German patriot"[70]

A more parsimonious explanation is that Müntzer's frequent references to God and scripture stem from sincere Christian beliefs. As the earlier overview of Müntzer's thought makes clear, a Christian apocalyptic worldview permeates his writings. It is true that Müntzer calls for radical change on earth, as Engels notes. But for Müntzer, such change is possible only because God is empowering the elect to realize his kingdom. Nothing in Müntzer's writings suggests that he abandons his Christian faith in favor of atheism. So rather than give the most accurate account of Müntzer's thought, Engels molds it to make it compatible with Marxism.

THE INADEQUACY OF UTOPIAN SOCIALISM

Engels secularizes Müntzer by downplaying the Christian elements in his thought and reinterpreting his conception of the kingdom of God. Below we will explore *why* Engels would interpret Müntzer in this way. But to answer that question, first it is important to understand parallels between Marxism and Christian apocalyptic thought. The goal here is not to repeat the facile criticism that Marxism lacks originality and just repackages Christian apocalyptic beliefs. It rather is to identify

---

[70] The stamp is from the American Philatelic Society's reference collection and the photo is by Mackenzie Jones.

points of convergence between Marxism and apocalyptic thought so as to highlight what makes Müntzer's thought appealing to Engels.

The parallels between Marxism and cataclysmic apocalyptic thought emerge most prominently in Marx and Engels's criticism of what they call utopian socialism. In the *Communist Manifesto*, they describe utopian socialists as rejecting "all political, and especially all revolutionary, action; they wish to attain their ends by peaceful means, and endeavour, by small experiments, necessarily doomed to failure, and by the force of example, to pave the way for the new social Gospel."[71] In their view, utopian socialism takes a naïve understanding of social change: someone just needs to come up with the right idea and implement it peacefully and gradually, starting with small experiments, then the ideal society will follow. This approach, warn Marx and Engels, ignores the decisive role that economic forces play in shaping history.

In *Socialism: Utopian and Scientific*, Engels contrasts utopian socialism with scientific socialism, which for him is Marxism. He dismisses utopian socialists for seeing no connection between their theories and "the chain of historical development." From their perspective, they "might just as well have been born 500 years earlier, and might then have spared humanity 500 years of error, strife, and suffering."[72] This understanding of social change, which takes a reformer's eureka moment as the impetus for such change, strikes Engels as hopelessly simplistic. He instead stresses that society advances toward the ideal as a result of changing economic forces. For theorists committed to scientific socialism, their duty is to understand those forces, how they develop, and what impact their future development will have. When economic forces are examined through a Marxist lens, the transition to the ideal society ceases to be as convenient and smooth as utopian socialism suggests.

Marxism offers a scientific approach to understanding socialism and its development, argues Engels, grounded in two concepts: historical materialism and surplus value.[73] Historical materialism expresses the idea that "the final causes of all social changes and political revolutions are to be sought, not in men's brains, not in man's better insight into eternal truth and justice, but in changes in the modes of production and exchange."[74] Importantly, Marxism takes economic and political crisis as an inescapable part of the transition to socialism.

Why is crisis inevitable? The answer lies in the other concept Engels singles out: surplus value. Capitalists amass wealth by extracting surplus value from

[71] Marx and Engels, *Manifesto of the Communist Party*, in *Marx and Engels: Collected Works*, vol. 6 (London: Lawrence & Wishart, 1976), 515.
[72] Engels, *Socialism: Utopian and Scientific*, 288.
[73] Engels, *Socialism: Utopian and Scientific*, 305.
[74] Engels, *Socialism: Utopian and Scientific*, 306.

their workers – that is, the value of workers' labor that exceeds their pay.[75] Competition puts pressure on capitalists to increase their profits and technology makes each worker more productive, which together lead to the extraction of more and more surplus value from the workers. This exploitation ensures an increasingly impoverished proletariat relative to the bourgeoisie, as the wealth gap and antagonism between the two classes grow. These economic developments set in motion a crisis for capitalism – the rise of the bourgeoisie's "own grave-diggers," as the *Communist Manifesto* puts it.[76] The growing wealth gap that comes with modern industry produces a proletariat more acutely aware of its exploitation. Moreover, proletarians work closely together in factories, which makes it easier for them to organize. Eventually, the power of the proletariat overwhelms the capitalist system, resulting in a revolution where the *"proletariat seizes political power and turns the means of production into State property."*[77]

There is, of course, much debate in Marxist theory on what exactly the crisis and revolution leading to capitalism's collapse will look like. At the time of the *Communist Manifesto* in 1848, Marx and Engels envisioned socialism coming "only by the forcible overthrow of all existing social conditions."[78] Within Marxism, Vladimir Lenin's theory of revolution – outlined on the eve of the Russian Revolution in *The State and Revolution* – argues perhaps most strongly that socialism only comes through violence. The "liberation of the oppressed class," writes Lenin, is possible only with a "violent revolution" and *"the destruction* of the apparatus of state power which was created by the ruling class."[79] The crisis giving birth to the communist state, in Lenin's view, is necessarily a violent revolution led by the vanguard of the proletariat. Regardless of whether Leninism is a perversion of Marxism or its fullest realization, it is hard to deny that there are resources in Marx and Engels's writings – which Lenin cites at length – for making the case that the communist revolution comes violently.

A few passages by Marx and Engels leave open the possibility of a peaceful transition to socialism, at least in some places. Speaking in 1872, Marx identifies several nations – America, England, and perhaps Holland – "where the workers may achieve their aims by peaceful means."[80] Similarly, Engels speaks

---

[75] Engels, *Socialism: Utopian and Scientific*, 305.
[76] Marx and Engels, *Manifesto of the Communist Party*, 496.
[77] Engels, *Socialism: Utopian and Scientific*, 320.
[78] Marx and Engels, *Manifesto of the Communist Party*, 519.
[79] Vladimir Lenin, *The State and Revolution*, trans. Robert Service (New York: Penguin Books, 1992), 9.
[80] Marx, "On the Hague Congress," in *Marx and Engels: Collected Works*, vol. 23 (London: Lawrence & Wishart, 1988), 255.

glowingly of advances made by communism in the wake of universal suffrage. He notes the irony of communists – "the 'revolutionaries,' the 'overthrowers' " – "thriving far better on legal methods than on illegal methods and overthrow."[81] So there also are resources in Marxist theory for the view that nonviolent revolution can bring about socialism.

Still, granting the possibility of nonviolent revolution does not eliminate crisis's role in Marxism. According to Marxist theory, human welfare does not improve gradually and steadily. Instead, social, political, and economic conditions must worsen before they can get better. Exploitation of the workers increases as capitalism develops, before culminating in a crisis that brings the communist ideal within reach. Regardless of whether the revolution is peaceful or violent, crisis is unavoidable in the Marxist understanding of how history unfolds.

Marxism's reliance on crisis to explain social change gives it a structure with similarities to cataclysmic apocalyptic thought. From the Marxist perspective, corruption infects capitalist society in the form of widespread exploitation of the working class. This exploitation ultimately proves unsustainable, as the antagonism between the proletariat and bourgeoisie reaches a crisis point that sets in motion capitalism's collapse. What ensues is more than mere chaos, since economic forces empower the proletariat to take the reins of political power. The dictatorship of the proletariat ends economic exploitation and brings to a close the long history in which one class oppressed another. With the arrival of communism, the state eventually withers away and the Marxist vision of utopia becomes a reality. In sum, the Marxist understanding of social change – corruption, crisis, economic forces guiding crisis to its intended end, and utopia – contains all the elements of cataclysmic apocalyptic thought in secular form.

ENGELS, MARXISM, AND APOCALYPTIC HOPE

To suggest that Marxism shares features with Christianity – in particular, apocalyptic thought – is by no means a new claim. Numerous interpreters make this claim, which often serves the goal of criticizing Marxism. With varying levels of sophistication, political theorists, theologians, and others make the case that Marxism's ties to religion are deep and inescapable. The diverse charges leveled against Marxism include that it is a philosophy motivated by apocalyptic hope,[82] the exhortations of

---

[81] Engels, "Introduction to Karl Marx's *The Class Struggles in France 1848 to 1850*," in *Marx and Engels: Collected Works*, vol. 27, 522.

[82] Richard Arneson, "Marxism and Secular Faith," *American Political Science Review* 79, no. 3 (1985): 639; Nicolas Berdyaev, *The Russian Idea* (New York: Macmillan, 1948), 200; Norman Cohn, *The Pursuit of the Millennium: Revolutionary Millenarians and Mystical*

a prophet,[83] a secularized religion,[84] a Christian heresy,[85] and the god that failed.[86] Abraham Friesen sums up the perceived connection between Marxism and Christian apocalyptic thought, evident in the former's fascination with figures like Müntzer: "The ultimate goal of Müntzer and Marx were identical, but the means of arriving at the goal were different. Would God or man overcome tensions in society and establish the Kingdom of God on earth? ... One could quibble over the means, but the goal remained the same."[87] At its heart, argues Friesen, Marxism is a utopian philosophy like apocalyptic Christianity. It only departs from Christianity in its belief that human forces, not divine ones, will realize the ideal society.

Some object to this characterization of Marxism. Roland Boer rejects the notion that there are significant ties between Marxism and apocalyptic thought.[88] This "infamous" charge (in Boer's words) certainly catches people's attention.[89] As "soon as one raises the question of Marxism and religion in a gathering," writes Boer, "at least one person will jump at the bait and insist that Marxism is a form of secularised eschatology.... These proponents argue that Jewish and Christian thought has influenced the Marxist narrative of

Anarchists of the Middle Ages, rev. ed. (New York: Oxford University Press, 1970), 251; Friesen, *Reformation and Utopia*, 236–39; John Hall, *Apocalypse: From Antiquity to the Empire of Modernity* (Malden, MA: Polity, 2009), 134–42; Karl Löwith, *Meaning in History* (Chicago: University of Chicago Press, 1949), 33–51; Reinhold Niebuhr, "Introduction," in *Karl Marx and Friedrich Engels on Religion* (New York: Schocken Books, 1964), vii–xiv; John Roberts, "The 'Returns to Religion': Messianism, Christianity and the Revolutionary Tradition. Part I: 'Wakefulness to the Future,'" *Historical Materialism* 16, no. 2 (2008): 59–84; Rothbard, "Karl Marx: Communist as Religious Eschatologist"; and David Rowley, "'Redeemer Empire': Russian Millenarianism," *American Historical Review* 104, no. 5 (1999): 1592.

[83] Leszek Kolakowski, *Main Currents of Marxism: Its Rise, Growth, and Dissolution. Volume 1: The Founders*, trans. P. S. Falla (New York: Oxford University Press, 1978), 375.

[84] Rudolf Bultmann, *The Presence of Eternity: History and Eschatology* (New York: Harper & Brothers, 1957), 68–70; Gregory Claeys, *Dystopia: A Natural History: A Study of Modern Despotism, Its Antecedents, and Its Literary Diffractions* (New York: Oxford University Press, 2017), 245; Gareth Jones, "How Marx Covered His Tracks: The Hidden Link between Communism and Religion," *Times Literary Supplement* 5175 (2002): 14; and David McLellan, *Marxism and Religion: A Description and Assessment of the Marxist Critique of Christianity* (New York: Harper & Row, 1987), 161.

[85] Alasdair MacIntyre, *Marxism and Christianity*, 2nd ed. (London: Duckworth Publishers, 1995), vi.

[86] Richard Crossman, ed., *The God that Failed* (New York: Harper & Brothers, 1949).

[87] Friesen, *Reformation and Utopia*, 239.

[88] Boer is not the first to object to this characterization of Marxism. See also Hans Blumenberg, *The Legitimacy of the Modern Age*, trans. Robert Wallace (Cambridge, MA: MIT Press, 1983), 14–15.

[89] Boer, *Criticism of Earth: On Marxism and Theology IV* (Chicago: Haymarket Books, 2013), 289.

history, which is but a pale copy of its original." That argument, he continues, usually "is used as ammunition in the hands of conservative and liberal critics."[90]

In Boer's reading of Marx and Engels, such criticism has little textual basis. Of the two, Engels shows more interest in apocalyptic thought, evident in his writings on Revelation and Müntzer. But once you dig into these texts, contends Boer, it becomes clear that "Engels was not the conduit for eschatological or apocalyptic themes in Marxism." As evidence, Boer cites Engels's conclusions on the book of Revelation: "By the 1850s, Engels ... argued that [Revelation] was a purely historical text, giving us a window into early Christianity."[91] So according to Boer, Revelation for Engels amounts to nothing more than a historical artifact, which has little influence on his philosophy.

Boer makes several compelling points when casting doubt on the idea that Marxism is apocalyptic Christianity in secular garb. He is right that such criticisms often are reactionary attacks with little interest in better understanding Marxism.[92] Given Marxism's claims to be scientific, comparing it to religious belief is an easy way to discredit it. Boer is also right to emphasize that there is no evidence that Marx and Engels appropriate elements from Christian apocalyptic thought when formulating Marxism. The suggestion that Christian apocalyptic thought provides the foundation for Marxism is speculation with little textual evidence. Marx and Engels never explicitly draw on Revelation or other apocalyptic writings when developing Marxism's core concepts. There are good reasons, then, for Boer's skepticism.

But in expressing this skepticism, Boer defends conclusions that prove too strong. He argues that the apocalyptic beliefs of Revelation are merely historical artifacts with little relevance to Engels's understanding of politics in the Industrial Age. For Boer, Engels's real interest in Revelation lies in identifying the book as the earliest Christian writing, which best captures Christianity's revolutionary nature.[93] It is here that Boer's interpretation goes awry, for he assumes that Engels sees the revolutionary elements in Revelation and early Christianity as *distinct from* their apocalyptic elements. If Revelation best captures the heart of early Christianity in Engels's view, that suggests he understands early Christianity as fundamentally apocalyptic in its outlook.

---

[90] Boer, *In the Vale of Tears: On Marxism and Theology V* (Chicago: Haymarket Books, 2014), 219.
[91] Boer, *In the Vale of Tears*, 225.
[92] See, e.g., Rothbard, "Karl Marx: Communist as Religious Eschatologist."
[93] Boer, *Criticism of Earth*, 290.

In fact, for Engels, it is precisely Christianity's apocalyptic outlook that made it revolutionary. He makes that argument in "On the History of Early Christianity." This work notes that Revelation relentlessly attacks the ruling powers, whose corruption stands in sharp contrast to God's ideal kingdom. By urging people to reject the corrupt present and set their sights instead on the ideal to come, early Christianity inspired masses of followers in the midst of crisis and persecution. This feature of early Christianity, argues Engels, resembles the process by which modern socialism achieves explosive growth. Despite being persecuted, socialists – like the early Christians – are thriving and positioning themselves to take over society.[94]

He echoes this point in his introduction to Marx's *Class Struggles in France*, one of Engels's last writings before his death in 1895. The text concludes by discussing Christianity's ability to flourish in the midst of crisis, while suggesting that the socialist movement has this same strength. The passage captures Engels's fascination with the power of apocalyptic hope:

> It is now, almost to the year, sixteen centuries since a dangerous party of overthrow was likewise active in the Roman empire. It undermined religion and all the foundations of the state; it flatly denied that Caesar's will was the supreme law; it was without a fatherland, was international; it spread over the whole empire, from Gaul to Asia, and beyond the frontiers of the empire. It had long carried on seditious activities underground in secret; for a considerable time, however, it had felt itself strong enough to come out into the open. This party of overthrow, which was known by the name of Christians, was also strongly represented in the army .... The Emperor Diocletian ... stepped in with vigour, while there was still time. He promulgated an anti-Socialist – I beg your pardon, I meant to say anti-Christian – law. The meetings of the overthrowers were forbidden, their meeting halls were closed or even pulled down, the Christian emblems, crosses, etc., were, like the red handkerchiefs in Saxony, prohibited. Christians were declared ineligible for holding public office; they were not to be allowed to become even corporals .... Christians were forbidden out of hand to seek justice before a court. Even this exceptional law was to no avail. The Christians tore it down from the walls with scorn; they are even supposed to have set fire to the Emperor's palace in Nicomedia in his presence. Then the latter revenged himself by the great persecution of Christians in the year 303 A.D. It was the last of its kind. And it was so effective that seventeen years later the army consisted overwhelmingly of Christians, and the succeeding autocrat of the whole Roman empire, Constantine, called the Great by the priests, proclaimed Christianity the state religion.[95]

---

[94] Engels, "On the History of Early Christianity," 447.
[95] Engels, "Introduction to Karl Marx's *The Class Struggles in France, 1848 to 1850*," 523–24.

Engels highlights how socialism mirrors early Christianity. Despite constant attacks from the ruling powers, Christianity's apocalyptic message found a way to triumph. Socialism will also triumph, but its victory will be far more complete and lasting. For Engels, the key difference between these movements is that modern socialism, unlike early Christianity, is correct in its prescriptions and vision for social change. Whereas early Christianity ultimately failed, modern socialism will succeed in realizing its ideal.

If we are going to take seriously Marx and Engels's thought and not read into their writings Christian influences that are never mentioned, as Boer rightly suggests, we also have to take seriously their texts that *do* directly engage with Christian thought. Though Engels understands Christian apocalyptic beliefs as myths that generate false predictions, he also goes out of his way to draw parallels between such beliefs and socialism. It is not an offhand observation he makes once and quickly abandons. Rather, he repeatedly returns to this idea, from his account of Müntzer in 1850 to his writings on early Christianity in the 1890s just before his death. Clearly, Engels finds in Christian apocalyptic thought insights relevant to modern socialism.

Despite its errors, apocalyptic thought contains a kernel of truth from Engels's perspective: it identifies crisis as the vehicle through which the oppressed and powerless will finally triumph. This idea from early Christianity inspires many, but ultimately fails because Christianity sets its focus on heaven above rather than on earth below. In contrast, Engels finds in Marxism a scientific explanation for how crisis will liberate the oppressed classes. Marxism fully embodies a truth that only appears in incomplete and mistaken form in early Christianity.

So Christian apocalyptic thought does not serve as a hidden source of inspiration for Marxist thought – a position that Boer rightly rejects. A more accurate interpretation is that apocalyptic Christianity's understanding of social change shares features with Marxism. Engels appreciates these similarities without subordinating his philosophy to Christian thought.

Some may see Engels's interest in the Christian apocalyptic tradition as having little importance to his overall thought and Marxism generally – it represents little more than an idiosyncratic curiosity. But it is a mistake to dismiss Engels's engagement with apocalyptic thought too quickly, for it offers insights into Marxism. A vision for social change with parallels to apocalyptic thought offers a strategy for reconciling competing goals within Marxism – outlining a political theory that is both utopian and feasible. Marxism purports to present a vision of the ideal society that is actually achievable. Marxism, like Christian apocalyptic thought, solves the problem of the vast gap between the corrupt present and ideal future by identifying crisis as the vehicle for radically transforming society and bringing the ideal within reach.

Ultimately, hope in the power of crisis, like that found in apocalyptic thought, is an inescapable element of Marxism. Engels seems to recognize this point, noting the seeds of Marxism's truth and power in inchoate form in early Christianity. Engels sees within apocalyptic thought the power to inspire dramatic political action in pursuit of an ideal, even when it seems hopelessly far away. Perhaps for this reason, he continually returns to Christian apocalyptic thought as a source of insight for understanding the socialist movement of his day. When encountering such thought, he refuses to entirely reject it or temper its utopian aspirations. Instead, he transforms apocalyptic thought – most obvious in how he reinterprets Müntzer's understanding of the kingdom of God – and puts its ideas in the service of earthly rather than heavenly aims.

PART III
IMPLICATIONS FOR IDEAL THEORY

6

Ideal Theory as Faith

Chapter 2 suggested that we can understand apocalyptic thought as a form of ideal theory, since it identifies an ideal and theorizes a path to it. Apocalyptic thought and ideal theory, it turns out, share more in common than is often assumed. This chapter builds on that idea. In doing so, it doesn't cast aside earlier methodological recommendations and suggest, without explicit evidence, that apocalyptic thought exercises insidious influence over ideal theory today. But the chapter does explore parallels between ideal theory and apocalyptic thought, with a focus on what grounds people have for believing them.

The most influential understanding of ideal theory comes from John Rawls, who explains it as offering principles of justice that members of a liberal democratic society have reason to accept. Ideal theory, according to this view, has navigational value: it outlines a shared goal – what Rawls calls a "realistic utopia"[1] – for those in society to strive toward. Apocalyptic and other religious beliefs, on the other hand, are not based on reasons all can be expected to accept. Individuals can hold such beliefs on faith, but unlike ideal theory, it would be unreasonable to demand the rest of society to adopt and pursue their goals. For Rawls, then, there is a neat distinction between ideal theory and religious belief: the former is based on plausible reasons that others should accept, whereas the latter is unsuitable to guide society as a whole.[2]

This distinction proves too neat. The grounds for ideal theory turn out to be shakier than ideal theorists tend to admit. Indeed, in recent years, there have been growing concerns over ideal theory. What has resulted is intense debate over the topic in political philosophy, which at times has grown insular and

---

[1] John Rawls, *The Law of Peoples* (Cambridge, MA: Harvard University Press, 1999), 12. See also Rawls, *Justice as Fairness: A Restatement*, ed. Erin Kelly (Cambridge, MA: Harvard University Press, 2001), 13.

[2] Rawls, *Justice as Fairness*, 26–29.

arcane, as understandings of ideal theory have multiplied.[3] This chapter suggests that a less insular approach, in dialogue with social science and other research, stands the best chance of advancing the current debate over ideal theory and its limitations.[4]

Specifically, my argument builds off criticisms of ideal theory by Gerald Gaus,[5] and draws on social science research to put them on firmer ground. To plausibly defend an ideal theory, it is necessary to show that its principles would have normative force in the future society it envisions. But research on human prediction undermines the claim that we can plausibly know societal conditions in the distant future and what principles of justice would look like under those conditions. The immense complexity of social phenomena and the occurrence of Black Swans – rare, difficult-to-predict events with transformative effects[6] – severely constrain human predictive capacities. Evidence for this point comes from forecasting studies, which suggest no reason for confidence in predictions about society for the distant future.[7] Since defenses of ideal theory *depend* on such predictions, they necessarily fail. Similar to religious and apocalyptic belief, ideal theory lacks plausible grounds and ultimately rests on faith. So contrary to Rawls's view, people do not have compelling reason to accept any proposed account of ideal theory.

Though Rawls's approach runs into insurmountable problems, it is important to appreciate its normative appeal. Too often, critics fail to grasp the moral instincts that motivate ideal theory. When ideal theory aims to identify the

---

[3] See, e.g., Alan Hamlin and Zofia Stemplowska, "Theory, Ideal Theory and the Theory of Ideals," *Political Studies Review* 10, no. 1 (2012): 48–62; Zofia Stemplowska and Adam Swift, "Ideal and Nonideal Theory," in *The Oxford Handbook of Political Philosophy*, ed. David Estlund (New York: Oxford University Press, 2012), 373–88; Laura Valentini, "Ideal vs. Non-ideal Theory: A Conceptual Map," *Philosophy Compass* 7, no. 9 (2012): 654–64; and Kwame Appiah, *As If: Idealization and Ideals* (Cambridge, MA: Harvard University Press, 2017), 112–72.

[4] A similar recommendation comes from Lisa Herzog, "Ideal and Non-ideal Theory and the Problem of Knowledge," *Journal of Applied Philosophy* 29, no. 4 (2012): 271–88. The goal here is to put this recommendation into practice by examining findings from empirical research, specifically on prediction, to better understand limits to ideal theorizing. This analysis leads to a conclusion far more skeptical than Herzog's on ideal theory's potential to guide collective action.

[5] Gerald Gaus, *The Tyranny of the Ideal: Justice in a Diverse Society* (Princeton, NJ: Princeton University Press, 2016). See also David Wiens, "Against Ideal Guidance," *Journal of Politics* 77, no. 2 (2015): 433–46; and "Political Ideals and the Feasibility Frontier," *Economics and Philosophy* 31, no. 3 (2015): 447–77.

[6] Nassim Taleb, *The Black Swan: The Impact of the Highly Improbable* (New York: Random House, 2010).

[7] Philip Tetlock, *Expert Political Judgment: How Good Is It? How Can We Know?* (Princeton, NJ: Princeton University Press, 2005); and Philip Tetlock and Dan Gardner, *Superforecasting: The Art and Science of Prediction* (New York: Crown Publishers, 2015).

most just society possible, it seeks information relevant for guiding action in a complex world where the path to greater justice is far from straightforward. Knowing the ideal helps avoid paths that, though appealing in isolation, lead away from the ideal. Without a plausible ideal to guide action, political philosophy is left with deep uncertainty over how best to advance justice long term. One never knows if certain actions move society closer to or further from its most just form possible. Even efforts that advance justice *now* risk taking society down paths that close off greater justice *later*.

Regrettably, ideal theory finds itself unable to escape this dilemma. There is perhaps, though, still a role for it in advancing justice. One function of ideal theory is to offer hope in the possibility of a just society.[8] Both ideal theory and apocalyptic thought offer *utopian hope*, which gives meaning to imperfect, partial efforts to advance justice by understanding them as steps toward the ideal within the long arc of history. Utopian hope goes beyond desiring and believing in the possibility of justice in the short term, which even if realized can often be fleeting in the face of new political developments that threaten to overturn progress. Utopian hope sets its sights on a far loftier goal: a future that *ultimately* proves hospitable to justice and the ideal society. Ideal theory offers such hope to sustain people when the immediate prospects of justice seem bleak.

Utopian hope offers psychological benefits and, understandably, some embrace it. For those who do so by turning to either religion or ideal theory, it is important to be honest that such beliefs rely on faith. The chapter closes with a look at Rawls's writings to show that, though its role is often downplayed, faith has been an inextricable part of contemporary ideal theory from the start. Once we recognize that point, it becomes clear that political philosophy must rethink ideal theory's role in advancing justice.

IDEAL THEORY'S NORMATIVE APPEAL

Before getting into ideal theory's limitations, let's first look at what draws people to it. Ideal theory takes different meanings, and here the focus is on

---

[8] Rawls, *The Law of Peoples*, 128; *Justice as Fairness*, 37–38; and *Political Liberalism*, exp. ed. (New York: Columbia University Press, 2005), lx. See also Paul Weithman, *Why Political Liberalism? On John Rawls's Political Turn* (New York: Oxford University Press, 2010), 367–69; Benjamin McKean, "Ideal Theory after Auschwitz? The Practical Uses and Ideological Abuses of Political Theory as Reconciliation," *Journal of Politics* 79, no. 4 (2017): 1177–90; and Dana Howard, "The Scoundrel and the Visionary: On Reasonable Hope and the Possibility of a Just Future," *Journal of Political Philosophy* 27, no. 3 (2019): 294–317.

what I call *navigational ideal theory*.⁹ This conception of ideal theory seeks to outline the best and most just society with the potential of being realized at some future point.¹⁰ I focus on this conception because, among competing understandings of ideal theory, it is the best candidate to serve as a normative guide to action.

To explain navigational ideal theory's normative appeal, it helps to contrast it with a conception less suited to serve as a moral guide. Sometimes ideal theory refers to *idealization*, meaning that it assumes ideal conditions that are rare or impossible in order to isolate and explain a concept. This manner of theorizing is common in science. Isaac Newton explains gravity by introducing an ideal pendulum, which experiences no friction or air resistance. This pendulum does not represent the perfect pendulum engineers should aim to build. Rather, the term ideal conveys that the pendulum functions under simplified conditions, which put the focus on gravitational force.¹¹ A similar rationale motivates thought experiments in philosophy that assume ideal conditions to better understand our intuitions about a normative concept. For instance, though others do not always contribute their fair share, imagining that they do illuminates basic intuitions about what fairness demands.

Ideal theorists sometimes construct idealizations with bolder normative ambitions: to present an end goal, ideal justice, to strive for. This approach specifies a goal under conditions that rarely if ever hold in reality. Constraints in the real world, but absent from an idealization, can make the ideal impossible. Ideal theory thus can send people chasing after utopia in one sense of the word – "nowhere," an ideal that doesn't exist now and is impossible to ever realize. Ideal theory that sets forth an impossible ideal raises concerns because it risks having perverse normative effects when the ideal looks much different from the best possible option.

To illustrate, imagine a perfect society. Many envision a place free from injustice where everyone always acts justly. But suppose weakness of will and other shortcomings prevent this ideal from ever being realized regardless of what society does – there always will be some who act unjustly. The perfect society imagined is what some call a "hopeless" ideal, meaning that the ideal

---

⁹ Some use the term "realistic utopianism," which comes from Rawls, to communicate a similar idea. See Ben Laurence, "Constructivism, Strict Compliance, and Realistic Utopianism," *Philosophy and Phenomenological Research* 97, no. 2 (2018): 433–53.

¹⁰ This understanding of ideal theory focuses on what is possible indefinitely into the future, not just now, so as to determine an ultimate goal. For a defense of this assumption, see the Appendix and specifically the response to Objection 1.

¹¹ Jenann Ismael, "A Philosopher of Science Looks at Idealization in Political Theory," *Social Philosophy and Policy* 33, nos. 1–2 (2016): 11–31.

requires action that each individual has the ability to do, yet collectively there is virtually no chance that everyone will do their part to realize the ideal.[12] If a society characterized by perfect compliance is indeed a hopeless ideal, it likely would be unwise to pursue it. Though some measures to increase compliance advance justice, beyond a certain point they backfire – like draconian surveillance to combat noncompliance. Indeed, such surveillance often backfires and leads to racially disparate outcomes.[13] We thus should be cautious of pursuing hopeless and unattainable ideals since they can lead away from the best possible option.[14]

There are legitimate concerns, then, regarding ideal theory's normative value. Yet this common criticism – ideal theory fails as a normative guide because it embraces unattainable ideals – is not a flaw inherent to it. Navigational ideal theory avoids this pitfall by focusing on what is collectively feasible and identifying the most just society possible. In this way, it steers clear of unattainable ideals that would undermine its normative value.

But this approach still has its critics.[15] It is helpful to differentiate common objections against navigational ideal theory so as to be clear why it might fail as a normative guide:

(a) There is no such thing as the most just society possible.[16]
(b) Ideal theory seeks information – what is the most just society possible – irrelevant to advancing justice.[17]
(c) Ideal theory cannot identify the most just society possible.[18]

According to (a) and (b), ideal theorists ask the wrong question – what is the most just society possible? – when formulating a theory of justice. That

---

[12] David Estlund, "Utopophobia," *Philosophy and Public Affairs* 42, no. 2 (2014): 117–18.
[13] See James Forman Jr., *Locking Up Our Own: Crime and Punishment in Black America* (New York: Farrar, Straus and Giroux, 2017), 185–215.
[14] This concern applies to Rawls's ideal theory, which assumes strict compliance – that is, everyone upholds the principles of justice. See Rawls, *A Theory of Justice*, rev. ed. (Cambridge, MA: Harvard University Press, 1999), 8. This idealization seems incompatible with his intention of offering a *feasible* goal, and thus may result in a theory that directs people toward an unattainable ideal when the best feasible option looks much different. See Colin Farrelly, "Justice in Ideal Theory: A Refutation," *Political Studies* 55, no. 4 (2007): 844–64; and Laurence, "Constructivism, Strict Compliance, and Realistic Utopianism."
[15] See, e.g., Amartya Sen, "What Do We Want from a Theory of Justice?" *Journal of Philosophy* 103, no. 5 (2006): 215–38; Amartya Sen, *The Idea of Justice* (Cambridge, MA: Harvard University Press, 2009); David Schmidtz, "Nonideal Theory: What It Is and What It Needs to Be," *Ethics* 121, no. 4 (2011): 772–96; and Jacob Levy, "There's No Such Thing as Ideal Theory," *Social Philosophy and Policy* 33, nos. 1–2 (2016): 312–33.
[16] See, e.g., Schmidtz, "Nonideal Theory," 774.
[17] See, e.g., Sen, "What Do We Want from a Theory of Justice?" 221–22.
[18] See, e.g., Gaus, *The Tyranny of the Ideal*, 139–44.

question is the wrong place to start because there is no such thing as the ideal society and, even if there were, knowledge of it would prove useless for advancing justice. In contrast, (c) avoids the strong claim that ideal theory is fundamentally misguided, and instead argues that ideal theory cannot answer the question it poses, no matter how valuable the answer would be. We'll examine (c) later in the chapter, but the remainder of this section focuses on the more fundamental critiques of ideal theory, (a) and (b).

Some find (a) compelling, uneasy with the idea that justice takes one perfect, platonic form. These critics believe the focus should be on eliminating injustice rather than climbing toward some illusory peak form of justice. As Amartya Sen puts it, we care about preventing famine, less so about whether a 45 or 46 percent tax rate for top earners best represents justice.[19]

Without question, ending grave injustice deserves priority. But that view is compatible with ideal theory. Ending the world's many injustices is no small feat, and constitutes its own lofty ideal that can serve as an end goal in efforts to advance justice. The interconnected nature of society demands that we look for an optimal approach, since ending one injustice can exacerbate others. As an example, consider Abraham Lincoln who secretly promised government jobs and other perks to Democrats to ensure passage of the Thirteenth Amendment abolishing slavery.[20] The injustice of slavery likely justified such bribery, but most would be uncomfortable with its continuing indefinitely. Ideal theory keeps in view the many aspects of justice worth striving for. Rather than necessarily condemning all compromises, it reminds us to consider how compromises impact efforts to advance toward an ideal goal.

So ideal theory emphasizes that advancing justice demands more than tackling one injustice at a time: it requires a holistic view focused on what social arrangements best eliminate various injustices. For the pursuit of that goal, there is reason to hang on to the climbing metaphor common to ideal theory. Societies are not simply just or unjust, but exhibit degrees of injustice. Efforts against injustice often are intergenerational and build off past successes with an ideal in mind, which is why the metaphor of climbing toward a peak is apt.

Sen is perhaps right that fine distinctions about perfect justice are not critical. Society could take various forms, whose comparative levels of justice vary slightly, but which all eliminate significant injustices. We want to reach

---

[19] Sen, "What Do We Want from a Theory of Justice?" 223.
[20] See James McPherson, *Battle Cry of Freedom: The Civil War Era* (New York: Oxford University Press, 1988), 839; and John Parrish, "Benevolent Skullduggery," in *Corruption and American Politics*, ed. Michael Genovese and Victoria Farrar-Myers (Amherst, NY: Cambria Press, 2010), 78–79.

one of those ideals and care less about reaching the absolute best one. That point implies revising, not abandoning, ideal theory. In efforts to advance justice, what is important is not necessarily ending up atop Everest, so to speak, but aiming for an eight-thousander – one of those rare peaks over 8,000 meters – free from the injustices of lesser peaks and valleys. This view opens the door to a pluralist approach to ideal theory, where there is a set of most just options and any one is worth striving for. That revision still leaves the core normative function of ideal theory in place: offering a lofty goal to guide action, while recognizing that many injustices must be overcome on the way to it.

Instead of denying existence of the ideal, (b) doubts that knowing it helps advance justice. Sen takes this view: "[T]he existence of an identifiably inviolate, or best, alternative does not indicate that it is necessary (or indeed useful) to refer to it in judging the relative merits of two other alternatives."[21] Here he overstates his case by suggesting that ideal theory would be irrelevant to guiding action *even if it gained the information it seeks*. Imagine that ideal theorists succeeded in compiling a volume that accurately details the most just society (or societies) possible. Contrary to Sen, there is reason to believe that such a work would offer insights into how best to advance justice.

The uneven and path-dependent nature of social change helps explain why. If the path to advancing justice were always smooth and gradually ascending – like a hike up Mount Fuji, as Gaus puts it[22] – knowing the ideal would be unnecessary. The option that leads to *greater justice* also would lead toward the *most just* possibility. But the path to advancing justice sometimes is more rugged with peaks and valleys: the option promising greater justice now leads to a local peak but away from the most just possibility. Knowledge of the ideal helps identify and avoid paths that, though appealing in isolation, lead away from and can preclude the ultimate goal.[23]

This strategy of bypassing opportunities to advance justice in the short term to do so in the long term does not mean that ideal theory *always* permits an action as long as it takes society closer to the ideal. Some ideal theories categorically prohibit certain actions – say restrictions of basic liberties – even if they represent the only path to an ideal. In this case, the ideal is morally infeasible. We could achieve it, but not through morally permissible actions. This complication does not undermine the normative value of an ideal goal. It rather adds another layer of feasibility to consider – moral feasibility – when determining the most just society to strive for.

---

[21] Sen, "What Do We Want from a Theory of Justice?" 222.
[22] Gaus, *The Tyranny of the Ideal*, 62.
[23] Rawls, *The Law of Peoples*, 89–90; A. John Simmons, "Ideal and Nonideal Theory," *Philosophy and Public Affairs* 38, 1 (2010): 5–36; and Gaus, *The Tyranny of the Ideal*, 61–67.

In many contexts, we readily recognize the value of a long-term goal like ideal theory provides. A medical student who wants to serve the poor as a doctor forgoes volunteering full-time at a homeless shelter, even though doing so would lead to greater justice now. Full-time volunteer work would force the student to abandon their studies and goal of advancing justice as a doctor. Leaders of social movements often make similar judgments. Rather than pursue *every* opportunity to advance justice, they strategically dedicate energy and resources to court cases, legislative campaigns, and protests best suited to advance their long-term goal.[24] Likewise, ideal theory offers an objective to orient action away from paths that diverge from our ultimate goal.

Despite these points in ideal theory's favor, perhaps the ideal is too far off to offer meaningful guidance. Admittedly, ideal theory cannot provide complete guidance on how to act by specifying an ideal – knowing a goal is distinct from knowing how to achieve it. Nevertheless, knowledge of a goal is often informative in evaluating paths to it. If a core principle of the ideal society were a ban on nuclear technology, that would tell us that the goal of banning nuclear weapons and power is not a fool's errand but worth pursuing. Though ideal theory cannot provide complete guidance, it offers information that merits consideration and has potential value in advancing justice.

In sum, valid moral instincts lie behind wanting to identify the most just society possible. Navigational ideal theory seeks information relevant to guiding action in a complex world where the path to greater justice is far from clear. The critical question, which we consider next, is whether ideal theory can attain this information.

WHAT A PLAUSIBLE DEFENSE OF IDEAL THEORY REQUIRES

This section identifies a necessary condition for a plausible defense of navigational ideal theory as part of an argument for why, unfortunately, such a defense fails. The argument builds on criticisms of ideal theory by Gaus in his book *Tyranny of the Ideal*. There he raises doubts that we have the information necessary to determine the most just society possible. Since the ideal likely lies far in the future, describing it requires predictions about far-off worlds. Gaus assumes we are less accurate in judgments about justice for the distant future than the present.[25] Though a reasonable claim, not all political

---

[24] See, e.g., David Garrow, *Bearing the Cross: Martin Luther King, Jr., and the Southern Christian Leadership Conference* (New York: HarperCollins Publishers, 2004).
[25] Gaus, *The Tyranny of the Ideal*, 78.

philosophers share it.[26] Some have more confidence in their predictions and descriptions of distant ideal worlds, which Gaus dismisses as "sheer delusion."[27]

The disagreement between Gaus and ideal theorists reflects a long-standing split among political philosophers: some are deeply suspicious of ideal and utopian theorizing, while others embrace it. Social science research on prediction can help overcome this impasse by shedding light on the uncertainty inherent in ideal theorizing. Given the sharp divide over ideal theory, there is value in detailing this evidence.

Let's start with premise (1) of my argument drawing on this evidence:

(1) Defenses of navigational ideal theory are plausible only if they show that the theory's principles would have normative force in the society it envisions.

This premise identifies a necessary condition to plausibly defend navigational ideal theory. It is modest in that it does not require a defense to show that an ideal theory's principles would have *more* normative appeal than all other proposals, leaving open the possibility discussed earlier that the ideal society could take various forms. The basic intuition of premise (1) is that, since ideal theory outlines principles for a *future* society, these principles cannot just have normative force now. They must have normative force in the ideal society. We do not want to embrace an ideal theory, pursue its ideal, arrive at it, and then discover its principles of justice are ill-suited for the society we find ourselves in.

Another way of expressing this point is that ideal theory must consider the social realizations of its principles. Ideal theory involves not just theorizing about principles of justice, but also thinking through what those principles would look like in society when implemented.[28] Many ideal theorists are sensitive to this point, even if they do not explicitly say so. Ideal theories usually include background social conditions – that is, they specify the context in which ideal principles of justice would be implemented. Knowing that context helps in imagining what an ideal theory's principles would look like when realized and whether they would have normative appeal in that form.

Rawls's theory of justice, for example, includes background social conditions. Its principles are adopted under "favorable circumstances,"[29] where

---

[26] Gaus, *The Tyranny of the Ideal*, 102.
[27] Gaus, *The Tyranny of the Ideal*, 106.
[28] Sen, *The Idea of Justice*, 18–22; and Gaus, *The Tyranny of the Ideal*, 23.
[29] Rawls, *A Theory of Justice*, 216.

there is moderate scarcity but conditions are not so harsh as to preclude cooperation or democratic institutions.[30] Rawls also takes pluralism as a given in the ideal society, assuming that individuals hold different religious and philosophical views.[31]

Such background conditions play a key role in Rawls's method of defending ideal theory. In his view, simply reflecting on a theory's principles in the abstract is insufficient for evaluating them. He instead recommends evaluating ideal principles against our judgments at all levels of generality – from abstract conceptions of justice to its demands in concrete situations – in search of a reflective equilibrium, where the principles and all our judgments align. This method does not privilege judgments at one level of generality over others.[32] It thus ensures a place for normative judgments on how an ideal theory's principles would fare in potential circumstances where they would be realized. By adopting this method for evaluating ideal theory, Rawls shows an appreciation for the concerns of premise (1).[33]

Other approaches are less congenial to premise (1). G. A. Cohen, for instance, criticizes Rawls for outlining a theory too closely tied to particular social conditions and recommends instead identifying more general principles of justice.[34] According to this view, a theory of justice need not provide background social conditions. But even for that approach, background social conditions remain relevant. Evaluating principles of justice in isolation, detached from their application in social settings, severely limits our ability to form and be confident in our normative judgments. We develop and refine such judgments by considering the application of principles in concrete contexts – a point Cohen himself recognizes.[35] If ideal theory fails to give background social conditions, evaluating it still involves bringing to mind likely conditions in the ideal society so as to determine what the theory's principles would look like in practice.

A more direct challenge to premise (1) comes from the idea that some principles of justice are so self-evident that no social realization of them – no matter how disastrous – could give us reason to rethink them. Like Sen and Gaus, I find this claim implausible.[36] To deny that *any* social realization could

---

[30] Rawls, A Theory of Justice, 110; and Justice as Fairness, 47.
[31] Rawls, Justice as Fairness, 84.
[32] Rawls, A Theory of Justice, 17–18; and Justice as Fairness, 29–32.
[33] See Gaus, The Tyranny of the Ideal, 21–22. Concern about the social realizations of principles of justice also comes up, at least in passing, in Robert Nozick's account of ideal theory. He leaves open whether we should reject principles of justice that cause "catastrophic moral horror." See Nozick, Anarchy, State, and Utopia (New York: Basic Books, 1974), 30.
[34] G. A. Cohen, "Facts and Principles," Philosophy and Public Affairs 31, no. 3 (2003): 241–42.
[35] Cohen, "Facts and Principles," 227.
[36] Sen, The Idea of Justice, 21; and Gaus, The Tyranny of the Ideal, 26–29.

challenge an ideal theory before even considering it betrays a lack of epistemic humility. It is impossible to know the full implications of principles we propose, so it is important to remain open to encountering considerations that could prompt us to revise them.[37] When moral reasoning closes that possibility and holds on to principles despite their troubling and absurd implications, it becomes rigid dogmatism – like Immanuel Kant's doubling down on the claim that it's wrong to lie to a murderer at the door looking for a friend.[38] Ideal theorists can claim that their principles of justice are true even if they cause the world to perish.[39] But they will encounter stiff resistance – and for good reason.

PREDICTION AND IDEAL THEORY

So considering the social realizations of an ideal theory's principles is key to evaluating and defending them. Now to the next step of the argument:

(2) Showing that navigational ideal theory's principles would have normative force in the society it envisions requires reliably accurate predictions about science, technology, economics, and politics for the distant future.

Given today's pervasive and entrenched injustices, few expect the ideal society to appear any time soon. Ending society's most significant injustices requires collective efforts that span generations. Since advancing justice is a long-term project, the potential arrival of the ideal society lies in the distant future. The ideal theorist interested in defending their theory must make predictions about society far into the future to show what their theory's principles would look like and that they would have normative force under those conditions.

Premise (2) perhaps seems misguided since ideal theory's purpose is to *prescribe* a goal, not *predict* whether it will be reached. That is right, but prescribing a feasible goal – navigational ideal theory's focus – requires prediction. Specifically, the ideal theorist must predict what is possible in the future, and from that feasible set identify the most just option.[40]

---

[37] See Elizabeth Anderson, "Moral Bias and Corrective Practices: A Pragmatist Perspective," *Proceedings and Addresses of the American Philosophical Association* 89 (2015): 21–47.
[38] Immanuel Kant, "On the Supposed Right to Lie from Philanthropy," in *Practical Philosophy*, trans. and ed. Mary Gregor (New York: Cambridge University Press, 1996), 605–15.
[39] This phrase is altered from a line, not surprisingly, in Kant's writings. See Kant, "Toward Perpetual Peace," in *Practical Philosophy*, trans. and ed. Mary Gregor (New York: Cambridge University Press, 1996), 8:378.
[40] There is much debate over how to define possible or feasible. See Juha Räikkä, "The Feasibility Condition in Political Theory," *Journal of Political Philosophy* 6, no. 1 (1998):

It is not enough, then, for the ideal theorist to predict what their proposed principles of justice would look like if implemented now. Before the ideal has any hope of arriving, much in society could change that would provide legitimate grounds for reconsidering our principles of justice.[41] Most obviously, society could cease to reflect background economic and political conditions assumed by ideal theory and render the theory's principles obsolete. If Rawls's assumption of moderate scarcity no longer held and new technology brought an overabundance of widely distributed resources, previous debates over distributive justice could look quaint, while other issues moved to the fore. Accurate predictions about future economic and political conditions are necessary to avoid a theory that becomes dated and vulnerable to challenges.

Defending ideal theory also calls for accurate predictions about science and technology. Though we use existing normative principles to evaluate innovations, the interaction between the two proves more complex. Technological and scientific discoveries can raise valid reasons to rethink

27–40; Geoffrey Brennan and Philip Pettit, "The Feasibility Issue," in *The Oxford Handbook of Contemporary Philosophy*, ed. Frank Jackson and Michael Smith (New York: Oxford University Press, 2007), 258–80; Mark Jensen, "The Limits of Practical Possibility," *Journal of Political Philosophy* 17, no. 2 (2009): 168–84; David Estlund, "Human Nature and the Limits (if any) of Political Philosophy," *Philosophy and Public Affairs* 39, no. 3 (2011): 207–37; Pablo Gilabert and Holly Lawford-Smith, "Political Feasibility: A Conceptual Exploration," *Political Studies* 60, no. 4 (2012): 809–25; Anca Gheaus, "The Feasibility Constraint on the Concept of Justice," *Philosophical Quarterly* 63, no. 252 (2013): 445–64; Holly Lawford-Smith, "Understanding Political Feasibility," *Journal of Political Philosophy* 21, no. 3 (2013): 243–59; David Wiens, "'Going Evaluative' to Save Justice from Feasibility—a Pyrrhic Victory," *Philosophical Quarterly* 64, no. 255 (2014): 301–7; David Wiens, "Motivational Limitations on the Demands of Justice," *European Journal of Political Theory* 15, no. 3 (2016): 333–52; Nicholas Southwood, "Does 'Ought' Imply 'Feasible'?" *Philosophy and Public Affairs* 44, no. 1 (2016): 7–45; Zofia Stemplowska, "Feasibility: Individual and Collective," *Social Philosophy and Policy* 33, nos. 1–2 (2016): 273–91; Emily McTernan, "Justice, Feasibility, and Social Science as It Is," *Ethical Theory and Moral Practice* 22, no. 1 (2019): 27–40; and David Estlund, *Utopophobia: On the Limits (if any) of Political Philosophy* (Princeton, NJ: Princeton University Press, 2020). For many issues – from the minimal probability level needed to deem an outcome realistically possible to whether psychological factors like weakness of will represent unchangeable feasibility constraints – there is no consensus and I take no position on them here. Doing so is unnecessary for my argument. What stands out in current debates is how much about future feasibility is unknown. Clearly, future scientific, technological, economic, and political developments will alter what is feasible. The ideal theorist is in no position to make reliably accurate predictions regarding those developments and thus what will be feasible in the future. That limitation poses an insurmountable obstacle for making a plausible defense of navigational ideal theory, as I explain later.

[41] Shmuel Nili raises this point and its complications. See Nili, "The Moving Global Everest: A New Challenge to Global Ideal Theory as a Necessary Compass," *European Journal of Political Theory* 17, no. 1 (2018): 87–108.

moral judgments.[42] If the ideal theorist fails to account for that, they risk specifying principles that appear just today but would be incomplete and mistaken in the ideal society.

Past innovations illustrate this point by expanding the realm of what's possible and giving rise to new rights and liberties. Consider developments in medicine. Previously, society had few options for healing the sick and injured, and thus a right to healthcare made little sense. Now in a world with effective methods for treating many injuries and diseases, access to such care has come to be seen as a right. People disagree on how extensive this right is, but most accept that wealthy societies have *some* obligation to treat the critically injured, regardless of whether they can pay for care. Likewise, the invention of the printing press contributed to the emergence of a freedom now widely recognized – freedom of the press. Today the Internet is having transformative effects, as it becomes more essential for communication, learning, and political engagement. Some believe access to it should be a basic right.[43] Future innovations will further shape conceptions of justice. The ideal theorist who enumerates basic rights and liberties for the ideal society without considering future innovations risks giving an incomplete list that neglects concerns at the center of tomorrow's debates about justice.

Beyond expanding conceptions of justice, scientific and technological discoveries sometimes unsettle them. Consider advances in our understanding of nonhuman animals. Research has overturned the view, most famously defended by René Descartes, that animals are machines lacking a variety of capacities believed to be distinct to humans.[44] Studies show animals to be creatures far more complex than previously believed, which experience pain and emotion, use language and tools, engage in problem solving, cooperate, and aid others. Such discoveries prompt us to rethink animals' place in the moral universe and suggest that they deserve stronger consideration in theories of justice than they traditionally receive.[45]

---

[42] See Hans Jonas, "Technology and Responsibility: Reflections on the New Tasks of Ethics," *Social Research* 40, no. 1 (1973): 31–54; and Marianne Boenink, Tsjalling Swierstra, and Dirk Stemerding, "Anticipating the Interaction between Technology and Morality: A Scenario Study of Experimenting with Humans in Biotechnology," *Studies in Ethics, Law, and Technology* 4, no. 2 (2010): Article 4, https://doi.org/10.2202/1941-6008.1098.

[43] Merten Reglitz, "The Human Right to Free Internet Access," *Journal of Applied Philosophy* 37, no. 2 (2020): 314–31.

[44] René Descartes, *Discourse on Method*, 3rd ed., trans. Donald Cress (Indianapolis: Hackett Publishing Company, 1998), 55–59 (page numbers refer to Adam and Tannery edition of Descartes's works).

[45] See Lori Gruen, *Ethics and Animals: An Introduction* (New York: Cambridge University Press, 2011).

In response to these examples, some may still resist premise (2). Rather than show the need for long-term prediction in ideal theory, perhaps these examples show the importance of specifying principles of justice that remain valid across contexts. For instance, instead of making a sharp distinction between humans and animals, a normative theory is better off identifying capacities that merit moral consideration, without predicting in advance what life forms possess them. Ideal theorists, in other words, need more theory.

In a sense that is right. Innovations and discoveries highlight blind spots in normative theories, and it would be best to formulate them free from errors to begin with. The problem, though, is that we often recognize errors in our theories only *after* confronting concrete counterexamples. Beforehand, it is difficult to know the specific refinements and qualifications that principles of justice require. For that reason, the ideal theorist cannot afford to neglect major technological and scientific advancements in a future hospitable to the ideal society, which may be radically different from our own. Given how often new discoveries influence conceptions of justice, we have little reason to assume that proposed principles of ideal justice that look appealing today are suited for future worlds. We also need an accurate account of what those worlds could look like.

WHY DEFENSES OF IDEAL THEORY (REGRETTABLY) FAIL

To review, the ideal theorist wanting to plausibly defend their theory must explain what their proposed principles of justice would look like when implemented in the ideal society, which is unlikely to arrive soon. That forces the ideal theorist to make predictions for the distant future about science, technology, economics, and politics, since these factors impact what form ideal principles would take when realized. Unfortunately for the ideal theorist, they cannot accurately make these predictions with any consistency, which is my next claim:

(3) We cannot make reliably accurate predictions about science, technology, economics, and politics for the distant future.[46]

---

[46] Karl Popper raises a similar concern. See Popper, *The Open Universe: An Argument for Indeterminism*, ed. W. W. Bartley, III (New York: Routledge, 1992), 68–77; and *The Poverty of Historicism* (New York: Routledge, 2002), xi–xiii. I share Popper's skepticism, but premise (3) does not rely on his claim that it is *logically* impossible to make such predictions, which may be too strong. See E. Lagerspetz, "Predictability and the Growth of Knowledge," *Synthese* 141, no. 3 (2004): 445–59.

Those who study prediction overwhelmingly agree on this point. Social science research offers nothing to suggest that we come close to having the predictive capacities necessary to formulate a defensible account of navigational ideal theory.

Philip Tetlock, a leading researcher on prediction, conducts forecasting tournaments to measure how well individuals – including professors, journalists, and intelligence analysts[47] – predict future societal events (e.g., who will win an election or whether two countries will go to war). These studies find that some individuals are better forecasters than others and that certain interventions and ways of thinking improve forecasting.[48] But they also find severe limitations on human predictive capacities. When making predictions five years out, forecasters' accuracy declines and approaches random chance – or, as Tetlock puts it, a dart-throwing chimp.[49] Tetlock and others conclude that even the best forecasters cannot make accurate predictions about society a decade from now, besides the occasional lucky guess and generalities (e.g., there will be interstate conflicts).[50] So if someone makes detailed claims about what society will look like in fifty years, we have little reason to take their arguments seriously.

These limitations reflect how difficult it is to predict outcomes of complex systems involving many variables in nonlinear relationships, as is the case with society. Weather forecasting offers a helpful analogy. Weather patterns are extremely complex. Small variations in initial conditions – beyond what we can accurately measure – lead to vastly different outcomes as time elapses.[51] So though meteorologists generally can predict the weather for the next few days, their longer-term forecasts are far less accurate. The complexity of the social world creates similar challenges. Skilled forecasters predict events in the short term with some accuracy, but their predictive powers fail them when trying to foretell events further out.

Some may accept these limits on human prediction while denying that they pose problems for ideal theory. After all, ideal theory only makes *general* predictions about the distant future (e.g., there will be moderate scarcity and

---

[47] Tetlock, *Expert Political Judgment*.
[48] Tetlock, *Expert Political Judgment*; Barbara Mellers et al., "The Psychology of Intelligence Analysis: Drivers of Prediction Accuracy in World Politics," *Journal of Experimental Psychology: Applied* 21, no. 1 (2015): 1–14; and Tetlock and Gardner, *Superforecasting*.
[49] Tetlock and Gardner, *Superforecasting*, 4.
[50] Tetlock and Gardner, *Superforecasting*, 243–44.
[51] Edward Lorenz, *The Essence of Chaos* (Seattle, WA: University of Washington Press, 1993), esp. 181–84.

pluralism), not the detailed predictions studied by Tetlock (e.g., the euro will hit this value by this date).

This defense fails to save ideal theory, however. Our inability to predict many small events can add up and lead to dramatic, unforeseen changes in society that are relevant to ideal theory. Relatedly, failures in forecasting sometimes result from the intervention of rare, difficult-to-predict, transformative events in society – what Nassim Taleb calls Black Swans.[52] These events, like the invention of the printing press, reshape society and alter its course in ways hard to foresee. Black Swans are especially relevant to ideal theory because their transformative effects can unsettle our considered views, causing us to rethink conceptions of justice. In other words, these societal developments are exactly the ones ideal theorists must predict to show that their principles of justice would have normative force in a future radically different from today. Yet the same feature that makes Black Swans transformative – radically departing from the status quo – also makes them difficult to predict. Predictions often extrapolate from the past, but that method fails to predict outliers like Black Swans. Such events pose a thorny dilemma for ideal theory: events with great impact on the world, which we desperately would like to predict, often are ones we are least likely to. Black Swans throw a wrench into predictive models, and give us little reason to believe that we can make reliably accurate predictions about society for the distant future.

Occasional predictions of Black Swans fail to provide much hope to ideal theorists. Pundits, academics, and others make many claims about the future – inevitably, some seemingly improbable predictions end up being right by chance. But that doesn't mean their predictions are *reliably* accurate. Forecasting studies put successful predictions, which grab our attention, into context by also tracking failed ones. And as research shows, people are poor predictors of future societal developments beyond the short term.

Such limitations severely hinder ideal theorizing. Since we cannot predict future possibilities for society, we don't know what an ideal theory's principles would look like when implemented, which prevents us from plausibly defending them. Here is a review of the argument so far and the conclusion that follows:

(1) Defenses of navigational ideal theory are plausible only if they show that the theory's principles would have normative force in the society it envisions.

---

[52] Taleb, *The Black Swan*.

(2) Showing that navigational ideal theory's principles would have normative force in the society it envisions requires reliably accurate predictions about science, technology, economics, and politics for the distant future.
(3) We cannot make reliably accurate predictions about science, technology, economics, and politics for the distant future.
(4) So, by (2) and (3), we cannot show that navigational ideal theory's principles would have normative force in the society it envisions.
(5) So, by (1) and (4), no defense of navigational ideal theory is plausible.[53]

There are two points worth noting. First, this argument is not based on radical skepticism about moral truth. I assume we can identify clear examples of unjust societies and make plausible claims about what the ideal society *is not* – for instance, one with the horrors of slavery like the antebellum South. But such claims alone cannot get us to a determinate answer about what the ideal society *specifically is*, especially given the vast array of future possibilities, some of which we would have difficulty even imagining today.

Second, the argument never rejects out of hand the concept of the ideal society. It grants to ideal theorists the possibility of an ideal that represents the most just society with the potential to be realized. The problem, though, is that we lack the predictive capacities to plausibly identify and defend this ideal. That is what makes ideal theorists' plight so frustrating. They believe in the possibility of the ideal, perhaps rightly so, but prove unable to identify it with any certainty.

IMPLICATIONS FOR POLITICAL PHILOSOPHY

One of the most famous critiques of religious belief comes from Bertrand Russell. He compares such belief to claiming that a tiny teapot, imperceptible by telescope, orbits the sun. Though no one can disprove this claim, it would be nonsense to accuse those who doubt it of being unreasonable. The onus is on those making the claim about the teapot to show its plausibility. If they fail to, we dismiss their claim as absurd. For Russell, religious belief has a similar status: it lacks plausible grounds, even if it cannot be falsified. His analogy emphasizes that those making religious claims cannot expect others to believe simply because it is impossible to disprove their claims.[54]

---

[53] See the Appendix for an expansion of this argument, which considers and responds to further potential objections.

[54] Bertrand Russell, "Is There a God?" in *The Collected Papers of Bertrand Russell, Vol. 11: Last Philosophical Testament, 1943–68*, ed. John Slater and Peter Köllner (New York: Routledge, 1997), 547–48.

Russell's analogy is relevant because it equally applies to navigational ideal theory. Though ideal theorists like Rawls distinguish ideal theory from religious belief, the former is no more immune from Russell's critique than the latter. The ideal theorist claims to give plausible grounds that a particular ideal should serve as a collective guide. Skeptics may run into difficulties disproving that claim, given deep uncertainty over the distant future. Yet for that same reason, the ideal theorist cannot make a compelling case *for* their ideal – they cannot show that it would have normative force in far-off contexts where it could be realized. Rawls's method aspires to offer an ideal that others in society have reason to accept, but ultimately fails to do so. That raises the question: Where does political philosophy go next?

Some suggest that political philosophy should abandon its focus on ideal theory. Charles Mills argues that, by placing its attention on far-off ideals, ideal theory distracts from today's most pressing injustices and has perverse effects on political philosophy's priorities.[55] Burke Hendrix raises the additional worry that ideal theory risks doing more harm than good by championing ideals whose full consequences cannot be known. Ideal theory often has unintended effects and can exacerbate the very injustices it seeks to remedy.[56] Such criticisms of ideal theory reflect underlying discontent with the dominant approach to justice in political philosophy.

Skeptics of ideal theory offer alternatives, which share the feature of rejecting a single ideal to guide efforts toward greater justice. Sen argues that we can advance justice without a perfect ideal by instead identifying the most pressing injustices and using a comparative approach to evaluate options for addressing them.[57] David Wiens also prefers to focus on specific injustices. He suggests institutional failure analysis, which identifies societal failures resulting in injustice and then formulates feasible measures to avoid them.[58] This interest in addressing injustice rather than striving after an ideal is nothing new and resembles sentiments common after the Second World War, whose horrors dashed utopian hopes.[59] Karl Popper reflects this mindset in a 1947 lecture on

---

[55] Charles Mills, "'Ideal Theory' as Ideology," *Hypatia* 20, no. 3 (2005): 165–84; and *Black Rights/White Wrongs: The Critique of Racial Liberalism* (New York: Oxford University Press, 2017), esp. 139–60, 201–16.

[56] Burke Hendrix, "Where Should We Expect Social Change in Non-ideal Theory?" *Political Theory* 41, no. 1 (2013): 116–43; and *Strategies of Justice: Aboriginal Peoples, Persistent Injustice, and the Ethics of Political Action* (New York: Oxford University Press, 2019).

[57] Sen, *The Idea of Justice*.

[58] David Wiens, "Prescribing Institutions without Ideal Theory," *Journal of Political Philosophy* 20, no. 1 (2012): 45–70.

[59] See Judith Shklar, *After Utopia: The Decline of Political Faith* (Princeton, NJ: Princeton University Press, 1957).

the ills of utopian projects, which recommends advancing justice through "the elimination of concrete evils rather than ... the realization of abstract goods."[60] Popper's influence today is most evident in Gaus's work to develop an alternative to ideal theory. Drawing on Popper's idea of the Open Society,[61] as well as John Stuart Mill's idea of experiments in living,[62] Gaus argues that society should encourage its members to pursue *different* ideals and that such experimentation gives insight into what social arrangements best promote justice.[63]

These proposals deserve consideration as potential paths forward in theorizing about justice without navigational ideal theory. It is important, though, to recognize the aspirations that these alternatives leave behind. Without an ideal to guide action, efforts to advance justice face deep uncertainty. Even when we advance justice, there always is the worry that our efforts lead away from greater justice later. Navigational ideal theory looks to be an antidote to such uncertainty by assuring us that we're on the right path when reforms move society closer to the ideal. Recent proposals by Sen, Wiens, and Gaus offer no such assurance. They leave open the very danger that ideal theory seeks to avoid: ending up on lesser peaks of justice because there is no end goal pointing to the highest peak. They fail to solve the problem at the heart of ideal theory – what ultimate aim should we strive for? In fact, they give up trying to solve it.[64]

I note this limitation not to recommend that political philosophy stubbornly defend the claims of navigational ideal theory. As we have seen, it is in no position to offer a plausible goal to guide action given future uncertainty. But recognizing this limitation helps avoid unrealistic hopes for alternatives to ideal theory. In particular, it is a mistake to claim there are reasonable grounds for believing that these alternatives lead to a society that is in any sense ideal. Despite his criticisms of ideal theory, Gaus makes this mistake when discussing his hopes for an open and diverse society. He writes: "[W]e cannot know

---

[60] Karl Popper, "Utopia and Violence," in *Conjectures and Refutations: The Growth of Scientific Knowledge* (New York: Routledge, 2002), 485.
[61] Karl Popper, *The Open Society and Its Enemies* (Princeton, NJ: Princeton University Press, 2013).
[62] John Stuart Mill, *On Liberty*, in *On Liberty and Other Essays*, ed. John Gray (New York: Oxford University Press, 1991), 63. For more on this idea in Mill, see Elizabeth Anderson, "John Stuart Mill and Experiments in Living," *Ethics* 102, no. 1 (1991): 4–26; and Ryan Muldoon, "Expanding the Justificatory Framework of Mill's Experiments in Living," *Utilitas* 27, no. 2 (2015): 179–94.
[63] Gaus, *The Tyranny of the Ideal*.
[64] Wiens explicitly concedes this point. See Wiens, "Political Ideals and the Feasibility Frontier," 472.

what such an ideal [society] would be – unless we disagree about it. Only those in a morally heterogeneous society have a reasonable hope of actually understanding what an ideal society would be like, but in such a society we will never be collectively devoted to any single ideal."[65] Gaus suggests that understanding the ideal comes through an indirect process where different individuals and groups seek their own ideal and learn from social experimentation.

Gaus's optimism is understandable. Experimentation has been the engine behind remarkable advances, transforming fields like medicine, which cures a host of ailments it was impotent against not long ago.[66] Perhaps Gaus is right, and applying this approach to justice will unleash similar advances. But even if he is right, suggesting that this approach leads to the ideal overlooks the often haphazard and imperfect nature of experimentation. Chance and timing impact how knowledge from experimentation grows. Successful experiments spark interest in a hypothesis, the study of which then enjoys disproportionate attention and resources. Yet after many years, we sometimes discover that the hypothesis was wrong. Knowledge eventually grows, but along the way some experimental results direct our attention away from more promising ideas that go neglected. Far from always triumphant, the experimental approach also leads society down paths that are less than ideal.

So abandoning the aspirations of navigational ideal theory comes with real losses. Political philosophy finds itself in a tough spot without any clear ideal to light the way regarding which path best advances justice long term. We are left stumbling about in the dark, with political philosophy unable to allay doubts that actions taken to advance justice may in fact lead away from the most just possibility.

That uncertainty can create motivational hurdles to engaging in the difficult work of advancing justice. For many, a critical component of such work is hope – that the future is not condemned to the same injustices plaguing the present. Alternatives to ideal theory can foster hope in short-term progress by identifying clear injustices, outlining ways to address them, and encouraging people to take action that will bring about marginal advances in justice. But it is unclear that such hope is always enough. Steps to advance justice today can be overturned tomorrow as administrations, lawmakers, and judges change. That reality renders hope in short-term progress fragile and fleeting. Even when marginal advances endure, we cannot know if they represent steps toward the most just society. Together, these factors undermine short-term

---

[65] Gaus, *The Tyranny of the Ideal*, xix.
[66] See Druin Burch, *Taking the Medicine: A Short History of Medicine's Beautiful Idea, and Our Difficulty Swallowing It* (London: Random House, 2010).

hope's potency as a source of motivation. If short-term hope is all we have, the arduous task of advancing justice risks resembling a random walk rather than a journey up a majestic peak.

That image of a random walk is far less inspiring and, for some, deeply unsettling. The difficult work of advancing justice entails sacrifices, setbacks, and frustration. Understandably, many look for reassurance that these struggles are worth it – that they lead to a goal worth striving for. Ideal theory offers that by infusing current hardships with moral significance and linking them to a far more hopeful future. So there are real worries that the loss of ideal theory leads to despair and, as a result, some resist simply leaving it behind. Whether ideal theory still has a role to play, despite its limitations, is what we explore next.

PRESERVING UTOPIAN HOPE

Defenses of navigational ideal theory fall short. But does that failure of ideal theory force us to abandon utopian hope? Even if there are not plausible grounds to accept a proposed ideal, one could accept it on faith. That point suggests a path forward for ideal theory, albeit with tempered ambitions: concede our inability to identify the most just society possible with any confidence, yet embrace hope for an ideal on faith. In the absence of strong evidence for an ideal, faith sustains hope in it. Faith has a close relation to hope, a point that the Christian tradition has long recognized: "[F]aith is the assurance of things hoped for, the conviction of things not seen" (Hebrews 11:1).[67] Guided by that principle, one strategy for preserving ideal theory and utopian hope is to recognize their reliance on faith.

This approach makes explicit ideal theory's parallels with religious belief. The apocalyptic tradition, in particular, envisions a future ideal society and fosters hope that it will be realized. In a pluralistic society, it would be unreasonable to expect everyone to accept these religious beliefs based on faith. Still, for those who have such faith, it is a source of meaning and instills hope for greater justice in a world marred by injustice. Ideal theory has the potential to play a similar role. Just as individuals in pluralistic societies practice different religions, they also can embrace different ideal theories (or none at all). According to this view, no ideal serves as a collective goal for society to pursue. Rather, individuals embrace different ideals, which help assure them that their efforts to advance justice are meaningful steps toward a more perfect world.

---

[67] New Revised Standard Version.

Some will see little point in hanging on to ideal theory and reach a conclusion similar to Russell's regarding religious belief. Beyond just claiming that arguments for religious belief lack plausible grounds, Russell treats such beliefs as nonsense – like believing a tiny teapot is orbiting the sun. Admitting religious belief's reliance on faith doesn't change that fact. Belief in ideal theory is vulnerable to the same criticism. From the critic's perspective, we should treat any account of ideal theory as absurd, since so much about the future is unknown and the forms society could take are virtually endless. We have no idea what a proposed ideal would look like in practice and whether it would have normative appeal under conditions that could be radically different from today's world. Even if we avoid defending ideal theory, belief in it is nonsense.

One can arrive at this conclusion while still caring about justice. For some, progress against concrete injustices and suffering provides sufficient assurance that their efforts are worth it. To continue in this work, they do not need the further assurance that their efforts move society toward the *most just* possibility.

Others, though, yearn for this more robust hope. That is evident from its persistent expressions in religion, philosophy, literature, and popular culture. Utopian hope expresses the desire to realize an ideally just society and belief in its possibility. Such hope often looks beyond the immediate future for inspiration, an idea evident in Martin Luther King Jr.'s maxim that "the arc of the moral universe is long, but it bends toward justice."[68] Even if the present is not hospitable to justice, the long arc of history is. Utopian hope instills partial, imperfect steps toward justice with meaning by situating them within a longer development toward the ideal. According to this view, human efforts over time move society closer to the ideal, which once achieved will be stable and lasting – otherwise it wouldn't be a true utopia. After all, a society that quickly falls into decline after achieving its goal fails to count as utopia. Because it is meant to endure, utopia represents an end goal. For this reason, utopian hope has close links to teleological views of history, which understand history as having a purpose and moving toward a particular end. Even if there are at times setbacks, the overall course of history is moving toward utopia – or at least that is the hope – and this future ideal informs the significance of all that comes before it.

[68] Martin Luther King Jr., "The Current Crisis in Race Relations," in *A Testament of Hope: The Essential Writings and Speeches of Martin Luther King, Jr.*, ed. James Washington (New York: HarperCollins Publishers, 1986), 88. For a qualified defense of this view, based on the idea that injustice is inherently unstable, see Joshua Cohen, "The Arc of the Moral Universe," *Philosophy and Public Affairs* 26, no. 2 (1997): 91–134.

The goal here is not to argue that morality or reason demands utopian hope. In a world long filled with injustice, where horrific suffering seems to fall at random on the undeserving, it is both understandable and defensible to reject utopian hope. There is plenty of room in political philosophy and social movements for those who work against injustice without hoping for utopia. My modest goal is to carve out space for utopian hope and explain how someone can embrace it without falling into error.

It turns out that the same factor that undermines defenses of ideal theory – future uncertainty – ensures a place for utopian hope. The nature of hope helps explain why. Though conceptions of hope vary, most understand it as involving, at the very least, the desire for an outcome believed to be neither guaranteed nor impossible.[69] The desired outcome need not be likely. After all, people often hope for very unlikely things, like an experimental drug that will cure their cancer. The desired outcome just has to be *possible*. As Adrienne Martin explains in her study *How We Hope*, the mere possibility of an outcome, no matter how unlikely, provides permission to hope and act on that hope. So hope does not require inflating the odds of an outcome, and there is nothing inherently irrational about "hoping against hope" – that is, hoping for an outcome with extremely long odds. Such hope emphasizes an outcome's possibility, which can have practical value by sustaining individuals as they pursue goals under incredibly trying circumstances, like a terminal illness.[70]

We can apply these insights to utopian hope. The deep uncertainty surrounding the future opens the door for such hope. Future uncertainty makes it impossible to establish what the utopian society would look like and whether it will be realized, so utopian hope must rely on faith. Yet this same uncertainty functions as a bulwark to protect faith in utopian hope. Because so much about the future is uncertain, we cannot entirely preclude the possibility of achieving the ideal society at some point. Though realizing the ideal is difficult to imagine, it still is possible, which frees people to embrace utopian hope without committing any obvious error. This hope offers needed assurance, at least for some, that the arduous work to make the world more just leads

---

[69] See R. S. Downie, "Hope," *Philosophy and Phenomenological Research* 24, no. 2 (1963): 248–49; J. P. Day, "Hope," *American Philosophical Quarterly* 6, no. 2 (1969): 89; Luc Bovens, "The Value of Hope," *Philosophy and Phenomenological Research* 59, no. 3 (1999): 673; Philip Pettit, "Hope and Its Place in Mind," *Annals of the American Academy of Political and Social Science* 592 (2004): 154; Ariel Meirav, "The Nature of Hope," *Ratio* 22, no. 2 (2009): 218–20; and Adrienne Martin, *How We Hope: A Moral Psychology* (Princeton, NJ: Princeton University Press, 2014), 62.

[70] Martin, *How We Hope*, 11–71.

to more than just fleeting progress. From the perspective of utopian hope, such work – so often incomplete and imperfect – contributes to an ideal truly worth striving for.

Here some might object that the analogy between ideal theory and religious faith breaks down. This description of utopian hope, aware of its own uncertainty, seems to stand in contrast to more dogmatic forms of hope often found in religious faith. Indeed, it is common for religious believers to describe their faith as providing hope for an ideal future that is certain.[71]

But that view is not universal. In today's secular age, as Charles Taylor points out, religious beliefs and hopes no longer seem as self-evident as they once did. Religious belief in many contemporary societies does not enjoy the status of assumed truth, nor does the divine pervade shared perceptions of the world and the forces within it. For those who choose to embrace religious faith in this context, their faith often coexists with uncertainty and doubt.[72]

This variety of religious faith described by Taylor, which offers uncertain hope, serves as an apt analogy for ideal theory aware of its epistemic limitations. In both cases, beliefs grounded in faith rather than plausible evidence serve as a source of utopian hope. Ideal theory and utopian hope cannot escape this shortcoming, but can persist in spite of it. If we are to hang on to ideal theory and utopian hope with intellectual honesty, we must abandon the ambition of offering plausible grounds for others to accept our ideal and hope for it.

RAWLS'S FAITH

The idea that ideal theory relies on faith can be jarring, since it is not usually described in this way. Ideal theory often aims to provide a common goal to strive for in a pluralistic society where religious faith fails to fulfill that role. Political philosophy thus tends to treat ideal theory as resting on more solid ground than religious faith. That perspective has its roots in Rawls, whose thought inspired much of contemporary ideal theory. A close look at Rawls's writings serves as a reminder, however, that reliance on faith is at the heart of ideal theory.

In his account of ideal theory, Rawls assigns a central role for utopian hope. No historical figure impacted his thinking on this issue more than Kant.

---

[71] David Elliot, *Hope and Christian Ethics* (New York: Cambridge University Press, 2017), 72.
[72] Charles Taylor, *A Secular Age* (Cambridge, MA: Harvard University Press, 2007). See also David Newheiser, *Hope in a Secular Age: Deconstruction, Negative Theology, and the Future of Faith* (New York: Cambridge University Press, 2019).

Citing Kant, Rawls stresses the need to hold on to hope for a just society if life in this world is to be worth living.[73] This hope strikes him as necessary, especially when individuals take on the difficult task of working to advance justice. Rawls believes ideal theory can "banish the dangers of resignation and cynicism" and meet the challenge of preserving utopian hope. "By showing how the social world may realize the features of a realistic utopia," he writes, "political philosophy provides a long-term goal of political endeavor, and in working toward it gives meaning to what we can do today."[74]

Rawls's *Lectures on the History of Moral Philosophy* illustrate in greater detail his interest in the utopian element in Kant's philosophy, as well as his debt to it.[75] His final lecture on Kant focuses on the relation among faith, reason, and hope in Kant's thought.[76] As Rawls explains, Kant treats utopian hope as a necessary component of morality. Specifically, the moral law takes as its object the highest good, which for Kant is a world where happiness is proportional to and in harmony with virtue. And since the moral law only seeks ends that are possible, one of its presuppositions is that the highest good must be possible.[77] Without that presupposition, the moral law cannot get off the ground. "If ... the highest good is impossible," writes Kant, "then the moral law, which commands us to promote it, must be fantastic and directed to empty imaginary ends and must therefore in itself be false."[78]

---

[73] Rawls, *Political Liberalism*, lx; and *The Law of Peoples*, 128.
[74] Rawls, *The Law of Peoples*, 128.
[75] In his *Lectures*, Rawls notes that his purpose for studying Kant and other thinkers is to "bring out what is distinctive in their approach to moral philosophy" rather than find "some philosophical argument, some analytic idea that will be directly useful for our present-day philosophical questions." See Rawls, *Lectures on the History of Moral Philosophy*, ed. Barbara Herman (Cambridge, MA: Harvard University Press, 2000), 329. We should keep that caveat in mind, but it does not mean that the *Lectures* are irrelevant to understanding Rawls's normative theory. In the case of Kant, Rawls explicitly and favorably cites him in his major works of political philosophy – in particular, when discussing the need to hope for a just future. The *Lectures* prove valuable in gathering a fuller picture of how Rawls understands this idea from Kant and what about it appeals to him.
[76] Rawls, *Lectures on the History of Moral Philosophy*, 309–25.
[77] Kant, *Critique of Practical Reason*, in *Practical Philosophy*, trans. and ed. Mary Gregor (New York: Cambridge University Press, 1996), 5:108–14; *Religion within the Boundaries of Mere Reason*, in *Religion and Rational Theology*, trans. and ed. Allen Wood and George di Giovanni (New York: Cambridge University Press, 1996), 6:3–6; and "On the Common Saying: That May Be Correct in Theory, But It Is of No Use in Practice," in *Practical Philosophy*, trans. and ed. Mary Gregor (New York: Cambridge University Press, 1996), 8:279–80. For more on this idea in Kant, see Loren Goldman, "In Defense of Blinders: On Kant, Political Hope, and the Need for Practical Belief," *Political Theory* 40, no. 4 (2012): 497–523.
[78] Kant, *Critique of Practical Reason*, 5:114.

Kant goes on to argue that further presuppositions are necessary for the highest good to be possible. It is here that he introduces tenets of religious faith – immortality of the soul and the existence of an omnipotent and benevolent God – along with freedom of will as necessary presuppositions of morality.[79] Without these presuppositions, the highest good as Kant sees it would be impossible. Only a good and all-powerful God ensures that virtue and happiness ultimately will correspond. Only immortality ensures that individuals can make continual progress in conforming their will to the moral law. And only freedom of will ensures the possibility of moral action to begin with. Together, the presuppositions of morality answer a question Kant poses to himself: "What may I hope for?"[80] They fill in the content of what he considers reasonable faith.[81] Kant avoids claiming that we can prove God's existence or immortality. But there is also no way to disprove these religious beliefs, so reason *permits* them. Moreover, since these beliefs are necessary presuppositions of the moral law, morality *requires* them.[82] As Kant puts it, "Morality ... inevitably leads to religion."[83]

Rawls's conception of utopian hope never looks as robust as Kant's, since it lacks hope for God and immortality. But despite these departures, Rawls treats Kant's account of utopian hope and reasonable faith with great sympathy. To distinguish between which elements are worth preserving and which to discard, Rawls uses the German term "*Vernunftglaube*" for some of Kant's beliefs and the English term "reasonable faith" for others. *Vernunftglaube* just means reasonable faith, but Rawls specifically uses it to refer to Kant's hope for achieving the highest good and the related presuppositions of God and immortality. Rawls then uses the term reasonable faith to refer to Kant's hope for a "realm of ends," a society where individuals live under conditions of justice.[84] This realm of ends closely resembles the realistic utopia that Rawls outlines in his ideal theory and defends as a goal to strive for. Notably, he calls the "realm of ends ... a secular ideal."[85]

Not surprisingly, Rawls sees the reasonable faith required for this ideal as more essential than Kant's *Vernunftglaube*. He asks: "[W]hat is the content of

---

[79] Kant, *Critique of Practical Reason*, 5:122–34.
[80] Kant poses this question in his letter to C. F. Stäudlin from May 4, 1793. See George di Giovanni, "Translator's Introduction," in *Religion and Rational Theology*, trans. and ed. Allen Wood and George di Giovanni (New York: Cambridge University Press, 1996), 49.
[81] Notably, hope for the kingdom of God is part of Kant's conception of reasonable faith. See Kant, *Religion within the Boundaries of Mere Reason*, 6:134–36.
[82] Kant, *Critique of Practical Reason*, 5:122–34.
[83] Kant, *Religion within the Boundaries of Mere Reason*, 6:6.
[84] Rawls, *Lectures on the History of Moral Philosophy*, 310.
[85] Rawls, *Lectures on the History of Moral Philosophy*, 312.

practical faith once we take a realm of ends as the object of the moral law?" Here Rawls essentially describes the move that he makes in his political philosophy, so his response to the question proves illuminating for understanding faith's role in his ideal theory. He writes:

> I suggest that while [taking a realm of ends as the object of the moral law] does not require the postulates of God and immortality, it does require certain beliefs about our nature and the social world . . . . For we can believe that a realm of ends is possible in the world only if the order of nature and social necessities are not unfriendly to that ideal. For this to be so, it must contain forces and tendencies that in the longer run tend to bring out, or at least support, such a realm and to educate mankind so as to further this end.[86]

For Rawls, Kant's religious beliefs are unnecessary as presuppositions for working toward an ideal society, but other presuppositions *are* necessary. Namely, we must hold on to the hope that such an ideal is possible and, relatedly, that the future is hospitable to its realization.

This hope for the future reflects aspects of a teleological view of history. Kant stresses our practical need to "hope for better times" and see history as progressing toward greater perfection.[87] Rawls's remarks on Kant's view suggest an affinity for it: "We must believe . . . that the course of human history is progressively improving, and not becoming worse, or that it does not fluctuate in perpetuity from bad to good and from good to bad. For in this case we will view the spectacle of human history as a farce that arouses loathing of our species."[88] Even as he leaves behind Kant's religious beliefs, Rawls expresses greater openness to other leaps of faith seen as necessary presuppositions of working toward the ideal society.[89]

The essay "On My Religion," written by Rawls near the end of his life, provides insight into why he cannot hang on to the religious elements in Kant's concept of reasonable faith, which he otherwise finds appealing. Rawls points to three events during his service in the Second World War that led him to

---

[86] Rawls, *Lectures on the History of Moral Philosophy*, 319.
[87] Kant, "On the Common Saying: That May Be Correct in Theory, But It Is of No Use in Practice," 8:309–10.
[88] Rawls, *Lectures on the History of Moral Philosophy*, 319–20.
[89] For clarity, it is helpful to distinguish Rawls's views on different forms of teleology. Rawls rejects teleological theories of ethics, which prioritize the good over the right, in favor of his conception of justice as fairness. See Rawls, *A Theory of Justice*, 21–30. Teleological theories of ethics are distinct from teleological views of history, which understand history as moving toward a particular end. Rawls's remarks on Kant and hope for a future hospitable to justice suggest a greater sympathy toward a teleological view of history. Specifically, he *hopes* that such a conception of history, in which society continually progresses toward ideal justice, is true.

abandon his Christian faith: (1) a sermon to him and other U.S. troops claiming that God would aid them in killing the Japanese; (2) the death of his friend Deacon on an expedition that Rawls almost went on instead; and (3) learning about the horrors of the Holocaust.[90] It became impossible to maintain his faith, as Rawls explains:

> These incidents, and especially the third [the Holocaust] ..., affected me in the same way. This took the form of questioning whether prayer was possible. How could I pray and ask God to help me, or my family, or my country, or any other cherished thing I cared about, when God would not save millions of Jews from Hitler? When Lincoln interprets the Civil War as God's punishment for the sin of slavery, deserved equally by North and South, God is seen as acting justly. But the Holocaust can't be interpreted in that way, and all attempts to do so that I have read of are hideous and evil. To interpret history as expressing God's will, God's will must accord with the most basic ideas of justice as we know them. For what else can the most basic justice be? Thus, I soon came to reject the idea of the supremacy of the divine will as also hideous and evil.[91]

Though deeply religious before the war – Rawls at one point considered seminary[92] – the Holocaust and his experiences in combat dashed his faith that God ensures justice now or ever. In fact, for Rawls, to imagine an omnipotent God in a world marred by such evil only crushes hope in a just future, for it suggests that the ruler of the universe is a monster.

The horrors of the Second World War pushed Rawls to give up his religious faith, yet he held on to utopian hope and the conviction that the future is hospitable to justice. Not everyone held on to such hope in the wake of these horrors. Rawls, though, adamantly rejects political despair as an option. Even after the "the manic evil of the Holocaust," he stresses that we must start from the assumption that a realistic utopia is possible.[93] The thought of abandoning hope in that ideal strikes Rawls as intolerable. So a secular understanding of ideal theory steps in to be the source of utopian hope that religious faith can no longer provide.

The basis for this move lies in his distinction between forms of reasonable faith. In his lecture on Kant, Rawls makes a point to differentiate reasonable faith in an ideal society from reasonable faith (or *Vernunftglaube*) in religious

---

[90] Rawls, *A Brief Inquiry into the Meaning of Sin and Faith with "On My Religion,"* ed. Thomas Nagel (Cambridge, MA: Harvard University Press, 2009), 262–63.
[91] Rawls, *A Brief Inquiry into the Meaning of Sin and Faith with "On My Religion,"* 263.
[92] Rawls, *A Brief Inquiry into the Meaning of Sin and Faith with "On My Religion,"* 261.
[93] Rawls, *Political Liberalism*, lx.

beliefs like immortality and the existence of God. Rawls admits that Kant himself never makes this distinction,[94] but feels compelled to make it because "the plausibility of Kant's view in these two cases are quite different."[95] For Rawls, reasonable faith in a just and ideal society has greater plausibility since the object of such faith could be realized within the confines of the natural world, without any necessary reference to the supernatural.[96] So though hope for a future ideal society and hope in the divine both rest on faith, Rawls sees the former as the more reasonable of the two faiths.

This desire to distinguish the faith required for ideal theory as more reasonable and plausible than the faith required for religious belief is where Rawls runs into trouble. To preserve his utopian hope, Rawls must make leaps of faith no less considerable than those he eschews. His ideal theory rests on the convictions that we can identify the ideal and that the future is such that it fosters progress toward it. We already have seen earlier in this chapter that there are not plausible grounds to support the first claim. And the teleological view of history implicit in the second claim long has been criticized as wishful thinking rather than grounded in actual evidence. That seems even truer today as the world grapples with the legacies of slavery and colonialism, as well as the devastating consequences of human-induced climate change. Confronted with such overwhelming injustice from the present and recent past, some have no patience for "fairy tales that imply some irrepressible justice."[97] According to that view, only a tendentious and selective reading of history suggests that it continually progresses toward greater justice.

Now it would be too strong to say that Rawls errs in hoping for utopia and a future conducive to its realization. The future *could* radically depart from the present and bring about the ideal. That possibility, regardless of its likelihood, allows one to embrace ideal theory and utopian hope without violating basic principles of rationality. But it is a mistake to think that ideal theory rests on faith so qualitatively different than religious faith that it succeeds in providing plausible grounds to accept and pursue a shared ideal. By making distinctions between ideal theory and religious faith that fail to hold up under scrutiny, Rawls set contemporary ideal theory on the wrong track from the start.

Political philosophy long has taken seriously the notion that ideal theory can identify the most just society possible, give plausible arguments for this claim, and offer an end goal to guide collective action. Such ambitions far

---

[94] Rawls, *Lectures on the History of Moral Philosophy*, 317.
[95] Rawls, *Lectures on the History of Moral Philosophy*, 310.
[96] Rawls, *Lectures on the History of Moral Philosophy*, 312.
[97] Ta-Nehisi Coates, *Between the World and Me* (New York: Spiegel & Grau, 2015), 70.

outstrip human capacities and fail to appreciate the deep uncertainty in the world along with its full implications. We cannot predict future developments and innovations that will shape society, and thus cannot show what proposed principles of justice would look like in far-off worlds, let alone that they would constitute the most just society. Political philosophers would be wise to admit these limitations and stop expecting the impossible from ideal theory. If theorizing about the most just society possible persists, it is important to recognize it for what it is: hope for an ideal grounded in faith.

7

Limiting the Dangers of Utopian Hope

As Chapter 6 explored, it is highly doubtful that ideal theory can identify the ideal society with confidence and serve as a reliable guide to social action. Because of future uncertainty, ideal theory ultimately rests on faith, not plausible arguments for the ideal it proposes. So ideal theory ends up in a role similar to that of apocalyptic thought – a source of utopian hope for those who accept it on faith. Such hope can have benefits. It instills efforts to advance justice with meaning by interpreting them as steps toward an ideal that is both possible and worth striving for. But not all aspects of utopian hope prove beneficial. As the history of apocalyptic thought makes clear, such hope also comes with real dangers – in particular violence.

This chapter examines the dangers of utopian hope and ways to limit them. It builds on the idea, emphasized throughout this study, that ideal theory shares overlooked features with apocalyptic thought. One long-standing worry with apocalyptic thought is that it promotes violence.[1] That fear has lurked in the background in the previous case studies of Thomas Müntzer and the Fifth

---

[1] See Norman Cohn, *The Pursuit of the Millennium: Revolutionary Millenarians and Mystical Anarchists of the Middle Ages*, rev. ed. (New York: Oxford University Press, 1970); Abbas Amanat and John Collins, eds., *Apocalypse and Violence* (New Haven, CT: Yale Center for International and Area Studies and the Council on Middle East Studies, 2004); Bernard McGinn, "Apocalypticism and Violence: Aspects of Their Relation in Antiquity and the Middle Ages," in *Scripture and Pluralism: Reading the Bible in the Religiously Plural Worlds of the Middle Ages and Renaissance*, ed. Thomas Heffernan and Thomas Burman (Leiden: Brill, 2005), 209–29; James Rinehart, *Apocalyptic Faith and Political Violence: Prophets of Terror* (New York: Palgrave Macmillan, 2006); James Jones, *Blood that Cries Out from the Earth: The Psychology of Religious Terrorism* (New York: Oxford University Press, 2008), 40–55; Michael Sells, "Armageddon in Christian, Sunni and Shia Traditions," in *The Oxford Handbook of Religion and Violence*, ed. Mark Juergensmeyer, Margo Kitts, and Michael Jerryson (New York: Oxford University Press, 2013), 467–95; Jamel Velji, "Apocalyptic Religion and Violence," in *The Oxford Handbook of Religion and Violence*, ed. Mark Juergensmeyer, Margo Kitts, and Michael Jerryson (New York: Oxford University Press,

Monarchy Men, whose apocalyptic visions helped inspire violent rebellion. Today apocalyptic thought continues to be a motivating force for a range of violent groups, from Christian White nationalists to Muslim extremists.[2] Their shocking brutality makes it tempting to conclude that apocalyptic thought – and perhaps religion generally – is inherently violent. A closer look at apocalyptic thought, however, reveals that its greatest pitfall is one that also threatens ideal theory. Both apocalyptic thought and ideal theory can fall victim to false confidence regarding their ability to identify and achieve utopia. Purported knowledge of the path to utopia has justified all kinds of bloodshed and cruelty throughout history, yet the ideal never comes. When utopian hope turns into hubris, it can lead to disaster.

The apocalyptic tradition is incredibly diverse and, though strands of it encourage violence, others suggest strategies for minimizing that risk. In this way, the apocalyptic tradition offers unexpected insights to ideal theory on how to understand utopian hope. Partly in response to the explosive potential of apocalyptic belief, Jewish and Christian thought developed interpretations of such belief aimed at neutralizing its dangers. These religious traditions often stress the radical nature of human ignorance as it pertains to what exactly the ideal society looks like, how to bring it about, and when it might come. Such knowledge lies with God alone. Given the limits of human knowledge, it would be foolish and dangerous to try to force utopia into existence through our own efforts. That conclusion is in part discouraging, for it pushes utopia beyond our grasp. But there is also wisdom in it, for it captures the epistemic limitations that face utopian theorizing and the dangers of ignoring them.

Now in recommending epistemic humility, Jewish and Christian thought still hold on to utopian hope. This hope is grounded in faith and gives meaning to the difficult work of advancing justice under conditions far removed from utopia. By closely linking utopian hope *with* epistemic humility, the apocalyptic tradition – or at least certain strands of it – suggests an approach that ideal theory would be wise to imitate.

2013), 250–59; Frances Flannery, *Understanding Apocalyptic Terrorism: Countering the Radical Mindset* (New York: Routledge, 2016); and Matthias Riedl, "Apocalyptic Violence and Revolutionary Action: Thomas Müntzer's *Sermon to the Princes*," in *A Companion to the Premodern Apocalypse*, ed. Michael Ryan (Leiden: Brill, 2016), 260–96.

[2] For case studies of contemporary apocalyptic groups who engage in violence, see Catherine Wessinger, ed., *Millennialism, Persecution, and Violence: Historical Cases* (Syracuse, NY: Syracuse University Press, 2000); and Mark Juergensmeyer, *Terror in the Mind of God: The Global Rise of Religious Violence*, 4th ed. (Oakland, CA: University of California Press, 2017), 17–146.

FEAR OF APOCALYPTIC VIOLENCE

According to Bernard McGinn, a leading scholar of religious thought in the Middle Ages, the "apocalyptic worldview is inherently violent."[3] He qualifies this claim by noting that apocalyptic belief does not *always* lead to violence.[4] But he does emphasize the salient role of violence in ancient apocalyptic texts. On this particular point, there is truth to his claim. Readers of apocalyptic literature do not have to search long to find violent imagery. Revelation 9:15, for instance, speaks of four angels of death set loose "to kill a third of humankind" (see Figure 7.1).[5] Another passage describes in gruesome detail the fate of the wicked and idolatrous: "Those who worship the beast ... will also drink the wine of God's wrath, poured unmixed into the cup of his anger, and they will be tormented with fire and sulfur.... And the smoke of their torment goes up forever and ever" (Revelation 14:9–11). Such vivid accounts of violence appear frequently in Jewish and Christian apocalyptic texts.

Interestingly, these texts rarely call on believers to engage in violence. That responsibility almost always lies with God, who enacts vengeance on the enemies of the righteous. At the same time that apocalyptic thought calls on believers to refrain from violence and accept martyrdom in the face of persecution (e.g., Revelation 2:10, 20:4), it celebrates God's use of violence against the wicked. So in Jewish and Christian apocalyptic thought, violence occupies an ambiguous role not free from danger.[6] Even if an apocalyptic text explicitly cautions against engaging in violence, its celebrations of divine wrath can motivate some to see themselves as agents chosen to inflict punishment on the wicked – especially when God tarries.

Beyond its violent imagery, apocalyptic texts portray a world divided between good and evil. Eternal peace and salvation await the righteous, while suffering and punishment await the wicked. Such a mindset can encourage the demonization of outsiders and weaken prohibitions on violence against them. Indeed, many who carry out genocide and religious violence see their victims as irredeemably evil and less than human.[7] Apocalyptic thought, with its dichotomous view of the world, seems to promote a mindset prone to violence.[8]

---

[3] McGinn, "Apocalypticism and Violence," 209.
[4] McGinn, "Apocalypticism and Violence," 210.
[5] New Revised Standard Version. All subsequent biblical quotes come from this version.
[6] Amanat and Collins, "Introduction," in *Apocalypse and Violence*, ii.
[7] See Ervin Staub, *The Roots of Evil: The Origins of Genocide and Other Group Violence* (New York: Cambridge University Press, 1989); and Juergensmeyer, *Terror in the Mind of God*, 213–21.
[8] Jones, *Blood that Cries Out from the Earth*, 40–45.

FIGURE 7.1 Angels of death from Revelation 9
Engraving from sixteenth century by Jean Duvet[9]

Because of their celebrations of violence, apocalyptic texts can appear out of place in religious traditions that elsewhere emphasize peace. The book of Revelation almost didn't make it into the Christian canon – many early lists of

---

[9] This image is in the public domain and available on the National Gallery of Art's website at the following link: www.nga.gov/collection/art-object-page.33614.html.

the canon left it off[10] – and some believe Christianity would have been better off without it. John Dominic Crossan takes that view due to worries over Revelation's incompatibility with the gospel message of peace, nonviolence, and forgiveness. The book's "pornography of violence" and portrayal of Christ unleashing vengeance on his enemies horrifies Crossan. "To turn Jesus into a divine warrior," he writes, "allows once again – but now terminally in the last book of the Bible – the normalcy of human civilization's violent injustice to subsume the radicality of God's nonviolent justice."[11] According to this view, the apocalyptic text of Revelation subverts Christianity's core message.[12]

These risks, of course, extend beyond just the religious traditions that gave birth to apocalyptic thought. Nonbelievers also draw on apocalyptic ideas and use them to advance political ends. This development is especially worrying for critics of apocalyptic thought. Arthur Mendel notes that, though "the world could afford the fantasy of Apocalypse" in the past, it no longer is tolerable in a nuclear age where its influence could have cataclysmic results.[13] In his view, apocalyptic thought anticipates total destruction and risks becoming a self-fulfilling prophecy. Similarly, John Hall calls the migration of apocalyptic ideas from the religious to the secular realm an "ominous development."[14] Apocalyptic thought, he argues, makes violence sacred. As a result, "the sacred violence of the warring apocalypse became grafted onto secular politics and social movements."[15] So according to some, apocalyptic thought's continued influence in politics today poses grave risks – perhaps even an existential threat.

Apocalyptic thought has no shortage of critics and it is easy to see why. Its visions of utopia appear side by side with gruesome images of violence and scenes of mass destruction. These features suggest to many that apocalyptic thought is inherently violent and should have no place in religion or politics.

---

[10] Elaine Pagels, *Revelations: Visions, Prophecy, and Politics in the Book of Revelation* (New York: Viking, 2012), 160–61.

[11] John Dominic Crossan, *God and Empire: Jesus against Rome, Then and Now* (San Francisco: HarperCollins Publishers, 2007), 234.

[12] For an overview of how theologians and biblical scholars grapple with the challenge posed by Revelation's vivid descriptions of violence, see Rebecca Skaggs and Thomas Doyle, "Violence in the Apocalypse of John," *Currents in Biblical Research* 5, no. 2 (2007): 220–34.

[13] Arthur Mendel, *Vision and Violence* (Ann Arbor, MI: University of Michigan Press, 1992), 1.

[14] John Hall, *Apocalypse: From Antiquity to the Empire of Modernity* (Malden, MA: Polity, 2009), 108.

[15] Hall, *Apocalypse*, 131.

COEXISTING WITH APOCALYPTIC BELIEF

Religiously motivated violence grabs people's attention. Sometimes the means employed – crashing planes into building or beheading victims – are spectacular. Yet even if the means are more mundane, there still is something shocking about religious beliefs that push people to violence. It is easier to understand violence prompted by greed, lust, or revenge. These are emotions we all experience to some degree and can identify with. But killing someone over a 2,000-year-old apocalyptic prophecy? That is harder to understand – and thus an object of curiosity. When religious and apocalyptic beliefs motivate violence, it's difficult to look away. Because such violence receives outsized attention, it can seem more pervasive than it is.

In the vast majority of cases, of course, apocalyptic belief never turns violent. The widespread nature of such belief reminds us of that point. Polling finds that over a third of Americans believe Christ's Second Coming will occur before 2050.[16] So in the United States alone, tens of millions of people hold apocalyptic beliefs, and there are even more worldwide. Almost all of them coexist peacefully with their neighbors. Only in an incredibly small number of cases does apocalyptic belief spark violence. For this reason, many scholars of apocalyptic thought reject the view that it is inherently violent.[17]

That conclusion stands in tension with views common to political theory. Many modern thinkers have a strong suspicion of religious belief that divides the world between good and evil – which apocalyptic thought often does – due to worries that it breeds discord and violence. As Jean-Jacques Rousseau writes, "It is impossible to live in peace with people one believes are damned."[18] Recent work on the history of toleration, however, gives us reason to question this assumption.

In her study *Mere Civility*, Teresa Bejan examines the thought of Roger Williams, who in founding Rhode Island embarked on one of the most radical experiments in religious toleration the world had seen. His support of religious freedom for even the most despised sects at the time did not derive, as one

---

[16] Pew Research Center, "Life in 2050: Amazing Science, Familiar Threats: Public Sees a Future Full of Promise and Peril," June 22, 2010, www.pewresearch.org/wp-content/uploads/sites/4/legacy-pdf/625.pdf, 14.

[17] See, e.g., Rinehart, *Apocalyptic Faith and Political Violence*, 4; and Flannery, *Understanding Apocalyptic Terrorism*, 59.

[18] Jean-Jacques Rousseau, *On the Social Contract*, in *The Major Political Writings of Jean-Jacques Rousseau*, trans. and ed. John Scott (Chicago: University of Chicago Press, 2012), IV.8: 271. For the persistence of this idea in contemporary political theory, see Teresa Bejan, *Mere Civility: Disagreement and the Limits of Toleration* (Cambridge, MA: Harvard University Press, 2017), 153–57.

might assume, from a respect for all faiths. As Bejan stresses, Williams held fervent religious and apocalyptic beliefs that led him to see most of his neighbors as damned – and he wasn't afraid to tell them so. It was *because of*, not in spite of, these convictions that he embraced a conception of religious liberty far more expansive than his contemporaries did.[19]

For Williams, religious freedom was key for ensuring that individuals were at liberty to evangelize their faith. As he was keen to point out, those who are religious opponents today could become members of the body of Christ tomorrow.[20] The neighbor who appears damned is not necessarily irredeemable. The way to bring them into the church is to evangelize to them rather than employ the state to persecute them – a step that inevitably would corrupt the church in Williams's mind. The Rhode Island experiment and its continuation in the United States today remind us that strongly held religious beliefs, including apocalyptic ones, do not guarantee violence. Those anxiously awaiting the end may see the world as sharply divided between the righteous and the damned, and even find the latter deeply disagreeable, while still coexisting with them in conditions free from violence.[21]

In sum, apocalyptic belief, like religious belief generally, proves too diverse to broadly characterize as violent.[22] That characterization lacks nuance and fails to account for the simple fact that many hold apocalyptic beliefs without ever engaging in violence. To understand apocalyptic thought's relation to violence, it is necessary to identify more precisely what forms of it are linked to violence. We turn to that question next.

WHAT MAKES UTOPIAN HOPE DANGEROUS

Though there is often unease with apocalyptic belief's dichotomous view of the world, this feature alone is insufficient to spark violence. After all, people can see the world as divided between good and evil, while at the same time placing all responsibility on God to bring about the utopia promised.

---

[19] Bejan, *Mere Civility*, 50–81.
[20] Williams writes: "[H]e that is a *Briar*, that is, a *Jew*, a *Turke*, a *Pagan*, an *Anti-Christian* to day, may be (when the Word of the *Lord* runs freely) a member of *Jesus Christ* to morrow cut out of the wilde *Olive*, and planted into the true." See Williams, *The Bloudy Tenent of Persecution*, in *The Complete Writings of Roger Williams*, vol. 3 (Eugene, OR: Wipf and Stock Publishers, 2007), 95.
[21] Bejan, *Mere Civility*, esp. 80.
[22] For more on this point as it regards religion generally, see William Cavanagh, *The Myth of Religious Violence: Secular Ideology and the Roots of Modern Conflict* (New York: Oxford University Press, 2009); and Karen Armstrong, *Fields of Blood: Religion and the History of Violence* (New York: Knopf, 2014).

According to this view, one patiently waits for God to act. To inspire violence, apocalyptic thought needs something more – belief that the elect have an active role to play in realizing God's kingdom and should do so by any means necessary, including force.

Frances Flannery emphasizes this point in her study of apocalyptic groups that engage in terrorism. She makes a distinction between what she calls "passive" and "active eschatology," and describes the latter as "one of the clearest indicators that a group will be violent."[23] Passive eschatology counsels patience while waiting for divine intervention to bring about the ideal society, whereas active eschatology calls on believers to eliminate evil and realize the ideal society through their own efforts.[24] The latter mindset justifies action normally prohibited – like violence against others – since it serves the critical role of realizing the ideal.

This link between active eschatology and terrorism identified by Flannery highlights a key point: the same aspect of apocalyptic thought that makes it appealing for politics also makes it dangerous. Chapter 2 noted that apocalyptic thought's political appeal partly lies in offering an apparent solution to a challenge that plagues ideal theory. In response to the worry that a truly ideal society seems beyond reach, cataclysmic apocalyptic thought points to an imminent crisis as the vehicle to finally realize the ideal. This mindset has advantages for politics because of the urgency it creates – *now* is the time for bold action to take advantage of the unique opportunity at hand. If that idea gains hold, it can become a powerful motivating force in politics. But this strategy comes with shortcomings. Due to future uncertainty, those predicting utopia and calling for violence to realize it cannot give plausible grounds to back up their claims.

That limitation is good reason to be wary of justifications for violence that appeal to apocalyptic thought. Such appeals call for *certain* bloodshed in the hope of attaining a highly *uncertain* utopia. If there were compelling evidence that violent action would bring about utopia, then one could make a strong case for violence. But in reality, there never is plausible evidence that violence will lead to utopia. The history of political violence motivated by apocalyptic belief suggests far less hopeful outcomes. At its worst, apocalyptic violence results in senseless bloodshed, like when thousands of peasants died heeding Müntzer's call to realize God's kingdom through revolutionary action.[25] At its best, it helps improve society while leaving it deeply flawed, like when

---

[23] Flannery, *Understanding Apocalyptic Terrorism*, 133.
[24] Flannery, *Understanding Apocalyptic Terrorism*, 65–67.
[25] See especially Riedl, "Apocalyptic Violence and Revolutionary Action."

apocalyptic belief motivated Union soldiers during the American Civil War as they marched through the South and liberated slaves.[26]

Even in these best-case scenarios, utopian hope by itself appears insufficient to justify violence. Calls for violence in pursuit of utopia are always dubious, considering that *no* action has yet to succeed in bringing about the ideal. Given the horrors of violence, it is wise to demand that justifications for it, at the very least, appeal to more certain and attainable ends than utopia (e.g., ending a concrete injustice like slavery). We can formulate this principle as follows:

> *Principle against utopian violence:* Given deep uncertainty over the future, which makes it impossible to identify the ideal society with confidence, calls to engage in violence cannot be justified on the grounds that it will help realize utopia. Such an uncertain good cannot justify the evils of violence.

This principle does not demand pacifism. It leaves open the possibility that violence can be justified when there are plausible grounds to believe that it will achieve worthy ends (e.g., stopping an unjust aggressor from inflicting civilian casualties).[27] The principle does, however, treat all appeals to utopian goals as insufficient to justify violence.

So far we have focused on utopian hope's violent potential in the context of apocalyptic thought, but the principle against utopian violence highlights that this risk applies to ideal theory generally. What makes apocalyptic thought dangerous – a commitment to bringing about the ideal society through whatever means necessary – also can render other forms of ideal theory dangerous. Indeed, the danger of mixing utopian aspirations with politics is a recurring concern in political thought, expressed by various thinkers who embrace the principle against utopian violence or something close to it.

Atrocities during the twentieth century in particular prompted critiques of utopian political projects. Referencing the dangers embodied by the politics of Lenin, Trotsky, Mao, and Pol Pot, Isaiah Berlin writes: "[I]f one really believes that [a final] solution is possible, then surely no cost would be too high to obtain it: to make mankind just and happy and creative and harmonious for

---

[26] See Terrie Dopp Aamodt, *Righteous Armies, Holy Cause: Apocalyptic Imagery and the Civil War* (Macon, GA: Mercer University Press, 2002), 46–49, 94–99.

[27] One objection to violence is its unpredictability due to the unintended consequences it tends to unleash. Some categorically reject violence for that reason. See Karuna Mantena, "Another Realism: The Politics of Gandhian Nonviolence," *American Political Science Review* 106, no. 2 (2012): 455–70. My argument does not rest on the claim that violence can never be justified, but those who take that stronger view have all the more reason to reject violence in pursuit of utopia.

ever – what could be too high a price for that?"[28] Though he understands the rationale behind this approach, the "search for perfection" ultimately strikes Berlin as "a recipe for bloodshed."[29]

Karl Popper expresses similar concerns. In his view, utopian projects inevitably come with epistemic uncertainty over how to achieve them, which makes violence appealing as a tool to overcome uncertainty and ensure agreement on a common political goal. He writes:

> [T]he Utopian method, which chooses an ideal state of society as the aim which all our political actions should serve, is likely to produce violence .... [D]ifferences of opinion concerning what the ideal state should be like cannot always be smoothed out by the method of argument. They will at least partly have the character of religious differences. And there can hardly be tolerance between these different Utopian religions. Utopian aims are designed to serve as a basis for rational political action and discussion, and such action appears to be possible only if the aim is definitely decided upon. Thus the Utopianist must win over, or else crush, his Utopianist competitors who do not share his own Utopian aims and who do not profess his own Utopianist religion.[30]

This remark comes well before the flurry of interest in ideal theory sparked by John Rawls's *Theory of Justice*. Popper makes a point often absent from current debates, which this study has explored: utopian or ideal theorizing resembles religious belief in its inability to provide plausible grounds for the ideal it champions. He worries that, faced with this dilemma, utopian theory may turn to violence to mobilize the collective action needed to realize its ambitions.

Some may object to these worries and argue that future uncertainty justifies violence in pursuit of utopia. Since we cannot be sure what the future holds, who can say that a particular utopian project will fail? And given that uncertainty, who has the right to stand in the way of sincere attempts to not just theorize about utopia but also realize it? The problem, though, is that realizing a particular ideal on a societal scale usually requires much of society to strive for it – including those with dramatically different utopian hopes (or none at all). Given future uncertainty, people lack compelling reason to believe that any proposed ideal accurately captures utopia. Even if no one can show that a proposed ideal is mistaken, that is different from offering plausible grounds to believe in it. As a result, deep divisions over the ideal are

---

[28] Isaiah Berlin, "The Pursuit of the Ideal," in *The Crooked Timber of Humanity*, ed. Henry Hardy (Princeton, NJ: Princeton University Press, 2013), 15–16.
[29] Berlin, "The Pursuit of the Ideal," 19.
[30] Karl Popper, "Utopia and Violence," in *Conjectures and Refutations: The Growth of Scientific Knowledge* (New York: Routledge, 2002), 483.

likely. Perhaps violence could overcome some divisions by compelling individuals to pursue the same ideal, but that course of action has obvious downsides. It violates the principle against utopian violence and inflicts immense costs on society for a highly uncertain goal.

As critics of apocalyptic thought and ideal theory point out, utopian hope comes with real dangers. If hope in utopia pushes us to realize it at all costs, it poses severe harms without the assurance that the ideal will ever come. That raises the question: Can we preserve utopian hope and its benefits while avoiding its more destructive elements? The following section looks at how religious traditions grappling with apocalyptic thought's explosive nature have tried to answer that question.

A REMEDY FROM WITHIN THE APOCALYPTIC TRADITION

In light of the concerns raised earlier, the apocalyptic tradition seems limited in what it can offer ideal theory. By pointing to crisis as the way to utopia, apocalyptic thought proves appealing to ideal theorists looking to explain how an ideal can be both utopian and feasible. This appeal, though, turns out to be illusory. Apocalyptic thought tries to justify dramatic political action, even violence, as necessary to realize utopia, but ultimately cannot provide compelling reasons for that claim. Given that defect, it may seem that ideal theorists would be better off ignoring apocalyptic thought altogether.

It's true that apocalyptic thought fails to provide an understanding of the ideal suited to guide collective action for a society. *No form of ideal theory succeeds in that regard.* The apocalyptic tradition suffers from a limitation common to all forms of ideal theory. That limitation should come as no surprise and doesn't preclude the apocalyptic tradition as a potential source of wisdom. In fact, dangers within this tradition have spurred reflection on how to contain them, resulting in strategies that offer insights on how to preserve utopian hope while avoiding its pitfalls.

Notably, one finds in Jewish and Christian thought strands of eschatology that take a humble approach to utopian hope, which proves particularly suited to guard against the dangers of apocalyptic thought. Three core principles define this approach:

(1) embrace utopian hope;
(2) accept that humans are largely ignorant of the ideal and how to bring it about; and
(3) recognize the dangers of trying to force the ideal into existence.

With these principles, Jewish and Christian thought put forward a strategy that gives space for utopian hope but remains alert to its hazards. This strategy avoids having to abandon utopian hope because it approaches such hope with an attitude of epistemic humility.

Let's look first at the Jewish tradition, for which apocalyptic belief and utopian hope are central. Maimonides's Thirteen Principles, a popular summation of the Jewish faith, highlight this point. His final two principles state:

(12) I believe with full faith in the coming of the Messiah, and, though he tarry, I anticipate him, nonetheless, on every day, when he may come.
(13) I believe with full faith that there will be a resurrection of the dead at the time that the Creator, may His name be blessed, wills it.[31]

The Jewish tradition has long wrestled with how to understand these apocalyptic expectations. In particular, outbursts of messianic enthusiasm throughout Jewish history have made this task all the more urgent.

Two of the most famous examples are the revolt against Rome led by Simon bar Kokhba and the movement inspired by Sabbatai Zevi. In both cases, apocalyptic hopes ended in utter disaster. Heralded as the messiah, Bar Kokhba initially succeeded in achieving a short period of Jewish self-rule beginning in 132 C.E. Rome, however, struck back and within a few years destroyed Jerusalem, killed thousands of its inhabitants – including Bar Kokhba – and sent those Jews who survived into exile.[32] The movement led by Sabbatai also met a sad end. This self-proclaimed messiah attracted followers across Europe, Africa, and the Middle East as apocalyptic expectations reached a fever pitch in the year 1666. But rather than restore Israel as predicted, Sabbatai eventually would deny his faith and convert to Islam.[33]

Such disappointments have left a deep impact on Jewish eschatology.[34] Drawing on teachings from the Talmud and Midrash, some rabbis argue that

---

[31] The principles appear here in their shortened, liturgical form and come from Steven Schwarzschild, "On Jewish Eschatology," in *The Pursuit of the Ideal: Jewish Writings of Steven Schwarzschild*, ed. Menachem Kellner (Albany, NY: State University of New York Press, 1990), 209. For their original formulation, see Moses Maimonides, "Helek: Sanhedrin, Chapter Ten," in *A Maimonides Reader*, ed. Isadore Twersky (Springdale, NJ: Behrman House, 1972), 422.
[32] See Menahem Mor, *The Second Jewish Revolt: The Bar Kokhba War, 132–136 CE* (Leiden: Brill, 2016).
[33] See Gershom Scholem, *Sabbatai Sevi: The Mystical Messiah, 1626–1676*, trans. R. J. Zwi Werblowsky (Princeton, NJ: Princeton University Press, 1973).
[34] David Novak, "Jewish Eschatology," in *The Oxford Handbook of Eschatology*, ed. Jerry Walls (New York: Oxford University Press, 2008), 125–26.

there is a divine injunction against trying to force the end.³⁵ This warning captures the wariness in Jewish thought toward any human projects that aspire to realize apocalyptic hopes.

Isaac Bashevis Singer sums up this attitude at the end of *Satan in Goray*, his fictional account of Sabbatai Zevi. After detailing the many hopes that Sabbatai dashed, Singer closes with the moral of the story: "Let none attempt to force the Lord: To end our pain within the world: The Messiah will come in God's own time: And free men of Despair and crime: Then death will put away his sword: And Satan die abjured, abhorred."³⁶ So the lesson of Sabbatai's failure is not that we should abandon utopian hope. Instead, it teaches the importance of learning how to maintain such hope while also recognizing that its aims lie beyond our power.

An even more radical approach within Jewish thought for avoiding the danger of forcing the end is found in the idea of the eternal delay of the Messiah's return. According to this view, the Messiah is always coming and believers should continually anticipate his arrival, but his return remains forever located in future time. Because the arrival of God's kingdom exists perpetually in the *future*, there is no reason to believe that one can force its manifestation in the *present*. This feature of God's kingdom means that one should continually strive for it, free from the hubris that one can ever attain it. Theologian Steven Schwarzschild defends this understanding of Jewish eschatology and explains its ethical implications: "[S]ince humanity is to strive to imitate God ... and since they are to undertake these efforts in this world, the ultimate goal of ethics is to establish what is then called 'the (Messianic) kingdom of God' on earth. This is, of course, an infinite goal, infinitely ... to be approached."³⁷ Utopian hope – even when its aim is eternally delayed – gives meaning to partial steps toward the ideal, while cautioning against the presumption that we can fully achieve it.

Similar strategies appear in Christianity, which like Judaism has a long history of contending with apocalyptic hopes coming to naught.³⁸ Various passages from scripture lend support to a humble approach to utopian hope, such as the reminder that only God knows when he will bring about his kingdom. In the so-called Little Apocalypse from the Gospels, Jesus warns

---

[35] Aviezer Ravitzky, *Messianism, Zionism, and Jewish Religious Radicalism*, trans. Michael Swirsky and Jonathan Chipman (Chicago: Chicago University Press, 1996), 211–34.
[36] Isaac Bashevis Singer, *Satan in Goray* (New York: Avon Books, 1963), 160.
[37] Schwarzschild, "On Jewish Eschatology," 218.
[38] See Cohn, *The Pursuit of the Millennium*; and Paul Boyer, *When Time Shall Be No More: Prophecy Belief in Modern American Culture* (Cambridge, MA: Harvard University Press, 1992).

his disciples of wars, political upheaval, and persecution that will precede the coming of the Messiah. As to when this hope will be fulfilled, he cannot say: "But about the day or hour no one knows, neither the angels in heaven, nor the Son, but only the Father" (Mark 13:32). The only guidance he can give is "keep awake – for you do not know when the master of the house will come, in the evening, or at midnight, or at cockcrow, or at dawn" (Mark 13:35). By denying that anyone but God knows when his kingdom will arrive, these verses undermine all human claims about being on the verge of realizing utopia.

Augustine is the most influential Christian theologian in developing this line of thought. He stresses a sharp break between the earthly and heavenly kingdoms, and cautions against trying to calculate when God's ideal kingdom will come or looking for signs of it in the world.[39] One of his foremost interpreters, R. A. Markus, explains how this understanding of eschatology shapes views on hope and progress: "Christian hope deflates all ideologies and utopias: in their place it sets provisional goals, to be realised piecemeal, and to be kept flexible and perpetually subject to revision and renewal."[40] Augustine's interpretation of eschatology does not jettison hope for an ideal future, but rather counsels skepticism toward anyone who purports to have a plan for achieving it.

As these examples from Judaism and Christianity illustrate, some of the strongest critics of apocalyptic thought's violent manifestations come from voices that still identify with and operate within this tradition of thought. Because of this connection, they have a deep familiarity with the tradition and intimate understanding of its weaknesses. Some traditions may be so flawed that they are not worth preserving, but that is not the conclusion of theologians like Augustine and Schwarzschild. For they also see certain strengths in the apocalyptic tradition. Rather than scrap it, they focus on crafting the most compelling interpretation of apocalyptic thought – one that overcomes its most problematic features.[41]

On this goal, they have had some success. Both Jewish and Christian thought developed understandings of eschatology that encourage epistemic humility and warn against the hubris of believing that human agency can

---

[39] Augustine, *City of God*, trans. Henry Bettenson (New York: Penguin Books, 1984), esp. XX.7, XX.9, XXII.30.
[40] R. A. Markus, *Saeculum: History and Society in the Theology of St Augustine* (New York: Cambridge University Press, 1970), 171–72.
[41] For more on the role and value of criticism within rather than wholly outside a tradition, see Michael Walzer, *Interpretation and Social Criticism* (Cambridge, MA: Harvard University Press, 1987); and *The Company of Critics: Social Criticism and Political Commitment in the Twentieth Century* (New York: Basic Books, 1988).

force the arrival of utopia. Obviously, that humble approach has not always prevailed – there is no shortage of apocalyptic sects that have pursued utopia, sometimes through violence. Importantly, though, that upheaval gave way to strategies for containing it. These strategies involve, at their core, recognizing the deep uncertainty that plagues any human effort to identify the ideal and bring it about. Given that uncertainty, they take a wary view toward justifications for violence that appeal to utopian goals. By pairing utopian hope with epistemic humility, the apocalyptic tradition offers an approach to ideal theory that tempers its ambitions and keeps its most dangerous aspects in check.

UTOPIAN HOPE WITH EPISTEMIC HUMILITY

If not approached with epistemic humility, utopian hope can have violent and destructive consequences. Both the Jewish and Christian traditions understand this point given their histories, and in response have developed accounts of utopian hope to guard against its dangers. That is a laudable achievement, but some may ask what utopian hope looks like in practice when we abandon claims to knowledge regarding the object of such hope. If we concede that we cannot identify the ideal with any confidence, what if anything is left of utopian hope?

The humble approach defended here does not render utopian hope a wholly empty concept. Though a complete picture of the ideal is beyond human knowledge, our ability to identify with greater confidence certain practices that are clearly unjust provides a sense of what the ideal is *not*. One finds traces of this intuition in apocalyptic literature, which frequently condemns present injustices and emphasizes that they have no place in the ideal to come. For instance, the book of Revelation rails against the cruelty, greed, and human bondage of the Roman Empire (Revelation 18). A negative understanding of the ideal, which excludes certain injustices from it, provides a basis for critiquing the present and cultivating an attitude never content with its imperfections. Despite its vagueness and incompleteness, this vision still represents a radical departure from the entrenched injustice of the present – and, as such, a source of hope for those who choose to embrace it.

Inevitably, embracing utopian hope will prompt some to use their imagination to further fill in their vision of the ideal. There is nothing necessarily wrong with such flights of the imagination. They have the potential to inspire new ideas and experiments within society that prove beneficial. But it is important to always remember the tentative nature of these visions, given the epistemic limitations inherent to ideal theorizing. Appreciating that fact should keep us humble. Humility teaches us to coexist with other conceptions of utopian hope that we may not fully understand and to remain open to learning from them. That openness to revision, and refusal to accept any particular vision of utopia as the final word, is what a world of deep uncertainty ultimately demands of ideal theory and utopian hope.

Conclusion

Encounters with apocalyptic thought often obscure the richness of this tradition. Many have a difficult time getting past the strange and bizarre impression that apocalyptic belief leaves them with. It is as if beliefs in the rapture, Armageddon, the Last Judgment, and the like spring from an alien mindset that outsiders cannot access. At the same time, the apocalypse has become mundane. Portrayals of global catastrophe – whether through nuclear war, climate change, asteroid impact, or deadly pandemic – have proliferated in popular culture. Apocalypse is understood simply as catastrophe, and this flattened conception now shows up everywhere.

These encounters leave us with an incomplete picture of apocalyptic thought, one that makes it difficult to grasp its nuances and persistent role in political life. To overcome that barrier, this study looks at apocalyptic thought from a different perspective – the perspective of thinkers with secular conceptions of politics. Machiavelli, Hobbes, and Engels all reject apocalyptic hopes that God will soon intervene to perfect society, so one might expect these theorists to dismiss apocalyptic thought. Yet they opt for a different approach. Recognizing the power of apocalyptic thought, they engage with it in their political writings.

By examining what draws these thinkers to apocalyptic thought, we gain insight into its enduring appeal and impact on political philosophy. Though apocalyptic thought's catastrophic imagery gets all the attention, its emphasis on utopian hope is just as central to it – if not more so. Because of its strategies for cultivating and preserving utopian hope, the apocalyptic tradition remains a resource for those interested in fostering such hope today.

THREE TAKEAWAYS

By taking a closer look at secular apocalyptic thought, this book arrives at three main conclusions. They concern how to study apocalyptic thought, the source of its political appeal, and its lessons for political philosophy today. Let's briefly review each of these conclusions.

(1) *The study of secular apocalyptic thought would place itself on firmer ground by focusing on cases where secular thinkers explicitly reference religious apocalyptic texts, figures, or concepts.* This methodological recommendation comes in response to how loosely the term apocalypse is used, not just in popular culture, but also in academic research. Originally in the Jewish and Christian traditions, apocalypse referred to a divine revelation. So in the Bible, apocalyptic literature recounts a revelation, which in many cases explores the relation between crisis and utopia in God's plan for the end of time. Today apocalypse has taken the expansive meaning of referring to any catastrophe. Influenced by this trend, researchers often conclude that any discussion of catastrophe counts as evidence that it was influenced by religious apocalyptic thought. As a result, they see religious influences where the evidence for them is questionable, since catastrophic imagery and language also can come from nonreligious sources (e.g., accounts of war). An additional factor exacerbates this methodological problem: some use the label apocalyptic as a rhetorical weapon against ideologies and beliefs they find irrational and bizarre. To guard against drawing illusory connections in the history of ideas, I suggest more rigorous standards for identifying secular apocalyptic thought. Specifically, there should be evidence of secular thinkers explicitly referencing and drawing on religious apocalyptic thought.

(2) *Apocalyptic thought's political appeal partly lies in offering resources to navigate persistent challenges in ideal theory.* Ideal theory tackles the task of identifying the most just society, often with the aim of providing a goal to guide collective action. This aspiration to be a normative guide leaves ideal theory with a challenge: outlining a goal that is utopian *and* feasible. Its vision of the ideal society needs to be feasible, for it makes little sense to dedicate valuable resources to striving after a goal that isn't even attainable. Its goal also needs to be utopian so that it possesses sufficient moral appeal to justify the sacrifices needed to attain it. Unfortunately, a more utopian ideal tends to be less feasible, and vice versa. What I call *cataclysmic apocalyptic thought* provides an apparent solution to this catch-22: it embraces a thoroughly utopian ideal, seemingly out of reach, and declares it feasible by pointing to a coming crisis as the path to attain it. According to this view, crisis promises to open up possibilities previously closed off and offers a rare opportunity to make the ideal a reality. Apocalyptic thought thus proves appealing for those who want to realize the ideal and not merely theorize about it.

(3) *Ideal theory and apocalyptic thought both rest on faith and are best suited to be sources of utopian hope, not guides for collective action by a society.*

Apocalyptic thought sets forth an ideal and theorizes a path to it. Such thought thus has similarities to ideal theory that political philosophy often overlooks. Most notably, John Rawls sees the two as fundamentally distinct. In his view, ideal theory presents an ideal that individuals in a pluralistic society have reason to accept and collectively strive for, which religious belief cannot offer. That view runs into problems, though, because it fails to account for how future uncertainty undermines ideal theory's claims. Even if its proposed ideal seems morally appealing, there is no reason to be confident that it will retain its appeal under radically different future conditions that we cannot predict. Unable to provide plausible grounds for the ideal it proposes, ideal theory ultimately rests on faith. Despite this limitation, ideal theory can persist as a source of utopian hope, which gives meaning to imperfect efforts to advance justice by portraying them as steps toward the ideal. Such hope comes with risks, since it can motivate efforts to bring about utopia by any means possible – including violence. One strategy to reduce this risk, found in Jewish and Christian thought, embraces utopian hope while stressing human ignorance of the ideal and how to achieve it. Sensitive to our epistemic limitations, this strategy warns against believing that we can identify the ideal and a path to it. By pairing utopian hope with epistemic humility, religious traditions offer potential wisdom for ideal theory.

REVISITING THE PARABLE OF HILLSIDE

The parable of Hillside at the start of this study highlights how Machiavelli, Hobbes, and Engels respond to apocalyptic thought and its appeal, while also hinting at potential drawbacks in each of their approaches. Though Machiavelli recognizes the power of apocalyptic hope in politics, he resists the temptation to embrace it. An obstacle stands in his way of taking that leap: he simply cannot fathom a lasting utopia ever emerging due to the constant flux and inevitable decay that characterize politics. Hobbes opts for a different strategy, which focuses on tempering apocalyptic ideals. He makes the case that the Christian understanding of utopia – the kingdom of God – manifests itself on earth as the Leviathan state, despite its many imperfections in that form. Engels is the most unapologetic in his embrace of apocalyptic thought and utopian hope. He praises Thomas Müntzer's apocalyptic vision for politics while transforming his ideal of the kingdom of God into a secular goal to strive for.

None of these approaches prove well suited to sustain utopian hope. That is most obvious in the case of Machiavelli, who rejects such hope to begin with. Hobbes does hang on to a form of utopian hope, but one so anemic that it is hard to imagine its having much appeal for those yearning for utopia. He coopts the apocalyptic ideal of the kingdom of God and equates it with the deeply imperfect state outlined in *Leviathan*, all in an effort to warn against political projects that strive for perfection and cause continual upheaval. Instead of embracing the most ambitious forms of utopian hope, Hobbes wants his readers to set their sights lower. On its face, Engels's approach seems most conducive for preserving utopian hope. What attracts him to apocalyptic thought – its idea that crisis opens the way to utopia – proves appealing as a potential solution to challenges inherent in ideal theory. That solution, though, turns out to be illusory. Utopian hope that looks to realize its aims through crisis sets itself up for disappointment. No one can give plausible grounds that a particular crisis will actually deliver utopia. So though Engels embraces utopian hope, his understanding of it proves difficult to sustain in a world filled with uncertainty.

Each thinker's engagement with the apocalyptic tradition has its shortcomings, yet other approaches prove more promising for sustaining utopian hope. In particular, Jewish and Christian theologians struggling with the explosive potential of apocalyptic thought came to develop strategies that both limit its dangers and preserve utopian hope. The relevance of these strategies to current debates over ideal theory reminds us not to dismiss or ignore the apocalyptic tradition, despite its odd and bizarre features. Prominent figures throughout the history of political thought have taken a keen interest in the apocalyptic tradition. As is hopefully now clear, close study of this tradition, in all its richness, still has the potential today to offer novel perspectives and insights into challenges common to political life.

A CLOSING PARABLE

Just as it began, this study ends with a parable. It comes from the Christian apocalyptic tradition, specifically Matthew 25:31–46. In the passage, Jesus explains the fate of the sheep (righteous) and the goats (unrighteous) at the end of time. The Son of Man returns, takes his place on the throne, and welcomes the sheep into his kingdom (see Figure C.1). He proceeds to explain why they have been blessed and chosen to enter his kingdom: "I was hungry and you gave me food, I was thirsty and you gave me something to drink, I was a stranger and you welcomed me, I was naked and you gave me clothing, I was sick and you took care of me, I was in prison and you visited me" (Matthew 25:35–36). His explanation confuses the sheep. They cannot remember ever serving the king in these ways. With a simple response, the king dispels their confusion: "Truly I tell you, just as you did it to one of the least of these who are

FIGURE C.1 Separation of the sheep and the goats
Byzantine mosaic from the early sixth century[1]

members of my family, you did it to me" (Matthew 25:40).[2] Perhaps no other verse better sums up the gospel message.

The parable of the sheep and the goats has generated a wide range of interpretations. Here I'd like to offer an interpretation not with the goal of supplanting others, but to highlight the parable's potential wisdom for ideal theory – specifically, its subtle reminder of the virtue found in epistemic humility. Consider the ignorance of the sheep. When the king thanks them, they are at a loss to explain how they served him. They have a woefully incomplete understanding of how their actions fit into the broader project of advancing God's kingdom. Moreover, the actions for which they are praised highlight their limitations. They feed the hungry, which suggests that hunger is still a problem. They take in the stranger, which suggests that lack of shelter is still a problem. And they visit the prisoner, which suggests that crime and the need for prisons are still problems. In short, the sheep fail to fully solve many of the social ills they encounter. Unable to realize utopia through their own

---

[1] This image is in the public domain and available on the Metropolitan Museum of Art's website at the following link: www.metmuseum.org/art/collection/search/466573.
[2] New Revised Standard Version.

efforts, they work for partial steps to alleviate suffering and remedy injustice. Despite the imperfect nature of their efforts, the parable makes clear that they still have reason to hold on to utopian hope.

For some ideal theorists, the sheep may seem like odd – even perverse – role models. Shouldn't we aim higher? Beyond just alleviating suffering, we must address the systemic injustices that cause it. That point is absolutely correct. But ideal theory often goes beyond identifying systemic injustices and proposing measures to fight them. It purports to outline a harmonious vision that eliminates injustice, and argues that this proposal should guide society. In reality, though, ideal theorists have no special knowledge of what the ideal society would look like. Too much about the future is unknown to make claims about utopia with confidence – or at least justified confidence. Realizing that fact is disappointing, to be sure. But it is far worse to presume that we have knowledge of the ideal and then attempt to bring it about by any means necessary. In a complex world, such hubris usually has unintended and regrettable consequences.

Given that danger, the sheep in their humility serve as an instructive model. With their questions to the king, they admit their epistemic limitations. As they stumble around in an uncertain world to advance justice, they cannot offer a detailed path to utopia and do not feign such knowledge. They are not, of course, completely ignorant of what actions are likely to be effective in advancing justice, at least in the short term. After all, they do have some success in feeding the hungry, providing shelter to the stranger, and comforting the imprisoned. So the lesson of the parable is not that good intentions are all that matter and questions of effectiveness are irrelevant. Research, experimentation, and planning all have an important role to play in helping ensure that good intentions are paired with – to the best of our knowledge – effective practices.

We can grant this point while still rejecting the loftier ambitions of ideal theory. For there is a fundamental difference between, on the one hand, weaving together a unified theory that aspires to wholly eliminate injustice and, on the other, more piecemeal efforts to improve institutions and practices as we gain a deeper understanding of injustices and their causes. The latter approach holds greater promise in an uncertain world that frustrates the long-term predictions of ideal theory. Recognition of our epistemic limitations ultimately recommends a humble approach to advancing justice – one that involves trial and error, small experiments that can be expanded if they are fortunate enough to succeed.

Though that approach departs from many prominent understandings of ideal theory, it leaves one aspect of it in place: utopian hope. At the same time that future uncertainty undermines the idea that we can identify utopia, it carves out space to believe in its possibility should we choose. Since so much about the future is uncertain, we are free to hope that it will be far better, no longer marred by the injustices of the present. Such hope, in short, can be as ambitious as our imagination allows.

APPENDIX

Argument against Ideal Theory's Plausibility

This study focuses on what I call *navigational ideal theory* due to its normative appeal. That variety of ideal theory seeks to outline the best and most just society with the potential of being realized at some future point. Chapter 6 presents an argument for why, regrettably, no defense of navigational ideal theory is plausible:

(1) Defenses of navigational ideal theory are plausible only if they show that the theory's principles would have normative force in the society it envisions.
(2) Showing that navigational ideal theory's principles would have normative force in the society it envisions requires reliably accurate predictions about science, technology, economics, and politics for the distant future.
(3) We cannot make reliably accurate predictions about science, technology, economics, and politics for the distant future.
(4) So, by (2) and (3), we cannot show that navigational ideal theory's principles would have normative force in the society it envisions.
(5) So, by (1) and (4), no defense of navigational ideal theory is plausible.

Here I expand on that argument by considering and responding to potential objections.

OBJECTION 1: ARGUMENT DEPENDS ON AN IMPLAUSIBLE VIEW OF IDEAL THEORY

My definition of navigational ideal theory places no constraints on the time period relevant to the ideal theorist, implying that they must look indefinitely into the future when determining the most just society possible. Some will find this conception of ideal theory implausible because it makes impossible demands on political philosophers. No one can fathom what society could look like millennia from now. We therefore should understand ideal theory as proposing a goal for a more limited time horizon, which is often the case in practice. John Rawls, for instance, sets forth an ideal suitable for today's liberal democratic societies characterized by pluralism and moderate scarcity, wasting no time on futuristic scenarios. Ideal theorists typically offer a vision of the most just society possible with a medium-term time horizon in mind – one lasting a few decades, not millennia. According to this view, if ideal theory provides a medium-term goal, it is unfair to criticize it for failing to foresee further ahead.

This objection, though reasonable, fails for two reasons. First, it undermines a primary argument for ideal theory. Defenders of ideal theory argue that it provides a goal to guide action and avoid paths away from the most just possibility.[1] Ideal theory cannot fulfill that role, however, if it only offers a medium-term goal. The most just society possible in the next 25 years may look much different than the most just society possible in 250 years. The challenge of climate change illustrates this point. If we adopt a medium-term time horizon from the perspective of 1900, heavy reliance on fossil fuel seems compatible with the ideal society given industrialization's role in significantly reducing poverty and mortality rates. But if the time horizon is extended, that proposal becomes more problematic given the dangerous impacts on the climate that dependence on fossil fuels eventually causes.[2] In the long-term scenario, it is critical for ideal theory to consider questions related to climate justice, but they have less relevance in the medium-term scenario.[3] As this example shows, pursuing the most just society possible in the medium term can take us further from the most just society possible in the long term – an outcome at odds with ideal theory's purpose. To focus on

---

[1] A. John Simmons, "Ideal and Nonideal Theory," *Philosophy and Public Affairs* 38, no. 1 (2010): 5–36.

[2] Ideal theory, of course, does not require subordinating current interests entirely to those of future generations. Most accounts of ideal theory recognize the need to balance current and future interests. See, e.g., John Rawls, *A Theory of Justice*, rev. ed. (Cambridge, MA: Harvard University Press, 1999), 251–58; and *Justice as Fairness: A Restatement*, ed. Erin Kelly (Cambridge, MA: Harvard University Press, 2001), 159–60. The problem is that, given future uncertainty, ideal theory is not in a position to know what exactly justice will demand in future societies and thus the implications of those demands for how best to advance justice now.

[3] Notably, some see climate change as a blind spot for Rawls's ideal theory, which he first developed in the 1970s. See Stephen Gardiner, "Rawls and Climate Change: Does Rawlsian Political Philosophy Pass the Global Test?" *Critical Review of International Social and Political Philosophy* 14, no. 2 (2011): 125–51.

a medium-term ideal, while putting aside long-term considerations, involves abandoning a core commitment of ideal theory.

Second, even if ideal theorists limit their time horizon and focus on a medium-term ideal, there is little reason to believe they can plausibly defend this less ambitious ideal. As discussed in Chapter 6, human predictive capacities decline drastically when trying to make predictions about society as little as five to ten years into the future. A medium-term ideal for the coming decades and century still falls outside that narrow window. The ideal theorist trying to defend a medium-term ideal has to make predictions about the world at the time when their principles of justice could be implemented, but they cannot make these predictions with reliable accuracy. As a result, they cannot plausibly defend their theory. Ultimately, ideal theory focused on a medium-term ideal falls victim to the same problems plaguing more ambitious forms of it.

OBJECTION 2: ARGUMENT WRONGLY ASSUMES IDEAL SOCIETY CANNOT ARRIVE SOON

The argument against ideal theory's plausibility assumes the potential for greater justice in the distant future, which puts ideal theorists in the impossible spot of trying to predict what their principles of justice would look like in a future society. Perhaps, though, the ideal society could come much sooner. That possibility is more likely with ideal theories that take society to be perfectly just whenever it satisfies certain principles of justice, in contrast to consequentialist theories that allow justice in society to increase indefinitely as, say, happiness increases.[4] According to the former view, what makes society ideal is not dramatic innovations and discoveries that improve welfare, but meeting certain defined criteria (e.g., protection of basic liberties and fair distribution of wealth). Though major injustices must be overcome, the ideal society may not be *so* distant from the present. That attitude sometimes appears in Rawls when he describes ideal theory as offering a "reasonably just" society to strive and hope for.[5] Such language implies a modest goal potentially within reach. If so, ideal theory seems to be in a better position to defend itself, since explaining the social realizations of its principles would only require short-term predictions.

---

[4] Laura Valentini, "A Paradigm Shift in Theorizing about Justice? A Critique of Sen," *Economics and Philosophy* 27, no. 3 (2011): 305.
[5] Rawls, *Political Liberalism*, exp. ed. (New York: Columbia University Press, 2005), lx; *The Law of Peoples* (Cambridge, MA: Harvard University Press, 1999), 11, 128; and *Justice as Fairness*, 4.

Though this objection tries to absolve ideal theorists from having to make long-term predictions, it fails to. Even if an ideal theorist gives plausible grounds for accepting and striving after an ideal in the short term, that defense says nothing about its moral appeal for the long term. A society that best promotes justice now but leads away from greater justice in the future hardly counts as ideal. To be plausible and compelling, a defense of ideal theory must show that its ideal is an end goal that will possess moral appeal far into the future, which *does* require long-term predictions. So regardless of whether the ideal society can arrive soon or only in the distant future, the ideal theorist cannot avoid the need for long-term predictions. Since these predictions are unreliable, in both cases defenses of ideal theory lack plausibility.

OBJECTION 3: ARGUMENT FAILS IF PREDICTION IMPROVES

There is a certain irony in using evidence of our inability to predict the future to then predict the future, which in effect is what the argument against ideal theory's plausibility does. It relies on research showing limitations on human predictive capacities, and infers that those limitations will continue. Some may argue that, if we take research on prediction seriously, we recognize how dramatically the world can change and never assume that past trends will continue. Though people currently do little better than dart-throwing chimps in making long-term predictions about society, things could change. Perhaps the future holds the Black Swan to end all Black Swans – some unforeseen event that renders the world far more predictable. That change would put premise (3) of my argument in doubt and potentially open the door to plausible defenses of navigational ideal theory.

In response, it is tempting to argue that uncertainty is the one thing we can be certain about, given the world's complexity. But defending that position is unnecessary. It suffices to note that the Black Swan to end all Black Swans clearly has not arrived yet. Even if such an event occurs in the future, it does nothing to change our inability to plausibly defend ideal theory *now*. To defend ideal theory in the present, we first need an accurate understanding of future conditions where an ideal theory's principles could be realized. If we ever gain that, political philosophers will have reason to revisit the project of defending ideal theory. But as long as severe limitations on prediction persist, defenses of ideal theory necessarily fail.

OBJECTION 4: ARGUMENT DOES NOT APPLY TO ALL FORMS OF IDEAL THEORY

My argument applies specifically to navigational ideal theory, but leaves open the possibility of plausibly defending other forms of ideal theory. So perhaps the argument is not so damning. It is true that my argument does not apply to ideal theory that outlines justice in idealized worlds. If ideal theorists engage in thought experiments involving fictional worlds without Black Swans, it indeed becomes easier to explain the social realizations of their principles of justice and defend them.

It hopefully is clear that, in focusing on navigational ideal theory, I am not constructing a straw man to tear down. Ideal theory often attracts attention *because* it purports to have navigational value. If ideal theorists viewed their theories as intellectual pursuits irrelevant to guiding action, the stakes would be lower and their work would provoke less debate. But the most influential accounts of ideal theory do claim to have normative value. Rawls believes ideal theory offers an objective to guide social reform,[6] calling it a "realistic utopia" that "is feasible and might actually exist, if not now then at some future time under happier circumstances."[7] In its most normatively compelling form, ideal theory concerns itself not with impossible ideals irrelevant to advancing justice, but with ones suitable for guiding action in the real world. Navigational ideal theory, by focusing on a feasible end goal, represents the strongest candidate for fulfilling the normative ambitions that Rawls and others assign to ideal theory. The argument outlined here shows that, even in its most promising form, ideal theory fails to offer what so many want from it – a compelling and plausible ideal to guide collective efforts in advancing justice.

---

[6] Rawls, *A Theory of Justice*, 215.
[7] Rawls, *The Law of Peoples*, 12. See also Rawls, *Justice as Fairness*, 13.

Bibliography

Aamodt, Terrie Dopp. *Righteous Armies, Holy Cause: Apocalyptic Imagery and the Civil War*. Macon, GA: Mercer University Press, 2002.

Abizadeh, Arash. "Hobbes's Agnostic Theology before *Leviathan*." *Canadian Journal of Philosophy* 47, no. 5 (2017): 714–37.

———. "Hobbes's Conventionalist Theology, the Trinity, and God as an Artificial Person by Fiction." *Historical Journal* 60, no. 4 (2017): 915–41.

Agricola, Johann. "Letter 21." In *The Collected Works of Thomas Müntzer*, edited by Peter Matheson, 29–31. Edinburgh: T. & T. Clark, 1988.

Alighieri, Dante. *The Banquet*. Translated by Christopher Ryan. Saratoga, CA: Anma Libri, 1989.

Amanat, Abbas, and John Collins, eds. *Apocalypse and Violence*. New Haven, CT: Yale Center for International and Area Studies and the Council on Middle East Studies, 2004.

Anderson, Elizabeth. "John Stuart Mill and Experiments in Living." *Ethics* 102, no. 1 (1991): 4–26.

———. "Moral Bias and Corrective Practices: A Pragmatist Perspective." *Proceedings and Addresses of the American Philosophical Association* 89 (2015): 21–47.

Appiah, Kwame. *As If: Idealization and Ideals*. Cambridge, MA: Harvard University Press, 2017.

Armstrong, Karen. *Fields of Blood: Religion and the History of Violence*. New York: Knopf, 2014.

Arneson, Richard. "Marxism and Secular Faith." *American Political Science Review* 79, no. 3 (1985): 627–40.

Aspinwall, William. *A Brief Description of the Fifth Monarchy Men*. London: M. Simmons, 1653.

Augustine. *City of God*. Translated by Henry Bettenson. New York: Penguin Books, 1984.

Badaan, Vivienne, John Jost, Julian Fernando, and Yoshihisa Kashima. "Imagining Better Societies: A Social Psychological Framework for the Study of Utopian Thinking and Collective Action." *Social and Personality Psychology Compass* 14, no. 4 (2020): e12525.

Ball, Bryan. *A Great Expectation: Eschatological Thought in English Protestantism to 1660*. Leiden: Brill, 1975.

Barkun, Michael. "Divided Apocalypse: Thinking about the End in Contemporary America." *Soundings: An Interdisciplinary Journal* 66, no. 3 (1983): 257–80.
"Millennialism on the Radical Right in America." In *The Oxford Handbook of Millennialism*, edited by Catherine Wessinger, 649–66. New York: Oxford University Press, 2011.
"Religion, Militias and Oklahoma City: The Mind of Conspiratorialists." *Terrorism and Political Violence* 8, no. 1 (1996): 50–64.
Bates, Karen Grigsby. "'Rapists,' 'Huts': Trump's Racist Dog Whistles Aren't New." NPR, January 13, 2018, www.npr.org/sections/codeswitch/2018/01/13/577674607/rapists-huts-shitholes-trumps-racist-dog-whistles-arent-new.
Bauckham, Richard. *The Theology of the Book of Revelation*. New York: Cambridge University Press, 1993.
Baylor, Michael. "Introduction." In *Revelation and Revolution: Basic Writings of Thomas Müntzer*, translated and edited by Michael Baylor, 13–46. Bethlehem, PA: Lehigh University Press, 1993.
ed. *The Radical Reformation*. New York: Cambridge University Press, 1991.
Beauchamp, Zack. "ISIS Is Really Obsessed with the Apocalypse." *Vox*, April 6, 2015, www.vox.com/2015/4/6/8341691/isis-apocalypse.
Bejan, Teresa. *Mere Civility: Disagreement and the Limits of Toleration*. Cambridge, MA: Harvard University Press, 2017.
Bellarmine, Robert. *Dichiarazione piu copiosa della dottrina cristiana*. In *Opera omnia*, vol. 12, edited by Justinus Fèvre, 283–337. Paris: Vivès, 1874.
Disputationes de controversiis Christianae fidei. In *Opera omnia*, vol. 6, edited by Justinus Fèvre. Paris: Vivès, 1873.
On the Temporal Power of the Pope. Against William Barclay. In *On Temporal and Spiritual Authority*, edited and translated by Stefania Tutino, 121–405. Indianapolis, IN: Liberty Fund, 2012.
Berdyaev, Nicolas. *The Russian Idea*. New York: Macmillan, 1948.
Berlin, Isaiah. "The Pursuit of the Ideal." In *The Crooked Timber of Humanity*, edited by Henry Hardy, 1–20. Princeton, NJ: Princeton University Press, 2013.
Blau, Adrian. "How (Not) to Use the History of Political Thought for Contemporary Purposes." *American Journal of Political Science* 65, no. 2 (2021): 359–72.
Blumenberg, Hans. *The Legitimacy of the Modern Age*. Translated by Robert Wallace. Cambridge, MA: MIT Press, 1983.
Boenink, Marianne, Tsjalling Swierstra, and Dirk Stemerding. "Anticipating the Interaction between Technology and Morality: A Scenario Study of Experimenting with Humans in Biotechnology." *Studies in Ethics, Law, and Technology* 4, no. 2 (2010): Article 4, https://doi.org/10.2202/1941-6008.1098.
Boer, Roland. *Criticism of Earth: On Marxism and Theology IV*. Chicago: Haymarket Books, 2013.
In the Vale of Tears: On Marxism and Theology V. Chicago: Haymarket Books, 2014.
"Marxism and Eschatology Reconsidered." *Mediations* 25, no. 1 (2010): 39–59.
Borchardt, Frank. *Doomsday Speculation as a Strategy of Persuasion: A Study of Apocalypticism as Rhetoric*. Lewiston, NY: Edwin Mellen Press, 1990.
Bostrom, Nick. *Superintelligence: Paths, Dangers, Strategies*. New York: Oxford University Press, 2014.

Bottonio, Timoteo. "La Vita del Beato Ieronimo Savonarola." In *Selected Writings of Girolamo Savonarola: Religion and Politics, 1490–1498*, translated and edited by Anne Borelli and Maria Pastore Passaro, 212–21, 241–43, 256–58, 345–48. New Haven, CT: Yale University Press, 2006.
Bovens, Luc. "The Value of Hope." *Philosophy and Phenomenological Research* 59, no. 3 (1999): 667–81.
Boyer, Paul. *When Time Shall Be No More: Prophecy Belief in Modern American Culture*. Cambridge, MA: Harvard University Press, 1992.
Bradstock, Andrew. "Millenarianism in the Reformation and the English Revolution." In *Christian Millenarianism: From the Early Church to Waco*, edited by Stephen Hunt, 77–87. Bloomington, IN: Indiana University Press, 2001.
Bramhall, John. *The Catching of Leviathan*. In *The Collected Works of John Bramhall*, vol. 4, 507–97. Oxford: John Henry Parker, 1844.
Brennan, Geoffrey, and Philip Pettit. "The Feasibility Issue." In *The Oxford Handbook of Contemporary Philosophy*, edited by Frank Jackson and Michael Smith, 258–80. New York: Oxford University Press, 2007.
Brown, Alison. "Philosophy and Religion in Machiavelli." In *The Cambridge Companion to Machiavelli*, edited by John Najemy, 157–72. New York: Cambridge University Press, 2010.
——— "Savonarola, Machiavelli and Moses: A Changing Model." In *Florence and Italy: Renaissance Studies in Honour of Nicolai Rubinstein*, edited by Peter Denley and Caroline Elam, 57–72. London: Westfield College, 1988.
Bruce, Susan, ed. *Three Early Modern Utopias*. New York: Oxford University Press, 1999.
Bultmann, Rudolf. *The Presence of Eternity: History and Eschatology*. New York: Harper & Brothers, 1957.
Burch, Druin. *Taking the Medicine: A Short History of Medicine's Beautiful Idea, and Our Difficulty Swallowing It*. London: Random House, 2010.
Bury, Simon, Michael Wenzel, and Lydia Woodyatt. "Against the Odds: Hope as an Antecedent of Support for Climate Change Action." *British Journal of Social Psychology* 59, no. 2 (2020): 289–310.
Bush, George W. "Appendix B: George W. Bush, Address to the Nation, October 7, 2001." In *Holy Terrors: Thinking about Religion after September 11*, edited by Bruce Lincoln, 99–101. Chicago: Chicago University Press, 2003.
Byron, Michael. *Submission and Subjection in Leviathan: Good Subjects in the Hobbesian Commonwealth*. London: Palgrave Macmillan, 2015.
Capp, B. S. *The Fifth Monarchy Men: A Study in Seventeenth-Century English Millenarianism*. London: Faber & Faber, 1972.
——— "The Political Dimension of Apocalyptic Thought." In *The Apocalypse in English Renaissance Thought and Literature*, edited by C. A. Patrides and Joseph Wittreich, 93–125. Ithaca, NY: Cornell University Press, 1984.
Catholic Church. *Catechism of the Catholic Church*, 2nd ed. Washington, D.C.: United States Conference of Catholic Bishops, 2019.
——— *Catechism of the Council of Trent*. Translated by John McHugh and Charles Callan. New York: Joseph F. Wagner, 1934.
Cavanagh, William. *The Myth of Religious Violence: Secular Ideology and the Roots of Modern Conflict*. New York: Oxford University Press, 2009.

Christianson, Paul. *Reformers and Babylon: English Apocalyptic Visions from the Reformation to the Eve of the Civil War.* Toronto: University of Toronto Press, 1978.
Claeys, Gregory. *Dystopia: A Natural History: A Study of Modern Despotism, Its Antecedents, and Its Literary Diffractions.* New York: Oxford University Press, 2017.
— ed. *Utopias of the British Enlightenment.* New York: Cambridge University Press, 1994.
Coates, Ta-Nehisi. *Between the World and Me.* New York: Spiegel & Grau, 2015.
Cohen, G. A. "Facts and Principles." *Philosophy and Public Affairs* 31, no. 3 (2003): 211–45.
Cohen, Joshua. "The Arc of the Moral Universe." *Philosophy and Public Affairs* 26, no. 2 (1997): 91–134.
Cohen-Chen, Smadar, and Martijn Van Zomeren. "Yes We Can? Group Efficacy Beliefs Predict Collective Action, but only When Hope Is High." *Journal of Experimental Social Psychology* 77 (2018): 50–59.
Cohn, Norman. *The Pursuit of the Millennium: Revolutionary Millenarians and Mystical Anarchists of the Middle Ages*, rev. ed. New York: Oxford University Press, 1970.
Colish, Marcia. "Republicanism, Religion, and Machiavelli's Savonarolan Moment." *Journal of the History of Ideas* 60, no. 4 (1999): 597–616.
Collins, Adela Yarbro. *Crisis and Catharsis: The Power of Apocalypse.* Philadelphia, PA: Westminster Press, 1984.
Collins, John. *The Apocalyptic Imagination: An Introduction to Jewish Apocalyptic Literature*, 2nd ed. Grand Rapids, MI: Eerdmans, 1998.
— "Introduction: Towards the Morphology of a Genre." *Semeia* 14 (1979): 1–20.
Collins, John, Bernard McGinn, and Stephen Stein, eds. *The Encyclopedia of Apocalypticism.* New York: Continuum, 1998.
Coogan, Michael, ed. *The New Oxford Annotated Bible*, 3rd ed. New York: Oxford University Press, 2001.
Cooke, Paul. *Hobbes and Christianity: Reassessing the Bible in Leviathan.* Lanham, MD: Rowman & Littlefield Publishers, 1996.
Corcoran, Paul. *Awaiting Apocalypse.* New York: St. Martin's Press, 2000.
Coyle, J. Kevin. "Augustine and Apocalyptic: Thoughts on the Fall of Rome, the Book of Revelation, and the End of the World." *Florilegium* 9 (1987): 1–34.
Cranston, Maurice. "A Dialogue on the State between Savonarola and Machiavelli." In *Political Dialogues*, 1–21. London: British Broadcasting Corporation, 1968.
Crossan, John Dominic. *God and Empire: Jesus against Rome, Then and Now.* San Francisco: HarperCollins Publishers, 2007.
Crossman, Richard, ed. *The God that Failed.* New York: Harper & Brothers, 1949.
Curley, Edwin. "'I Durst Not Write so Boldly,' or How to Read Hobbes' Theological-Political Treatise." In *Hobbes e Spinoza*, edited by Daniela Bostrenghi, 497–593. Napoli: Bibliopolis, 1992.
Day, J. P. "Hope." *American Philosophical Quarterly* 6, no. 2 (1969): 89–102.
de Grazia, Sebastian. *Machiavelli in Hell.* Princeton, NJ: Princeton University Press, 1989.
Deigh, John. "Political Obligation." In *The Oxford Handbook of Hobbes*, edited by Al Martinich and Kinch Hoekstra, 293–314. New York: Oxford University Press, 2016.

Descartes, René. *Discourse on Method*, 3rd ed. Translated by Donald Cress. Indianapolis, IN: Hackett Publishing Company, 1998.
di Giovanni, George. "Translator's Introduction." In *Religion and Rational Theology*, translated and edited by Allen Wood and George di Giovanni, 41–54. New York: Cambridge University Press, 1996.
Dias, Elizabeth. "The Apocalypse as an 'Unveiling': What Religion Teaches Us about the End Times." *New York Times*, April 2, 2020, www.nytimes.com/2020/04/02/us/coronavirus-apocalypse-religion.html.
Downie, R. S. "Hope." *Philosophy and Phenomenological Research* 24, no. 2 (1963): 248–51.
Durham, Martin. "Preparing for Armageddon: Citizen Militias, the Patriot Movement and the Oklahoma City Bombing." *Terrorism and Political Violence* 8, no. 1 (1996): 65–79.
Eliade, Mircea. *The Myth of the Eternal Return: Cosmos and History*. Translated by Willard Trask. Princeton, NJ: Princeton University Press, 2005.
Elliot, David. *Hope and Christian Ethics*. New York: Cambridge University Press, 2017.
Engels, Friedrich. *Anti-Dühring*. In *Marx and Engels: Collected Works*, vol. 25, 1–309. London: Lawrence & Wishart, 1987.
"The Book of Revelation." In *Marx and Engels: Collected Works*, vol. 26, 112–17. London: Lawrence & Wishart, 1990.
Dialectics of Nature. In *Marx and Engels: Collected Works*, vol. 25, 311–588. London: Lawrence & Wishart, 1987.
"Engels to Joseph Bloch." In *Marx and Engels: Collected Works*, vol. 49, 33–37. London: Lawrence & Wishart, 2001.
"On the History of Early Christianity." In *Marx and Engels: Collected Works*, vol. 27, 445–69. London: Lawrence & Wishart, 1990.
"Introduction to the English Edition (1892) of *Socialism: Utopian and Scientific*." In *Marx and Engels: Collected Works*, vol. 27, 278–302. London: Lawrence & Wishart, 1990.
"Introduction to Karl Marx's *The Class Struggles in France 1848 to 1850*." In *Marx and Engels: Collected Works*, vol. 27, 506–24. London: Lawrence & Wishart, 1990.
The Peasant War in Germany. In *Marx and Engels: Collected Works*, vol. 10, 397–482. London: Lawrence & Wishart, 1978.
Socialism: Utopian and Scientific. In *Marx and Engels: Collected Works*, vol. 24, 281–325. London: Lawrence & Wishart, 1989.
Erman, Eva, and Niklas Möller. "Three Failed Charges against Ideal Theory." *Social Theory and Practice* 39, no. 1 (2013): 19–44.
Estep, William. *The Anabaptist Story: An Introduction to Sixteenth-Century Anabaptism*, 3rd ed. Grand Rapids, MI: Eerdmans, 1996.
Estlund, David. "Human Nature and the Limits (if any) of Political Philosophy." *Philosophy and Public Affairs* 39, no. 3 (2011): 207–37.
"Utopophobia." *Philosophy and Public Affairs* 42, no. 2 (2014): 113–34.
Utopophobia: On the Limits (if any) of Political Philosophy. Princeton, NJ: Princeton University Press, 2020.
"What Good Is It? Unrealistic Political Theory and the Value of Intellectual Work." *Analyse & Kritik* 33, no. 2 (2011): 395–416.

Evrigenis, Ioannis. *Fear of Enemies and Collective Action*. New York: Cambridge University Press, 2008.
  Images of Anarchy: The Rhetoric and Science in Hobbes's State of Nature. New York: Cambridge University Press, 2014.
Farrelly, Colin. "Justice in Ideal Theory: A Refutation." *Political Studies* 55, no. 4 (2007): 844–64.
Fernando, Julian, Nicholas Burden, Adam Ferguson, Léan O'Brien, Madeline Judge, and Yoshihisa Kashima. "Functions of Utopia: How Utopian Thinking Motivates Societal Engagement." *Personality and Social Psychology Bulletin* 44, no. 5 (2018): 779–92.
Fifth Monarchist Petitioners. "King Jesus." In *The English Civil War and Revolution: A Sourcebook*, edited by Keith Lindley, 174–76. New York: Routledge, 1998.
Firth, Katharine. *The Apocalyptic Tradition in Reformation Britain, 1530–1645*. New York: Oxford University Press, 1979.
Flannery, Frances. *Understanding Apocalyptic Terrorism: Countering the Radical Mindset*. New York: Routledge, 2016.
Fontana, Benedetto. "Love of Country and Love of God: The Political Uses of Religion in Machiavelli." *Journal of the History of Ideas* 60, no. 4 (1999): 639–58.
Forman Jr., James. *Locking Up Our Own: Crime and Punishment in Black America*. New York: Farrar, Straus and Giroux, 2017.
Friedman, Milton. *Capitalism and Freedom*, 40th anniversary ed. Chicago: University of Chicago Press, 2002.
Friesen, Abraham. "The Marxist Interpretation of Anabaptism." *Sixteenth Century Essays and Studies* 1 (1970): 17–34.
  Reformation and Utopia: The Marxist Interpretation of the Reformation and Its Antecedents. Wiesbaden: F. Steiner, 1974.
  Thomas Muentzer, a Destroyer of the Godless: The Making of a Sixteenth-Century Religious Revolutionary. Berkeley, CA: University of California Press, 1990.
  "Thomas Müntzer in Marxist Thought." *Church History* 34, no. 3 (1965): 306–27.
Galston, William. "Realism in Political Theory." *European Journal of Political Theory* 9, no. 4 (2010): 385–411.
Gardiner, Stephen. "Rawls and Climate Change: Does Rawlsian Political Philosophy Pass the Global Test?" *Critical Review of International Social and Political Philosophy* 14, no. 2 (2011): 125–51.
Garrow, David. *Bearing the Cross: Martin Luther King, Jr., and the Southern Christian Leadership Conference*. New York: HarperCollins Publishers, 2004.
Garsten, Bryan. "Religion and Representation in Hobbes." In *Thomas Hobbes, Leviathan*, edited by Ian Shapiro, 519–46. New Haven, CT: Yale University Press, 2010.
Gaus, Gerald. *The Tyranny of the Ideal: Justice in a Diverse Society*. Princeton, NJ: Princeton University Press, 2016.
Geerken, John. "Machiavelli's Moses and Renaissance Politics." *Journal of the History of Ideas* 60, no. 4 (1999): 579–95.
Geuss, Raymond. *Philosophy and Real Politics*. Princeton, NJ: Princeton University Press, 2008.
Gheaus, Anca. "The Feasibility Constraint on the Concept of Justice." *Philosophical Quarterly* 63, no. 252 (2013): 445–64.

Gilabert, Pablo, and Holly Lawford-Smith. "Political Feasibility: A Conceptual Exploration." *Political Studies* 60, no. 4 (2012): 809–25.
Gilbert, Felix. "Machiavelli's 'Istorie Fiorentine': An Essay in Interpretation." In *Studies on Machiavelli*, edited by Myron Gilmore, 73–99. Florence: Sansoni, 1972.
Gilchrest, Eric. *Revelation 21–22 in Light of Jewish and Greco-Roman Utopianism*. Leiden: Brill, 2013.
Glover, Willis. "God and Thomas Hobbes." *Church History* 29, no. 3 (1960): 275–97.
Goertz, Hans-Jürgen. *Thomas Müntzer: Apocalyptic Mystic and Revolutionary*. Translated by Jocelyn Jaquiery and edited by Peter Matheseon. Edinburgh: T. & T. Clark, 1993.
Goldman, Loren. "In Defense of Blinders: On Kant, Political Hope, and the Need for Practical Belief." *Political Theory* 40, no. 4 (2012): 497–523.
Goodwin, Barbara, and Keith Taylor. *The Politics of Utopia: A Study in Theory and Practice*. London: Hutchinson, 1982.
Goodwin, Thomas. *The Great Interest of States & Kingdomes*. London, 1646.
Gray, John. *Black Mass: Apocalyptic Religion and the Death of Utopia*. New York: Farrar, Straus and Giroux, 2007.
Grebel, Conrad, Andreas Kastelberg, Felix Manz, Hans Oggenfuss, Bartholomew Pur, and Heinrich Aberli. "Letter 69." In *The Collected Works of Thomas Müntzer*, edited by Peter Matheson, 121–30. Edinburgh: T. & T. Clark, 1988.
Greenaway, Katharine, Aleksandra Cichocka, Ruth van Veelen, Tiina Likki, and Nyla Branscombe. "Feeling Hopeful Inspires Support for Social Change." *Political Psychology* 37, no. 1 (2016): 89–107.
Gribben, Crawford. *The Puritan Millennium: Literature & Theology, 1550–1682*. Dublin: Four Courts Press, 2000.
Gruen, Lori. *Ethics and Animals: An Introduction*. New York: Cambridge University Press, 2011.
Guicciardini, Francesco. *The History of Florence*. In *Selected Writings of Girolamo Savonarola: Religion and Politics, 1490–1498*, translated and edited by Anne Borelli and Maria Pastore Passaro, 360–62. New Haven, CT: Yale University Press, 2006.
  The History of Italy. Translated and edited by Sidney Alexander. Princeton, NJ: Princeton University Press, 1984.
Guyatt, Nicholas. *Have a Nice Doomsday: Why Millions of Americans Are Looking forward to the End of the World*. New York: HarperCollins Publishers, 2007.
Hall, John. *Apocalypse: From Antiquity to the Empire of Modernity*. Malden, MA: Polity Press, 2009.
Hamlin, Alan, and Zofia Stemplowska. "Theory, Ideal Theory and the Theory of Ideals." *Political Studies Review* 10, no. 1 (2012): 48–62.
Hanson, Paul. *The Dawn of Apocalyptic: The Historical and Sociological Roots of Jewish Apocalyptic Eschatology*. Philadelphia, PA: Fortress Press, 1975.
Hay, Colin. "Narrating Crisis: The Discursive Construction of the 'Winter of Discontent.'" *Sociology* 30, no. 2 (1996): 253–77.
Hendrix, Burke. *Strategies of Justice: Aboriginal Peoples, Persistent Injustice, and the Ethics of Political Action*. New York: Oxford University Press, 2019.

"Where Should We Expect Social Change in Non-ideal Theory?" *Political Theory* 41, no. 1 (2013): 116–43.

Herzog, Lisa. "Ideal and Non-ideal Theory and the Problem of Knowledge." *Journal of Applied Philosophy* 29, no. 4 (2012): 271–88.

Hexter, J. H. "The Burden of Proof." *Times Literary Supplement* 3841 (1975): 1250–52.

Higgs, Robert. *Crisis and Leviathan: Critical Episodes in the Growth of American Government*. New York: Oxford University Press, 1987.

Hill, Christopher. *Antichrist in Seventeenth-Century England*. New York: Oxford University Press, 1971.

The World Turned Upside Down: Radical Ideas during the English Revolution. New York: Penguin Books, 1991.

Hobbes, Thomas. *Behemoth, or The Long Parliament*. Edited by Ferdinand Tönnies. Chicago: Chicago University Press, 1990.

On the Citizen. Edited and translated by Richard Tuck and Michael Silverthorne. New York: Cambridge University Press, 1998.

The Elements of Law. Edited by Ferdinand Tönnies. Cambridge: Cambridge University Press, 1928.

Historia Ecclesiastica. Edited and translated by Patricia Springborg, Patricia Stablein, and Paul Wilson. Paris: Honoré Champion 2008.

Leviathan. Edited by Noel Malcolm. New York: Oxford University Press, 2012.

Seven Philosophical Problems. In *The English Works of Thomas Hobbes of Malmesbury*, vol. 7, edited by William Molesworth, 1–68. London: Longman, Brown, Green, and Longmans, 1845.

Hoekstra, Kinch. "Disarming the Prophets: Thomas Hobbes and Predictive Power." *Rivista di storia della filosofia* 59, no. 1 (2004): 97–153.

Horsley, Richard. *Revolt of the Scribes: Resistance and Apocalyptic Origins*. Minneapolis, MN: Fortress Press, 2010.

Howard, Dana. "The Scoundrel and the Visionary: On Reasonable Hope and the Possibility of a Just Future." *Journal of Political Philosophy* 27, no. 3 (2019): 294–317.

Ismael, Jenann. "A Philosopher of Science Looks at Idealization in Political Theory." *Social Philosophy and Policy* 33, nos. 1–2 (2016): 11–31.

James, Scott. "From Oakland to the World, Words of Warning: Time's Up." *New York Times*, May 19, 2011, www.nytimes.com/2011/05/20/us/20bcjames.html.

Jensen, Mark. "The Limits of Practical Possibility." *Journal of Political Philosophy* 17, no. 2 (2009): 168–84.

Jonas, Hans. "Technology and Responsibility: Reflections on the New Tasks of Ethics." *Social Research* 40, no. 1 (1973): 31–54.

Jones, Ben. "The Challenges of Ideal Theory and Appeal of Secular Apocalyptic Thought." *European Journal of Political Theory* 19, no. 4 (2020): 465–88.

"The Natural Kingdom of God in Hobbes's Political Thought." *History of European Ideas* 45, no. 3 (2019): 436–53.

Jones, Gareth. "How Marx Covered His Tracks: The Hidden Link between Communism and Religion." *Times Literary Supplement* 5175 (2002): 13–14.

Jones, James. *Blood that Cries Out from the Earth: The Psychology of Religious Terrorism*. New York: Oxford University Press, 2008.

Jubb, Robert. "Tragedies of Nonideal Theory." *European Journal of Political Theory* 11, no. 3 (2012): 229–46.
Juergensmeyer, Mark. *Terror in the Mind of God: The Global Rise of Religious Violence*, 4th ed. Oakland, CA: University of California Press, 2017.
Jurdjevic, Mark. *A Great and Wretched City: Promise and Failure in Machiavelli's Florentine Political Thought*. Cambridge, MA: Harvard University Press, 2014.
Kant, Immanuel. "On the Common Saying: That May Be Correct in Theory, but It Is of No Use in Practice." In *Practical Philosophy*, translated and edited by Mary Gregor, 273–309. New York: Cambridge University Press, 1996.
    Critique of Practical Reason. In *Practical Philosophy*, translated and edited by Mary Gregor, 133–271. New York: Cambridge University Press, 1996.
    Religion within the Boundaries of Mere Reason. In *Religion and Rational Theology*, translated and edited by Allen Wood and George di Giovanni, 55–215. New York: Cambridge University Press, 1996.
    "On the Supposed Right to Lie from Philanthropy." In *Practical Philosophy*, translated and edited by Mary Gregor, 605–15. New York: Cambridge University Press, 1996.
    "Toward Perpetual Peace." In *Practical Philosophy*, translated and edited by Mary Gregor, 311–51. New York: Cambridge University Press, 1996.
Kavka, Gregory. *Hobbesian Moral and Political Theory*. Princeton, NJ: Princeton University Press, 1986.
Kenyon, Timothy. "Utopia in Reality: 'Ideal' Societies in Social and Political Theory." *History of Political Thought* 3, no. 1 (1982): 123–55.
Kermode, Frank. *The Sense of an Ending: Studies in the Theory of Fiction*. New York: Oxford University Press, 2000.
King Jr., Martin Luther. "The Current Crisis in Race Relations." In *A Testament of Hope: The Essential Writings and Speeches of Martin Luther King, Jr.*, edited by James Washington, 85–90. New York: HarperCollins Publishers, 1986.
Koester, Craig. *Revelation and the End of All Things*. Grand Rapids, MI: Eerdmans, 2001.
Kolakowski, Leszek. *Main Currents of Marxism: Its Rise, Growth, and Dissolution. Volume 1: The Founders*. Translated by P. S. Falla. New York: Oxford University Press, 1978.
Kyle, Richard. *Apocalyptic Fever: End-Time Prophecies in Modern America*. Eugene, OR: Cascade Books, 2012.
Lagerspetz, E. "Predictability and the Growth of Knowledge." *Synthese* 141, no. 3 (2004): 445–59.
Lamont, William. *Godly Rule: Politics and Religion, 1603–60*. New York: St. Martin's Press, 1969.
Landes, Richard. *Heaven on Earth: The Varieties of Millennial Experience*. New York: Oxford University Press, 2011.
Landucci, Luca. *A Florentine Diary*. In *Selected Writings of Girolamo Savonarola: Religion and Politics, 1490–1498*, translated and edited by Anne Borelli and Maria Pastore Passaro, 209–10, 238, 336, 351–52. New Haven, CT: Yale University Press, 2006.
Laurence, Ben. "Constructivism, Strict Compliance, and Realistic Utopianism." *Philosophy and Phenomenological Research* 97, no. 2 (2018): 433–53.

Lawford-Smith, Holly. "Understanding Political Feasibility." *Journal of Political Philosophy* 21, no. 3 (2013): 243–59.
Lazar, Nomi Claire. *Out of Joint: Power, Crisis, and the Rhetoric of Time.* New Haven, CT: Yale University Press, 2019.
Lenin, Vladimir. *The State and Revolution.* Translated by Robert Service. New York: Penguin Books, 1992.
Levitas, Ruth. *The Concept of Utopia.* Syracuse, NY: Syracuse University Press, 1990.
Levy, Jacob. "There's No Such Thing as Ideal Theory." *Social Philosophy and Policy* 33, nos. 1–2 (2016): 312–33.
Lincoln, Bruce. *Holy Terrors: Thinking about Religion after September 11.* Chicago: Chicago University Press, 2003.
Livy. *The Early History of Rome: Books I–V of The History of Rome from Its Foundation.* Translated by Aubrey de Sélincourt. Baltimore, MD: Penguin Books, 1960.
Lloyd, S. A. *Ideals as Interests in Hobbes's* Leviathan: *The Power of Mind over Matter.* New York: Cambridge University Press, 1992.
Lorenz, Edward. *The Essence of Chaos.* Seattle, WA: University of Washington Press, 1993.
Löwith, Karl. *Meaning in History.* Chicago: Chicago University Press, 1949.
Lupoli, Agostino. "Hobbes and Religion without Theology." In *The Oxford Handbook of Hobbes*, edited by Al Martinich and Kinch Hoekstra, 453–80. New York: Oxford University Press, 2016.
Luther, Martin. *Admonition to Peace: A Reply to the Twelve Articles of the Peasants in Swabia.* Translated by Charles Jacobs. In *Luther's Works*, vol. 46, edited by Robert Schultz, 3–43. Philadelphia, PA: Fortress Press, 1967.
Against the Robbing and Murdering Hordes of Peasants. Translated by Charles Jacobs. In *Luther's Works*, vol. 46, edited by Robert Schultz, 45–55. Philadelphia, PA: Fortress Press, 1967.
Letter to the Princes of Saxony Concerning the Rebellious Spirit. Translated by Conrad Bergendoff. In *Luther's Works*, vol. 40, edited by Conrad Bergendoff, 45–59. Philadelphia, PA: Muhlenberg Press, 1958.
Machiavelli, Niccolò. *Art of War.* Translated and edited by Christopher Lynch. Chicago: University of Chicago Press, 2003.
A Discourse on Remodeling the Government of Florence. In *Machiavelli: The Chief Works and Others*, vol. 1, translated by Allan Gilbert, 101–15. Durham, NC: Duke University Press, 1965.
Discourses on Livy. Translated by Harvey Mansfield and Nathan Tarcov. Chicago: University of Chicago Press, 1996.
First Decennale. In *Machiavelli: The Chief Works and Others*, vol. 3, translated by Allan Gilbert, 1444–56. Durham, NC: Duke University Press, 1965.
Florentine Histories. Translated by Laura Banfield and Harvey Mansfield. Princeton, NJ: Princeton University Press, 1988.
The [Golden] Ass. In *Machiavelli: The Chief Works and Others*, vol. 2, translated by Allan Gilbert, 750–72. Durham, NC: Duke University Press, 1965.
Machiavelli and His Friends: Their Personal Correspondence. Translated and edited by James Atkinson and David Sices. DeKalb, IL: Northern Illinois University Press, 1996.

The Prince, 2nd ed. Translated by Harvey Mansfield. Chicago: University of Chicago Press, 1998.
Tutte le opere. Edited by Mario Martelli. Florence: Sansoni, 1971.
MacIntyre, Alasdair. *Marxism and Christianity*, 2nd ed. London: Duckworth Publishers, 1995.
Maimonides, Moses. "Helek: Sanhedrin, Chapter Ten." In *A Maimonides Reader*, edited by Isadore Twersky, 401–23. Springdale, NJ: Behrman House, 1972.
Malcolm, Noel. *Leviathan: Introduction*. London: Oxford University Press. 2012.
Mantena, Karuna. "Another Realism: The Politics of Gandhian Nonviolence." *American Political Science Review* 106, no. 2 (2012): 455–70.
Manuel, Frank, and Fritzie Manuel, eds. *French Utopias: An Anthology of Ideal Societies*. New York: The Free Press, 1966.
Markus, R. A. *Saeculum: History and Society in the Theology of St Augustine*. New York: Cambridge University Press, 1970.
Martin, Adrienne. *How We Hope: A Moral Psychology*. Princeton, NJ: Princeton University Press, 2014.
Martines, Lauro. *Lawyers and Statecraft in Renaissance Florence*. Princeton, NJ: Princeton University Press, 1968.
Scourge and Fire: Savonarola and Renaissance Italy. London: Jonathan Cape, 2006.
Martinich, A. P. *The Two Gods of Leviathan: Thomas Hobbes on Religion and Politics*. New York: Cambridge University Press, 1992.
Marx, Karl. "On the Hague Congress." In *Marx and Engels: Collected Works*, vol. 23, 254–56. London: Lawrence & Wishart, 1988.
"Introduction to *Contribution to the Critique of Hegel's* Philosophy of Law." In *Marx and Engels: Collected Works*, vol. 3, 175–87, London: Lawrence & Wishart, 1975.
Marx, Karl, and Friedrich Engels. *The German Ideology*. In *Marx and Engels: Collected Works*, vol. 5, 19–539. London: Lawrence & Wishart, 1975.
Manifesto of the Communist Party. In *Marx and Engels: Collected Works*, vol. 6, 477–519. London: Lawrence & Wishart, 1976.
Mathis-Lilley, Ben. "The Last Trump Apocalypse Watch." *Slate*, November 9, 2016, https://slate.com/news-and-politics/2016/11/the-last-trump-apocalypse-watch.html.
Maynard, John. *A Shadow of the Victory of Christ*. London: F. Neile, 1646.
McCants, William. *The ISIS Apocalypse: The History, Strategy, and Doomsday Vision of the Islamic State*. New York: St. Martin's Press, 2015.
McClure, Christopher. "Hell and Anxiety in Hobbes's *Leviathan*." *Review of Politics* 73, no. 1 (2011): 1–27.
Hobbes and the Artifice of Eternity. New York: Cambridge University Press, 2016.
McGinn, Bernard. "Apocalypticism and Violence: Aspects of Their Relation in Antiquity and the Middle Ages." In *Scripture and Pluralism: Reading the Bible in the Religiously Plural Worlds of the Middle Ages and Renaissance*, edited by Thomas Heffernan and Thomas Burman, 209–29. Leiden: Brill, 2005.
McKean, Benjamin. "Ideal Theory after Auschwitz? The Practical Uses and Ideological Abuses of Political Theory as Reconciliation." *Journal of Politics* 79, no. 4 (2017): 1177–90.
McLellan, David. *Marxism and Religion: A Description and Assessment of the Marxist Critique of Christianity*. New York: Harper & Row, 1987.

McPherson, James. *Battle Cry of Freedom: The Civil War Era*. New York: Oxford University Press, 1988.
McQueen, Alison. "How to Be a Prophet of Doom." *New York Times*, May 11, 2018, www.nytimes.com/2018/05/11/opinion/nuclear-doomsday-denial.html.
   Political Realism in Apocalyptic Times. New York: Cambridge University Press, 2018.
McTernan, Emily. "Justice, Feasibility, and Social Science as It Is." *Ethical Theory and Moral Practice* 22, no. 1 (2019): 27–40.
Meirav, Ariel. "The Nature of Hope." *Ratio* 22, no. 2 (2009): 216–33.
Mellers, Barbara, Eric Stone, Pavel Atanasov, Nick Rohrbaugh, S. Metz, Lyle Ungar, Michael Bishop, Michael Horwitz, Ed Merkle, and Philip Tetlock. "The Psychology of Intelligence Analysis: Drivers of Prediction Accuracy in World Politics." *Journal of Experimental Psychology: Applied* 21, no. 1 (2015): 1–14.
Mendel, Arthur. *Vision and Violence*. Ann Arbor, MI: University of Michigan Press, 1992.
Mill, John Stuart. *On Liberty*. In *On Liberty and Other Essays*, edited by John Gray, 1–128. New York: Oxford University Press, 1991.
Mills, Charles. *Black Rights/White Wrongs: The Critique of Racial Liberalism*. New York: Oxford University Press, 2017.
   "'Ideal Theory' as Ideology." *Hypatia* 20, no. 3 (2005): 165–84.
Moltmann, Jürgen. *The Coming of God: Christian Eschatology*. Translated by Margaret Kohl. Minneapolis, MN: Fortress Press, 1996.
Moorhead, James. "Searching for the Millennium in America." *Princeton Seminary Bulletin* 8, no. 2 (1987): 17–33.
Mor, Menahem. *The Second Jewish Revolt: The Bar Kokhba War, 132–136 CE*. Leiden: Brill, 2016.
More, Thomas. *Utopia*. Translated by Paul Turner. New York: Penguin Books, 1965.
Mortimer, Sarah. "Christianity and Civil Religion in Hobbes's *Leviathan*." In *The Oxford Handbook of Hobbes*, edited by Al Martinich and Kinch Hoekstra, 501–19. New York: Oxford University Press, 2016.
Mortimer, Sarah, and David Scott. "*Leviathan* and the Wars of the Three Kingdoms." *Journal of the History of Ideas* 76, no. 2 (2015): 259–70.
Moser, Bob. "Welcome to the Trumpocalypse." *Rolling Stone*, April 11, 2020, www.rollingstone.com/politics/politics-features/trump-evangelicals-apocalypse-coronavirus-981995/.
Muldoon, Ryan. "Expanding the Justificatory Framework of Mill's Experiments in Living." *Utilitas* 27, no. 2 (2015): 179–94.
Müntzer, Thomas. *The Collected Works of Thomas Müntzer*. Translated and edited by Peter Matheson. Edinburgh: T. & T. Clark, 1988.
Najemy, John. *A History of Florence, 1200–1575*. Malden, MA: Blackwell Publishing, 2006.
   "Machiavelli and the Medici: The Lessons of Florentine History." *Renaissance Quarterly* 35, no. 4 (1982): 551–76.
   "Papirius and the Chickens, or Machiavelli on the Necessity of Interpreting Religion." *Journal of the History of Ideas* 60, no. 4 (1999): 659–81.
Newheiser, David. *Hope in a Secular Age: Deconstruction, Negative Theology, and the Future of Faith*. New York: Cambridge University Press, 2019.

Nickerson, Raymond. "Confirmation Bias: A Ubiquitous Phenomenon in Many Guises." *Review of General Psychology* 2, no. 2 (1998): 175–220.
Niebuhr, Reinhold. "Introduction." In *Karl Marx and Friedrich Engels on Religion*, vii–xiv. New York: Schocken Books, 1964.
Nili, Shmuel. "The Moving Global Everest: A New Challenge to Global Ideal Theory as a Necessary Compass." *European Journal of Political Theory* 17, no. 1 (2018): 87–108.
Novak, David. "Jewish Eschatology." In *The Oxford Handbook of Eschatology*, edited by Jerry Walls, 113–28. New York: Oxford University Press, 2008.
Nozick, Robert. *Anarchy, State, and Utopia.* New York: Basic Books, 1974.
O'Leary, Stephen. *Arguing the Apocalypse: A Theory of Millennial Rhetoric.* New York: Oxford University Press, 1994.
Olson, Theodore. *Millennialism, Utopianism, and Progress.* Toronto: University of Toronto Press, 1982.
Orwin, Clifford. "Machiavelli's Unchristian Charity." *American Political Science Review* 72, no. 4 (1978): 1217–28.
Ovid. *Fasti.* Translated and edited by A. J. Boyle and R. D. Woodard. New York: Penguin Books, 2000.
Pagels, Elaine. *Revelations: Visions, Prophecy, and Politics in the Book of Revelation.* New York: Viking, 2012.
Paine, Thomas. *The Crisis.* In *Thomas Paine: Collected Writings*, edited by Eric Foner, 91–176, 181–210, 222–52, 325–33, 348–54. New York: Library of America, 1995.
Palaver, Wolfgang. "Hobbes and the *Katéchon*: The Secularization of Sacrificial Christianity." *Contagion: Journal of Violence, Mimesis and Culture* 2, no. 1 (1995): 57–74.
Parrish, John. "Benevolent Skullduggery." In *Corruption and American Politics*, edited by Michael Genovese and Victoria Farrar-Myers, 65–98. Amherst, NY: Cambria Press, 2010.
Paul, Robert. *The Assembly of the Lord: Politics and Religion in the Westminster Assembly and the "Grand Debate".* Edinburgh: T. & T. Clark, 1985.
Perlstein, Rick. "Exclusive: Lee Atwater's Infamous 1981 Interview on the Southern Strategy." *The Nation*, November, 13, 2012, www.thenation.com/article/exclusive-lee-atwaters-infamous-1981-interview-southern-strategy/.
Pettit, Philip. "Hope and Its Place in Mind." *Annals of the American Academy of Political and Social Science* 592 (2004): 152–65.
Pew Research Center. "Life in 2050: Amazing Science, Familiar Threats: Public Sees a Future Full of Promise and Peril." June 22, 2010, www.pewresearch.org/wp-content/uploads/sites/4/legacy-pdf/625.pdf.
Plato. *The Republic.* Edited by G. R. F. Ferrari and translated by Tom Griffith. New York: Cambridge University Press, 2000.
Pocock, J. G. A. *The Machiavellian Moment: Florentine Political Thought and the Atlantic Republican Tradition*, 2nd ed. Princeton, NJ: Princeton University Press, 2003.
"Time, History and Eschatology in the Thought of Thomas Hobbes." In *Politics, Language, and Time: Essays on Political Thought and History*, 148–201. New York: Atheneum, 1971.

Polizzotto, Lorenzo. *The Elect Nation: The Savonarolan Movement in Florence, 1494–1545.* Oxford: Clarendon Press, 1994.
Popkin, Richard. "Seventeenth-Century Millenarianism." In *Apocalypse Theory and the Ends of the World*, edited by Malcolm Bull, 112–34. Oxford: Blackwell Publishers, 1995.
Popper, Karl. *The Open Society and Its Enemies.* Princeton, NJ: Princeton University Press, 2013.
  The Open Universe: An Argument for Indeterminism. Edited by W. W. Bartley, III. New York: Routledge, 1992.
  The Poverty of Historicism. New York: Routledge, 2002.
  "Utopia and Violence." In *Conjectures and Refutations: The Growth of Scientific Knowledge*, 477–88. New York: Routledge, 2002.
Portier-Young, Anathea. *Apocalypse against Empire: Theologies of Resistance in Early Judaism.* Grand Rapids, MI: Eerdmans, 2011.
Pratt, Kenneth. "Rome as Eternal." *Journal of the History of Ideas* 26, no. 1 (1965): 25–44.
Preus, Samuel. "Machiavelli's Functional Analysis of Religion: Context and Object." *Journal of the History of Ideas* 40, no. 2 (1979): 171–90.
Räikkä, Juha. "The Feasibility Condition in Political Theory." *Journal of Political Philosophy* 6, no. 1 (1998): 27–40.
Ravitzky, Aviezer. *Messianism, Zionism, and Jewish Religious Radicalism.* Translated by Michael Swirsky and Jonathan Chipman. Chicago: Chicago University Press, 1996.
Rawls, John. *A Brief Inquiry into the Meaning of Sin and Faith with "On My Religion."* Edited by Thomas Nagel. Cambridge, MA: Harvard University Press, 2009.
  Justice as Fairness: A Restatement. Edited by Erin Kelly. Cambridge, MA: Harvard University Press, 2001.
  The Law of Peoples. Cambridge, MA: Harvard University Press, 1999.
  Lectures on the History of Moral Philosophy. Edited by Barbara Herman. Cambridge, MA: Harvard University Press, 2000.
  Political Liberalism, exp. ed. New York: Columbia University Press, 2005.
  A Theory of Justice, rev. ed. Cambridge, MA: Harvard University Press, 1999.
Reglitz, Merten. "The Human Right to Free Internet Access." *Journal of Applied Philosophy* 37, no. 2 (2020): 314–31.
Riedl, Matthias. "Apocalyptic Violence and Revolutionary Action: Thomas Müntzer's *Sermon to the Princes*." In *A Companion to the Premodern Apocalypse*, edited by Michael Ryan, 260–96. Leiden: Brill, 2016.
Rinehart, James. *Apocalyptic Faith and Political Violence: Prophets of Terror.* New York: Palgrave Macmillan, 2006.
Roberts, John. "The 'Returns to Religion': Messianism, Christianity and the Revolutionary Tradition. Part I: 'Wakefulness to the Future.'" *Historical Materialism* 16, no. 2 (2008): 59–84.
Robeyns, Ingrid. "Ideal Theory in Theory and Practice." *Social Theory and Practice* 34, no. 3 (2008): 341–62.
Rooke, Deborah. "Prophecy." In *The Oxford Handbook of Biblical Studies*, edited by J. W. Rogerson and Judith Lieu, 385–96. New York: Oxford University Press, 2008.
Rossing, Barbara. "River of Life in God's New Jerusalem: An Eschatological Vision for Earth's Future." In *Christianity and Ecology: Seeking the Well-Being of Earth and*

Humans, edited by Dieter Hessel and Rosemary Radford Ruether, 205–24. Cambridge, MA: Harvard University Press, 2000.

Rothbard, Murray. "Karl Marx: Communist as Religious Eschatologist." *Review of Austrian Economics* 4, no. 1 (1990): 123–79.

Rousseau, Jean-Jacques. *On the Social Contract*. In *The Major Political Writings of Jean-Jacques Rousseau*, translated and edited by John Scott, 153–272. Chicago: University of Chicago Press, 2012.

Rowley, David. "'Redeemer Empire': Russian Millenarianism." *American Historical Review* 104, no. 5 (1999): 1582–1602.

Runciman, David. "What Is Realistic Political Philosophy?" *Metaphilosophy* 43, nos. 1–2 (2012): 58–70.

Russell, Bertrand. "Is There a God?" In *The Collected Papers of Bertrand Russell, Vol. 11: Last Philosophical Testament, 1943–68*, edited by John Slater and Peter Köllner, 542–48. New York: Routledge, 1997.

Savonarola, Girolamo. *The Compendium of Revelations*. In *Apocalyptic Spirituality*, translated and edited by Bernard McGinn, 192–275. New York: Paulist Press, 1979.

Girolamo Savonarola: A Guide to Righteous Living and Other Works. Translated and edited by Konrad Eisenbichler. Toronto: Centre for Reformation and Renaissance Studies, 2003.

Prediche sopra Aggeo. Edited by Luigi Firpo. Rome: Angelo Belardetti, 1965.

Prediche sopra i Salmi, vol. 1. Edited by Vincenzo Romano. Rome: Angelo Belardetti, 1969.

Selected Writings of Girolamo Savonarola: Religion and Politics, 1490–1498. Translated and edited by Anne Borelli and Marie Pastore Passaro. New Haven, CT: Yale University Press, 2006.

Schmidtz, David. "Nonideal Theory: What It Is and What It Needs to Be." *Ethics* 121, no. 4 (2011): 772–96.

Scholem, Gershom. *Sabbatai Sevi: The Mystical Messiah, 1626–1676*. Translated by R. J. Zwi Werblowsky. Princeton, NJ: Princeton University Press, 1973.

Schwarzschild, Steven. "On Jewish Eschatology." In *The Pursuit of the Ideal: Jewish Writings of Steven Schwarzschild*, edited by Menachem Kellner, 209–28. Albany, NY: State University of New York Press, 1990.

Scott, John. "The Fortune of Machiavelli's Unarmed Prophet." *Journal of Politics* 80, no. 2 (2018): 615–29.

Seib, Gerald. "In Crisis, Opportunity for Obama." *Wall Street Journal*, November 21, 2008, http://www.wsj.com/articles/SB122721278056345271.

Sells, Michael. "Armageddon in Christian, Sunni and Shia Traditions." In *The Oxford Handbook of Religion and Violence*, edited by Mark Juergensmeyer, Margo Kitts, and Michael Jerryson, 467–95. New York: Oxford University Press, 2013.

Sen, Amartya. *The Idea of Justice*. Cambridge, MA: Harvard University Press, 2009.

"What Do We Want from a Theory of Justice?" *Journal of Philosophy* 103, no. 5 (2006): 215–38.

Shklar, Judith. *After Utopia: The Decline of Political Faith*. Princeton, NJ: Princeton University Press, 1957.

"The Liberalism of Fear." In *Liberalism and the Moral Life*, edited by Nancy Rosenblum, 21–38. Cambridge, MA: Harvard University Press, 1989.

"The Political Theory of Utopia: From Melancholy to Nostalgia." *Daedalus* 94, no. 2 (1965): 367–81.
Simmons, A. John. "Ideal and Nonideal Theory." *Philosophy and Public Affairs* 38, no. 1 (2010): 5–36.
Singer, Isaac Bashevis. *Satan in Goray*. New York: Avon Books, 1963.
Skaggs, Rebecca, and Thomas Doyle. "Violence in the Apocalypse of John." *Currents in Biblical Research* 5, no. 2 (2007): 220–34.
Skinner, Quentin. "Meaning and Understanding in the History of Ideas." *History and Theory* 8, no. 1 (1969): 3–53.
  Reason and Rhetoric in the Philosophy of Hobbes. New York: Cambridge University Press, 1996
Sleat, Matt. "Realism, Liberalism and Non-ideal Theory or, Are There Two Ways to Do Realistic Political Theory?" *Political Studies* 64, no. 1 (2016): 27–41.
Smart, Ian. "The Political Ideas of the Scottish Covenanters. 1638–88." *History of Political Thought* 1, no. 2 (1980): 167–93.
Smith, Steven. *Modernity and Its Discontents: Making and Unmaking the Bourgeois from Machiavelli to Bellow*. New Haven, CT: Yale University Press, 2016.
Southwood, Nicholas. "Does 'Ought' Imply 'Feasible'?" *Philosophy and Public Affairs* 44, no. 1 (2016): 7–45.
Springborg, Patricia. "Thomas Hobbes and Cardinal Bellarmine: Leviathan and 'The Ghost of the Roman Empire.'" *History of Political Thought* 16, no. 4 (1995): 503–31.
Sreedhar, Susanne. *Hobbes on Resistance: Defying the Leviathan*. New York: Cambridge University Press, 2010.
Staub, Ervin. *The Roots of Evil: The Origins of Genocide and Other Group Violence*. New York: Cambridge University Press, 1989.
Stauffer, Devin. "'Of Religion' in Hobbes's *Leviathan*." *Journal of Politics* 72, no. 3 (2010): 868–79.
Steinberger, Peter. "Hobbesian Resistance." *American Journal of Political Science* 46, no. 4 (2002): 856–65.
Stemplowska, Zofia, "Feasibility: Individual and Collective." *Social Philosophy and Policy* 33, nos. 1–2 (2016): 273–91.
Stemplowska, Zofia, and Adam Swift. "Ideal and Nonideal Theory." In *The Oxford Handbook of Political Philosophy*, edited by David Estlund, 373–88. New York: Oxford University Press, 2012.
Strauss, Leo. *The Political Philosophy of Hobbes: Its Basis and Its Genesis*. Translated by Elsa Sinclair. Chicago: University of Chicago Press, 1952.
  Thoughts on Machiavelli. Chicago: University of Chicago Press, 1958.
Sullivan, Vickie. "Neither Christian nor Pagan: Machiavelli's Treatment of Religion in the *Discourses*." *Polity* 26, no. 2 (1993): 259–80.
Taleb, Nassim. *The Black Swan: The Impact of the Highly Improbable*. New York: Random House, 2010.
Taylor, Charles. *A Secular Age*. Cambridge, MA: Harvard University Press, 2007.
Tetlock, Philip. *Expert Political Judgment: How Good Is It? How Can We Know?* Princeton, NJ: Princeton University Press, 2005.
Tetlock, Philip, and Dan Gardner. *Superforecasting: The Art and Science of Prediction*. New York: Crown Publishers, 2015.

Thucydides. *The History of the Grecian War*. Translated by Thomas Hobbes. In *The English Works of Thomas Hobbes of Malmesbury*, vol. 8–9, edited by William Molesworth. London: John Bohn, 1843.
Tinder, Glenn. "Eschatology and Politics." *Review of Politics* 27, no. 3 (1965): 311–33.
Tuck, Richard. "The 'Christian Atheism' of Thomas Hobbes." In *Atheism from the Reformation to the Enlightenment*, edited by Michael Hunter and David Wootton, 111–30. Oxford: Clarendon Press, 1992.
  Hobbes. New York: Oxford University Press, 1989.
  "The Utopianism of *Leviathan*." In *Leviathan after 350 Years*, edited by Tom Sorrell and Luc Foisneau, 125–38. New York: Oxford University Press, 2004.
Tutino, Stefania. *Empire of Souls: Robert Bellarmine and the Christian Commonwealth*. New York: Oxford University Press, 2010.
Tuveson, Ernest. *Millennium and Utopia: A Study in the Background of the Idea of Progress*. Berkeley, CA: University of California Press, 1949.
Valentini, Laura. "On the Apparent Paradox of Ideal Theory." *Journal of Political Philosophy* 17, no. 3 (2009): 332–55.
  "Ideal vs. Non-ideal Theory: A Conceptual Map." *Philosophy Compass* 7, no. 9 (2012): 654–64.
  "A Paradigm Shift in Theorizing about Justice? A Critique of Sen." *Economics and Philosophy* 27, no. 3 (2011): 297–315.
Velji, Jamel. "Apocalyptic Religion and Violence." In *The Oxford Handbook of Religion and Violence*, edited by Mark Juergensmeyer, Margo Kitts, and Michael Jerryson, 250–59. New York: Oxford University Press, 2013.
Virgil. *The Aeneid*. Translated by David West. New York: Penguin Books, 1991.
Viroli, Maurizio. *Machiavelli's God*. Translated by Antony Shugaar. Princeton, NJ: Princeton University Press, 2010.
  Niccolò's Smile: A Biography of Machiavelli. Translated by Antony Shugaar. New York: Hill and Wang, 2002.
  Redeeming The Prince: The Meaning of Machiavelli's Masterpiece. Princeton, NJ: Princeton University Press, 2014.
Voegelin, Eric. *The Political Religions*. Translated by Virginia Ann Schildhauer. In *Modernity without Restraint*. The Collected Works of Eric Voegelin, vol. 5, edited by Manfred Henningsen, 19–73. Columbia, MO: University of Missouri, 2000.
Vondung, Klaus. *The Apocalypse in Germany*. Translated by Stephen Ricks. Columbia, MO: University of Missouri Press, 2000.
Walzer, Michael. *The Company of Critics: Social Criticism and Political Commitment in the Twentieth Century*. New York: Basic Books, 1988.
  Interpretation and Social Criticism. Cambridge, MA: Harvard University Press, 1987.
  The Revolution of the Saints: A Study in the Origins of Radical Politics. Cambridge, MA: Harvard University Press, 1965.
Warrender, Howard. *The Political Philosophy of Hobbes: His Theory of Obligation*. Oxford: Clarendon Press, 1957.
Weber, Michael, and Kevin Vallier, eds. *Political Utopias: Contemporary Debates*. New York: Oxford University Press, 2017.

Weber, Timothy. *Living in the Shadow of the Second Coming: American Premillennialism, 1875–1982*. Grand Rapids, MI: Academie Books, 1983.
Weinstein, Donald. "Machiavelli and Savonarola." In *Studies on Machiavelli*, edited by Myron Gilmore, 251–64. Florence: Sansoni, 1972.
   Savonarola and Florence: Prophecy and Patriotism in the Renaissance. Princeton, NJ: Princeton University Press, 1970.
   Savonarola: The Rise and Fall of a Renaissance Prophet. New Haven, CT: Yale University Press, 2011.
Weithman, Paul. *Why Political Liberalism? On John Rawls's Political Turn*. New York: Oxford University Press, 2010.
Wessinger, Catherine. "Introduction: The Interacting Dynamics of Millennial Beliefs, Persecution, and Violence." In *Millennialism, Persecution, and Violence: Historical Cases*, edited by Catherine Wessinger, 3–39. Syracuse, NY: Syracuse University Press, 2000.
   "Millennial Glossary." In *The Oxford Handbook of Millennialism*, edited by Catherine Wessinger, 717–24. New York: Oxford University Press, 2011.
   ed. *Millennialism, Persecution, and Violence: Historical Cases*. Syracuse, NY: Syracuse University Press, 2000.
Westminster Assembly. *The Westminster Confession of Faith*. In *Creeds and Confessions of Faith in the Christian Tradition*, vol. 2, edited by Jaroslav Pelikan and Valerie Hotchkiss, 601–49. New Haven, CT: Yale University Press, 2003.
Whitfield, J. H. *Discourses on Machiavelli*. Cambridge: W. Heffer & Sons, 1969.
Wiens, David. "Against Ideal Guidance." *Journal of Politics* 77, no. 2 (2015): 433–46.
   "'Going Evaluative' to Save Justice from Feasibility—a Pyrrhic Victory." *Philosophical Quarterly* 64, no. 255 (2014): 301–7.
   "Motivational Limitations on the Demands of Justice." *European Journal of Political Theory* 15, no. 3 (2016): 333–52.
   "Political Ideals and the Feasibility Frontier." *Economics and Philosophy* 31, no. 3 (2015): 447–77.
   "Prescribing Institutions without Ideal Theory." *Journal of Political Philosophy* 20, no. 1 (2012): 45–70.
Wilkinson, Henry. *Babylons Ruine, Jerusalems Rising*. London, 1643.
Williams, Bernard. *In the Beginning Was the Deed: Realism and Moralism in Political Argument*. Edited by Geoffrey Hawthorn. Princeton, NJ: Princeton University Press, 2005.
Williams, Roger. *The Bloudy Tenent of Persecution*. In *The Complete Writings of Roger Williams*, vol. 3. Eugene, OR: Wipf and Stock Publishers, 2007.
Williamson, Arthur. *Apocalypse Then: Prophecy and the Making of the Modern World*. Westport, CT: Praeger, 2008.
Wilson, John. *The Pulpit in Parliament: Puritanism during the English Civil Wars, 1640–1648*. Princeton, NJ: Princeton University Press, 1969.
Wood, Graeme. "What ISIS Really Wants." *The Atlantic*, March 2015, www.theatlantic.com/magazine/archive/2015/03/what-isis-really-wants/384980/.
Wood, Neal. "Sallust's Theorem: A Comment on 'Fear' in Western Political Thought." *History of Political Thought* 16, no. 2 (1995): 174–89.

Ypi, Lea. "On the Confusion between Ideal and Non-ideal in Recent Debates on Global Justice." *Political Studies* 58, no. 3 (2010): 536–55.
Zagorin, Perez. *Hobbes and the Law of Nature*. Princeton, NJ: Princeton University Press, 2009.
Zupan, Patricia. "Machiavelli and Savonarola Revisited: The Closing Chapter of *Il Principe*." *Machiavelli Studies* 1 (1987): 43–64.

Index

Acts, book of, 44, 111
Agricola, Johann, 124
Alexander VI, Pope, 62
Anabaptism, 121–22
anarchy, 117. *See also* state of nature.
Antichrist, 5, 21, 94–95, 103, 123
apocalyptic thought, cataclysmic, 7–8, 10, 40, 41, 45, 49, 54, 55–58, 72, 96, 123, 134, 136, 182, 192
Aristotle, 79
Armageddon, 191
Aspinwall, William, 96–97
atheism, 2, 119, 130, 133
Augustine, Saint, 39, 44, 69, 188
Augustus, Roman emperor, 68

Bacon, Francis, 115
Bar Kokhba, Simon, 186
Bathsheba, 116
Becchi, Ricciardo, 76, 80, 84, 88, 90
Bejan, Teresa, 180
Bellarmine, Robert, 99–100, 108
Berlin, Isaiah, 183
Bible, 15, 29, 39, 122, 130, 179, 192
Black Swan, 146, 160, 201–2
Blumenberg, Hans, 13–14, 25–27, 32, 36–37, 108
Boer, Roland, 137–40
bourgeoisie, 135, 136
Boyer, Paul, 21
Bush, George W., 29–31, 37

Caligula, Roman emperor, 116
capital punishment. *See* execution.
capitalism, 8, 58, 127, 134–36
catastrophe, 7, 11, 14, 17, 32–33, 34–35, 37, 136, 191

Catechism of the Catholic Church, 44
Catechism of the Council of Trent, 108
Catholicism, 44, 82, 99–100, 108, 130
Charles I, king of England, 95, 96, 97, 100, 105
Charles II, king of England, 99
Charles VIII, king of France, 61, 81–82
Christ. *See* Jesus.
Christianity, 2, 4–5, 7, 8, 10, 14–16, 17, 24, 30, 33, 35, 36, 39, 40–43, 44, 58, 68–70, 80–81, 82, 98, 110–13, 121, 122, 124, 128–29, 130, 131, 136–41, 165, 172, 176, 178–79, 187–89, 192, 193, 194
Church of England, 95, 100
City, Eternal. *See* Rome.
climate change, 12, 173, 191, 199
Cohen, G. A., 51, 54, 154
Cohn, Norman, 22, 24
Collins, Adela Yarbro, 69
Collins, John, 42
colonialism, 173
communism, 22, 23, 24, 25, 130, 136
Constantine, Roman emperor, 139
Covenanters, Scottish, 105
COVID-19, 12. *See* pandemic.
crisis, 1–2, 4, 7, 9, 17, 40, 41–43, 49, 55–56, 57–58, 64, 65–66, 72, 85, 88, 120, 121, 123, 124, 125, 132, 134–36, 139, 140–41, 182, 185, 192, 194
Cromwell, Oliver, 97
Crossan, John Dominic, 179
Cyrus, 66, 78, 83

Daniel, book of, 28, 35, 96, 124, 125
Dante, Alighieri, 70
David, king of Israel, 116
Descartes, René, 157

Deuteronomy, book of, 104
Diocletian, Roman emperor, 139
Dominic, Saint, 82

Emanuel, Rahm, 56
Engels, Friedrich, 1–4, 7–8, 14, 17, 23, 36, 119–21, 127–41, 191, 193–94
England, 92, 94–98, 99, 101, 135
Ephesians, book of, 122
eschatology, 14, 24, 26, 57, 75, 87, 93, 97–98, 108, 112, 120, 137, 182, 185–89
Estep, William, 122
Estlund, David, 50–51, 54
execution, 89–90, 96, 117
Exodus, book of, 67, 84, 104, 112
Ezekiel, book of, 126

faith, 10, 16, 17, 18, 24, 42, 44, 63, 72, 82, 85–86, 88, 98, 111–12, 114, 131, 145, 146, 147, 165–74, 175, 176, 192–93
 reasonable, 170–73
fear of enemies (*metus hostilis*), 118
feasibility, 7–8, 39–40, 47, 58, 115, 121, 127, 140, 149, 151, 155–56, 162, 185, 192, 202. *See also* ideal theory, feasibility objection to
Fifth Monarchy Men, 92, 96–98, 101, 176
Flannery, Frances, 182
Florence, 17, 61–64, 66, 68, 70–91
founders, 2, 66–67, 78–85, 86–88, 90–91
France, 61, 82
Francis, Saint, 82
Frankenhausen, Battle of, 119
Frederick III, Elector of Saxony, 125
Friedman, Milton, 56
Friesen, Abraham, 137

Gaus, Gerald, 46, 55, 146, 151, 152–55, 163–64
Genesis, book of, 34
Germany, 23, 34, 120, 130, 132
good, the greatest (*summum bonum*), 117
Goodwin, Thomas, 95
Gray, John, 31–32
Grebel, Conrad, 122
Guicciardini, Francesco, 61, 77–78, 83

Hall, John, 179
Harrison, Thomas, 97
Hebrews, book of, 165
Hendrix, Burke, 162
Hobbes, Thomas, 1–4, 7–8, 17, 33–35, 92–94, 96–118, 191, 193–94. *See also* kingdom of God, natural; kingdom of God, prophetic; and state of nature
Hoekstra, Kinch, 97, 103
Holland, 135
hope, 1, 6, 42–43, 56–58, 66, 67–68, 86, 114, 141, 164–65
 apocalyptic, 3, 4, 23, 30, 44, 63, 67, 73, 94, 97, 102–3, 136, 139, 186–88, 191, 193
 utopian, 4, 7–8, 9–10, 11, 13, 17, 18, 31, 57, 66, 67, 75, 88, 93, 115, 133–36, 147, 162, 165–74, 175–76, 182–86, 187, 189–90, 191, 192–94, 196
humility, 10, 81, 185, 187, 196
 epistemic, 18, 155, 176, 186, 188–90, 193, 195

ideal theory, 6–11, 16, 17–18, 39–40, 45–49, 54–58, 145–74, 175–76, 182, 183–85, 189–90, 192–97, 198–202
 catch-22 of, 7–8, 40, 55, 56, 58, 192
 feasibility objection to, 48, 49, 50–53, 54, 55
 navigational, 145, 148, 149, 152–53, 155, 159, 160–61, 162, 163–64, 165, 198, 201–2
 utopian objection to, 48, 49, 53–55
idealism, 4, 18, 114–15
idealization, 148
idolatry, 41–43, 93, 111–12, 177
immortality, 68, 86, 87, 115, 170–71, 173
Islam, 186
Islamic State (ISIS), 5
Israel, 67, 78, 84, 104, 106, 186
Italy, 64, 66–67, 70, 71, 72, 74, 80, 81–82, 86

James I, king of England, 94
Jerusalem, new, 41, 43, 55, 63, 67–70, 71, 73–75, 85, 107
Jesus, 39, 41, 43, 44, 74, 95, 96, 100, 101, 106, 107, 110, 112–13, 114, 179, 180, 187, 194
Job, book of, 115
John, Duke of Saxony, 125
Judaism, 7, 10, 15–16, 24, 40, 137, 176, 186–87, 189, 192, 193
Judgment, the Last, 191
Jurdjevic, Mark, 65, 75

Kant, Immanuel, 155, 168–73
Kermode, Frank, 28
King Jr., Martin Luther, 166
kingdom of God, 2, 3–4, 7, 15, 17, 30, 36, 39, 40, 41, 43, 58, 66, 68–70, 72, 81, 88, 92–94, 95–103, 105, 114, 115, 118, 119–20, 122, 123,

125, 126, 130, 131–33, 137, 139, 141, 182, 187–88, 193–95
natural, 93, 106, 107–13, 115, 118
prophetic, 106–7, 109, 111, 112–13
Kings, book of 2, 112

Landes, Richard, 27
Landucci, Luca, 90
Laud, William, 105
Lenin, Vladimir, 135, 183
Leo X, Pope, 86
Lincoln, Abraham, 150, 172
Lincoln, Bruce, 29–31
Livy, 68
Lloyd, Sharon, 115
Lord's Prayer, the, 107
Löwith, Karl, 22, 24, 26
Luther, Martin, 121, 122, 124, 125

Machiavelli, Niccolò, 1–4, 7–8, 17, 61–68, 70, 75–91, 191, 193
republic, perpetual (*republica perpetua*), 4, 63–64, 67–68, 86–87, 88
Maimonides, Moses, 186
Mark, book of, 188
Markus, R. A., 188
Martin, Adrienne, 167
Marx, Karl, 23, 121, 127–28, 134, 135, 137–39, 140
Marxism, 2, 58, 119–21, 130, 133–41
materialism, historical, 127, 134
Matthew, book of, 29, 72, 73, 123, 194–95
Maynard, John, 95
McGinn, Bernard, 177
McQueen, Alison, 10–11, 28–31, 33–35, 65, 66
McVeigh, Timothy, 5
Mede, Joseph, 95
Medici, Lorenzo de', 64–67, 78, 86
Medici, Piero de', 61
Mendel, Arthur, 179
methodology, 11, 17, 32, 35, 145, 192
Mill, John Stuart, 163
millennialism/millenarianism, 14, 15, 24, 25, 27–28, 31, 65, 67
Mills, Charles, 162
miracles, 67, 72, 81, 104
Moltmann, Jürgen, 43
Moorhead, James, 27
More, Thomas, 16, 46, 115
Moses, 66–67, 78, 83–84, 104, 106
Müntzer, Thomas, 4, 17, 36, 119–20, 121–27, 128, 130–34, 137–38, 140, 141, 175, 182, 193

Naaman, 111–12
Najemy, John, 72
Nazism, 23–24, 31
Nero, Roman emperor, 116
Newton, Isaac, 148
Nozick, Robert, 154

O'Leary, Stephen, 57

Paine, Thomas, 56
pandemic, 12, 191
COVID-19, 12
parable, 123
of Hillside, 1–2, 193–94
of the Sheep and the Goats, 194–97
Parliament of England, 94–97, 102
Plato, 9, 16, 46, 79, 115
Pocock, J. G. A., 43
Popper, Karl, 158, 162–63, 184
power, indirect (*potestas indirecta*), 99
preacher, 11, 65, 75
prediction, 4, 12, 13, 15, 18, 21, 39, 42, 55, 58, 61, 67, 73, 80, 81, 82, 98, 104, 113, 124, 126, 129, 140, 146, 152–53, 155–61, 174, 182, 186, 193, 196, 198–201
Presbyterianism, 99–101, 105
proletariat, 120, 131–32, 135–36
prophecy, 1–2, 3, 12, 14, 15–16, 21, 24, 33, 39, 44, 61, 65, 72–73, 75, 77, 78, 81–82, 84, 92, 93–94, 95, 96, 103–5, 129, 130, 132, 137, 180. *See also* kingdom of God, prophetic
Protestant, 99, 100

racism, 30
Räikkä, Juha, 53
rapture, 11, 21, 191
Rawls, John, 9, 18, 45–46, 47, 145–47, 149, 153–54, 156, 162, 168–73, 184, 193, 199, 200, 202
realism, political, 10–11
Reformation, 36, 125, 131, 132
Radical, 121
religion, 12–17, 23, 31, 39, 61, 63, 80, 81, 82–85, 89, 96, 98, 102, 104, 107, 127–29, 136, 137, 139, 147, 165–66, 170, 171, 176, 179, 184
Revelation, book of, 4, 5, 7, 12, 14–16, 17, 28–30, 35, 39–43, 55, 69, 70–71, 73–74, 85, 94–95, 107, 112, 120, 125, 128–29, 138–39, 177–79, 189
revolution, 2, 24, 56, 71, 72, 94, 119, 132, 134–36, 182

risk, 9, 10, 13, 18, 27, 35, 37, 53, 56–58, 87, 90, 102, 147, 148, 157, 162, 176, 179, 183, 193
Robeyns, Ingrid, 47, 49
Romans, book of, 125
Rome, 24, 41–42, 73–75, 76, 78, 82, 100, 118, 129, 139, 186, 189
 the Eternal City, 68–70
Romulus, 78, 83
Rossing, Barbara, 69
Rousseau, Jean-Jacques, 180
Russell, Bertrand, 161–62, 166
Russia, 135

Samuel, book of 2, 116
Savonarola, Girolamo, 3–4, 17, 61–67, 68, 70–86, 88–91
Schwarzschild, Steven, 187, 188
Scotland, 105. *See also* Covenanters, Scottish
secularization, 8, 13–14, 16, 23–27, 43–45, 120–21, 133, 136–38, 193
Sen, Amartya, 51–52, 150–51, 154, 162–63
September 11 attacks, 29, 37
Shklar, Judith, 13, 22–23, 25–27, 32, 36–37
Singer, Isaac Bashevis, 187
Skinner, Quentin, 92
slavery, 29, 66, 67, 150, 161, 172, 173, 182–83
socialism, 14, 17, 128–29, 139–41
 utopian, 75
state of nature, 33–35, 54, 118

Taleb, Nassim, 160
Taliban, 29–30
Talmud, 186
Taylor, Charles, 168
teleology, 166, 171, 173
terrorism, 5, 22, 29–30, 31, 182
Tetlock, Philip, 159–60
Theseus, 66, 78, 83
Thucydides, 35
Tinder, Glenn, 39
Trump, Donald, 12
Tuck, Richard, 114

United States, 5, 12, 21, 30, 135, 180
Uriah, 116–17
utopia, 2, 3, 4, 7, 11, 16, 17, 25, 31, 39–40, 41, 43, 45, 46–47, 49, 55–56, 58, 63, 66, 72, 74–75, 86, 89, 93, 114–15, 118, 121, 123, 126, 137, 140–41, 148, 153, 179, 181, 185, 188–89, 192, 193, 195–96
 realistic, 47, 145, 170, 172, 202. *See also* hope, utopian; ideal theory, utopian objection to; and socialism, utopian

Valentini, Laura, 53
value, surplus, 134–35
Vettori, Francesco, 84
violence, 2, 5–7, 10, 31, 34, 42, 45, 54, 58, 113, 116, 118, 122, 124–26, 135, 175–85, 189, 193
 principle against utopian, 183–85
Virgil, 68, 70
Viroli, Maurizio, 67
Voegelin, Eric, 22, 23–24

war, 5, 13, 28, 31, 33, 34–35, 42, 43, 44, 84, 95–96, 113, 117, 131, 159, 188, 192
 American Civil, 172, 183
 English Civil, 3, 17, 33, 92, 96, 98, 100–3, 105, 115, 118
 German Peasants', 4, 120, 130
 Iraq, 31
 nuclear, 12, 22, 191
 Second World, 162, 171–72
Weinstein, Donald, 64, 68, 70–71
Westminster Assembly, 100
Westminster Confession, 100
Wiens, David, 162–63
Wilkinson, Henry, 95
Williams, Roger, 180–81

Ypi, Lea, 46

Zevi, Sabbatai, 186–87
Zupan, Patricia, 65

For EU product safety concerns, contact us at Calle de José Abascal, 56–1°, 28003 Madrid, Spain or eugpsr@cambridge.org.

www.ingramcontent.com/pod-product-compliance
Lightning Source LLC
LaVergne TN
LVHW020344260326
834688LV00045B/1520